SATAN'S CON

CW01083881

SATAN'S CONSPIRACY

Magic and Witchcraft
in Sixteenth–Century Scotland

P.G.Maxwell-Stuart

TUCKWELL PRESS

For Liam and Duncan Stewart

First published in Great Britain in 2001 by
Tuckwell Press
The Mill House
Phantassie
East Linton
East Lothian EH40 3DG
Scotland

Copyright P.G.Maxwell-Stuart, 2001

ISBN 1 86232 136 1

British Library Cataloguing in Publication Data

A catalogue record for this book is available
on request from the British Library

The right of P.G. Maxwell-Stuart to be identified
as the author of this work has been asserted by him in
accordance with the Copyright, Design and Patent Act 1988

Typeset by Hewer Text Ltd, Edinburgh
Printed and bound by Bell & Bain Ltd., Glasgow

Satan this long tyme in his members hes so rageit and perturbit the good successe and proceeding of Chrysts religioun within this realme, be craftie meanes and subtill conspiracies, that the same from tyme to tyme doeth decay, in hazard altogether to be subvertit.

Booke of the Universall Kirk, 96

CONTENTS

PREFACE

The evidence for magic and witchcraft in sixteenth-century Scotland lies scattered in unpublished manuscripts, nineteenth and early twentieth-century transcriptions, and passing remarks in the histories of shires and burghs. Its constituent parts have never before been brought together or discussed as a whole, and my object in this study has been to lay the material in front of the reader and make some preliminary suggestions about how it can be interpreted, in the hope that future scholars of Scottish witchcraft in particular will be able the more easily to construct their theories with the bricks I have provided. I do not pretend to have uncovered all the existing material on this subject, for there are certainly caches of papers and further references still to be found. But there is a great deal here which has not been seen in print before, and the picture of Scottish witchcraft produced therefrom is very different from the one which is normally painted.

I am very grateful to the Manuscripts Department of the University of St Andrews where most of this book was written, to the staff of the Scottish Record Office, and to the archivists of Aberdeen, Dundee, and Montrose for their help and co-operation.

All dates in this book have been altered to the New Style.

GLOSSARY OF SCOTTISH LEGAL TERMS

Ask instruments have legal documents drawn up to record the verdict of the assize or the decision of the justice depute

Assize jury

Chancellor foreman of the jury

Clengit declared not guilty or innocent

Decern pass an opinion or judgement upon

Delate accuse or denounce judicially

Dittay indictment

Escheat forfeiture of property upon a person's conviction of certain crimes

Fylit declared guilty

Justice-air itinerant court

Justice depute trial judge

Panel defendant

roloquitor for the panel defence advocate

Pursuer prosecuting advocate

ABBREVIATIONS

APS	*Acts of the Parliaments of Scotland*
BUK	*Booke of the Universall Kirk*
CSP	*Calendar of State Papers*
CSPS	*Calendar of State Papers relating to Scotland*
ERS	*Exchequer Rolls of Scotland*
JC	*Records of the High Court of Justiciary*
JMH	*Journal of Mediaeval History*
JSPR	*Journal of the Society for Psychical Research*
RMS	*Registrum Magni Sigilli Regum Scotorum*
SCM	*Spalding Club Miscellany*
SHR	*Scottish Historical Review*
SJTh	*Scottish Journal of Theology*
TGSI	*Transactions of the Gaelic Society of Inverness*

1

Magic and Occult Powers in Sixteenth-Century Scotland

P eople in sixteenth-century Europe lived amid a multiplicity of inter-penetrating worlds. There was the physical earth over which, by God's dispensation, they had command; the celestial world in which God himself existed along with those beings of his creation called angels, archangels, cherubim, seraphim, and so forth; the demonic world of Satan and his army of evil spirits, many of whose names were known and could be used to summon them into the physical world by rituals of evocation; and the preternatural world of the planets and the stars with their tutelary spirits, pouring down influences upon the earth beneath by means of subtle rays.[1] There was Heaven above and Hell below, with Purgatory and Limbo between. Ghosts wandered the earth or haunted particular places or answered magicians' calls or acted as messengers. The sky could reveal strange, monitory signs – unexpected lights and comets, bizarre cloud-formations, showers of animals or blood; the air might be filled with noises and spectral sounds; nature might produce deformed monstrosities from humans or animals, or engrave significant marks upon plants and stones; dreams were not mere emanations from the brain but portents to be divined and messages to be interpreted; the very lines and excrescences upon the human face and hand did not appear there by chance, but were created as signs of character and inclination; the elements themselves had their attendant spirits – sala-manders for fire, gnomes for earth, nymphs for water, and sylphs for air – who might be encountered at any moment and who needed to be placated if disturbed, while fairies existed in realms usually hidden from human sight, but could cross over into the physical world at will, or draw humans into theirs.[2] Nothing existed or happened fortuitously, for everything in each of these worlds was connected in some fashion to everything else, as though creation were a great, intricate web streaming outwards from God who sat spider-like in the centre and governed the whole.

---

1 Cornelius Agrippa expressed it thus, 'There is a threefold world, elementary, celestial, and intellectual and every inferior is governed by its superior and receiveth the influence of the vertues thereof, so that the very original and chief worker of all doth by angels, the heavens, stars, elements, animals, plants, metals, and stones convey from himself the vertues of his omnipotency upon us for whose service he made and created all these things', *Three Books of Occult Philosophy*, Book 1, chapter 1.
2 For illustrations of these points, see Maxwell-Stuart: *The Occult in Early Modern Europe* (Macmillan 1999), Chapter 1, and McLean: *A Treatise on Angel Magic* (Phanes Press 1990).

But if human beings were dominant over the natural world, over the others they exercised no power by God-granted right. Yet they need not be altogether impotent, for anyone who understood the workings of creation and knew how each tiny part of the whole related to all the others was in possession of a key which might unlock for him or her control over the hidden forces of those other worlds. Spirits, demons, angels could be summoned and forced to obey one's will (so went the theory), and by making use of their superior knowledge of occult sympathies and antipathies, and their consequent ability to work wonders human power could never achieve by itself, men and women could come closer to an understanding of the mind of the Creator and thus participate, in a small but highly significant way, in the God-like work of manipulating the very warp and woof of nature and so weave a pattern other than that intended by God himself – a prospect fraught with peril and amazement, in which curiosity, excitement, and intense religious awareness rubbed shoulders with spiritual pride, blasphemy, sacrilege, and heresy.

Magic and Witchcraft

Magic, then, involves pursuit, discovery, and exercise of those techniques which can offer a human being control over the power revealed by occult knowledge, and the motive for the pursuit may be noble or base. It may be noble because, in the words of Agrippa, magic "contains the most profound contemplation of things which are most secret, together with their nature, power, quality, substance, and virtues, and the knowledge of the whole of nature . . . It is the most perfect and principal branch of knowledge, a sacred and more lofty kind of philosophy", or it may be base because, according to Ficino (and, indeed, to many others) it uses "a particular kind of worship to attract the favour of evil spirits and, relying on their co-operation, often fabricates abnormal phenomena".[3]

Early modern commentators, however, did not regard magic as a single entity, good or bad.[4] They divided it into several types: *ceremonial* or *angelic* magic which endeavoured by means of complex ritual to raise the practitioner's consciousness to a higher spiritual plane;[5] *natural magic* which relied upon the operator's knowledge of the workings of nature and his or her consequent ability to produce effects the non-initiated would find wonderful; *artificial magic* which was trickery in our sense of 'conjuring', dependent on prestidigitation and especially

---

3 Agrippa: *De Occulta Philosophia*, Book 1, chapter 2. Marsilio Ficino: *Apologia de medicina, astrologia, vita mundi*, Chapter 147.

4 Nor did they necessarily relate it, or any aspect of it, to a preconceived 'world-view'. Someone, for example, complaining that he or she was bewitched might well describe the experience in entirely different terms to a clergyman and to a neighbour or relative. See De Blécourt: 'On the continuation of witchcraft', in Barry, Hester, Roberts: *Witchcraft in Early Modern Europe*, 337–8.

5 This was often described as one of the aims of alchemy, too.

manufactured props; and *demonic magic* which worked because the human operator was in league with an evil spirit and relied upon the spirit's superior knowledge of and control over occult forces to work the required wonders.[6] It was this last type of magic which might easily be re-defined as 'witchcraft', because one of the features of witchcraft common to any attempted definition of the term is the intentional commission of *maleficium*, an act of harmful magic. Nevertheless, 'demonic magic' and 'witchcraft' are not synonymous since some-one may attempt an act of malefice without thereby necessarily putting him or herself within the category 'witch'. So defining the terms 'witch' and 'witchcraft' satisfactorily is not altogether straightforward; but an attempt to do so might produce the following; (a) 'witch': a witch is someone who practises witchcraft, and (b) 'witchcraft': witchcraft is what witches do. The circularity of these definitions may be irritating, but unfortunately it is almost unavoidable, partly at least because if one looks at the range of activities which might be labelled 'witchcraft', it rapidly becomes clear that the classic indications provided by early modern demonologists – pact with an evil spirit, flight through the air on the back of an animal, ability to change shape, attendance at a Sabbat during which blasphemy, idolatry, and sexual promiscuity were the behavioural norms – are not very helpful when it comes to understanding exactly what it was in sixteenth-century eyes that differentiated witchcraft from any other form of operative magic.

Let me give five examples of witches' activities:

1) John Ramsay in Newburgh was very ill and came to Helen Fraser for a cure. She told him to rise at dawn and eat some sorrel while the dew still lay upon it, make a meal of kail, and at evening to sit at his door while the birds were flying home to roost and bare his chest so that the wind of their wings might beat upon his heart.

2) Katharine MacFerries gave Elspeth Forbes an enchanted lamen which was to be worn by Elspeth's daughters as a means of ensuring they would get husbands; and Elspeth herself received a magic ring which, she was told, would reveal many things to her.

---

6 A convenient summary of these types is given by the Jesuit, Benito Pereira: *Adversus Fallaces et Superstitiosas Artes*, Book 1, Chapter 9. Not all early commentators used the same terminology. 'Necromancy', for example, might refer to a form of demonic magic or a type of divination. But the kinds of magic listed here will cover those generally discussed during the sixteenth and seventeenth centuries. A modern definition of 'occult' may be useful here by way of comparison. 'By "the occult" I understand intentional practices, techniques, or procedures which: a) draw upon hidden or concealed forces in nature or the cosmos that cannot be measured or recognised by the instruments of modern science, and b) which have as their desired or intended consequence empirical results, such as either obtaining knowledge of the empirical course of events, or altering them from what they would have been without this intervention', Tiryakian: 'Towards the sociology of esoteric culture', 498.

3) When Edward Donaldson told Katharine Gray he no longer wanted her as a tenant, she bewitched him. He fell sick and his business began to fail and things became so bad that he was obliged to go to Inverness to get himself unwitched by someone else.

4) Agnes Wobster asked Isobel Davidson for some milk. She was refused and Isobel's cow thereafter gave no more milk.

5) Janet Wishart envied John Pyet some land he had inherited, so she bewitched him to the effect that he lay for eighteen weeks sick of a fever and then died.[7]

What we see illustrated here is the exercise of magic to produce a number of desired results: effecting a cure, engineering success in love, removing a piece of witchcraft laid on by someone else, interfering with a domestic economy to the detriment of the housewife, and inflicting both sickness and death on a human being. All these, subject of course to a hundred possible minor variations, are typical themes of witchcraft, and since each of these examples has been chosen from Scottish cases of the 1590s, the witchcraft they describe is the witchcraft faced by the ministers and elders of the Kirk, the local community, and the organs of judicial authority at that time. Two things may strike us. First, there is no mention of flying through the air to a Sabbat, or sexual intercourse with the Devil or any other evil spirit, or banqueting followed by an indiscriminate orgy, or the formal renunciation of baptism and acceptance of a diabolical pact. Secondly, in spite of the variety apparent in the witches' activities, which range from the beneficent to the maleficent, there is a unifying factor: the exercise of power.

Now, it is often assumed that the nature of this power was, on the one hand supernatural, and on the other diabolical. With respect to the first, however, theorists of the period were very careful to distinguish between a *miraculum* and a *mirum*. A *miraculum* occurs as the result of a suspension of the laws of natural order, which are the laws of God, the creator of that order. A *mirum*, by contrast, is an event which appears to transcend those laws but does not, in fact, do so. Archangels, angels, planetary spirits, demons, and Satan himself, all being part of God's creation, are subject to the laws of that creation and cannot operate beyond them. Consequently the *mirum*, whether caused by a major or a minor angel or spirit, is an event whose cause is not supernatural and whose workings may therefore be understood. But because God's laws are extremely complex, there may be much that is beyond human understanding at present. Hence apparent miracles are performed by magicians and alchemists and witches, who may or may not operate with the aid of angels or evil spirits. If magicians and alchemists and witches *are* able to do such things, however, it is only because the angels or evil spirits, being cleverer than human

7 *SCM*, 105. *Aberdeen Press* 18–64. *SCM*, 128, 88.

beings and thus more privy to the hidden (i.e. occult) workings of nature, can manipulate natural laws in a fashion not yet understood by their human employers. Thus, the results of their manipulations may seem to be astonishing (*mira*). In reality, however, the angels and demons are limited in what they can do by the boundaries set by God when he created them as part of the *mundus universalis*, and so their power is not transcendent. True miracle, in a word, belongs to God alone; the rest of creation has to make do with astonishment.[8]

The performance of *mira*, then, constitutes magic which may be defined as the exercise, not of supernatural but of preternatural power, and it follows that whoever possesses the ability to exercise such power is stronger than – or, as we might say, has the psychological advantage of – anyone who does not possess it, and a demonstration of this power, or even a credible claim to possess it, will therefore set up a number of reactions in the immediate community. Those who have not yet been affected by it will tend to seek to avoid it rather than try to contact and use it, while those who have been affected by it will either suffer its consequences because they feel or believe themselves to be too weak to resist it; or will co-operate with it because they think it can be used for their benefit (in which case they acknowledge themselves subordinate to the will and force of the person exercising it); or they will perceive the power as malevolent and struggle against it and seek some kind of redress against its unwanted effects.[9]

This brings us back to witchcraft. Witchcraft is just such an exercise of preternatural power and a witch is someone with access to that power. But just as there is not a single type of magic, so there is more than one kind of witch. Eva Pócs has distinguished three: (1) the 'neighbourhood' or 'social' witch who is identified with conflicts among neighbours or within the wider community, and who can be, and indeed is seen as someone who breaks the norms of social co-existence; (2) the 'magical' or 'sorcerer' witch who has a special expertise in one or more magical techniques, and may cure illnesses, divine the future, provide good luck in fortune or love, or wreak the opposite of any of these should circumstance or the witch's wishes seem to require it; and (3) the 'supernatural' or 'night' witch who appears during the hours of darkness and attacks human beings or animals

---

8 'Whatever the intricacies of its vocabulary demonology was, therefore, a form of natural knowledge – to be exact, a form of natural philosophy specialising in preternatural phenomena', Clark: *Thinking With Demons*, 161. Cf. 'One of the principal aims of demonological enquiry was precisely that of establishing what was supernatural and what was not; and there was scarcely an author who did not state categorically that demonism was an aspect of the natural world. The devil lacked just those powers to overrule the laws of nature that constituted truly miraculous agency', *Ibid.*, 168.

9 See Favret-Saada: *Deadly Words*, 70–1.

out of simple maleficence.[10] Now, if we return to the five examples of witchcraft I gave above and compare them with these three types, it is clear that each belongs to category 2. Does this mean that the 'witchcraft' with which the local minister and elders and then the justice deputes and assizes were faced was what is often referred to as 'folk' or 'popular' magic: and if so, is there a distinction between 'popular magic' and 'witchcraft': and if so, what would it have been that caused the operations of which these panels were accused to be labelled 'witchcraft' rather than 'magic', and the operator 'witch' rather than 'magician'?[11]

It is worth noting here that the trial-records of those accused of being witches regularly indict them not merely of witchcraft but at the least of sorcery and witchcraft, and in the sixteenth century the records actually make a list of the separate magical offences. Thus, Elizabeth Dunlop was accused in 1576 of "sorcery, witchcraft, incantations, and invocations of spirits of the Devil, dealing with charms, [and] abusing the people thereby", an echo of the wording of the 1563 Witchcraft Act which distinguished "witchcraft, sorcery, [and] necromancy".[12] By the seventeenth century this had become formulaic. "Ye and ilk ane of yow ar endyted and accused fforsameikle as (*in as much as*) notwithstanding both be the divyne law of the omnipotent and almyghty god and be the lawes and actis of parliament of this kingdome the cryme of sorcirie and witchcraft is expreslie forbidden and discharged", etc.[13] The offence is always expressed in the singular: the *crime* of sorcery and witchcraft *is* . . . So these two were clearly regarded as one. Is "sorcery and witchcraft", then, merely lawyers' verbosity, or does the phrase represent a real distinction,

---

10 *Between the Living and the Dead*, 10–11. Obviously, these categories are not hard and fast, and a witch may be seen to have occupied any or all of them at any given time. Witches may also be subdivided further according to their activities. When it comes to witches who attack children, for example, Kieckhefer gives us (a) witches as vampires who kill children by sucking away their blood; (b) conspiratorial witches who take children's bodies to the Sabbat and there eat them in an act of gratuitous malice and blasphemy, a malice arising from their common, sectarian desire to subvert humanity's impulse to goodness and thus to increase the amount of evil in the world; and (3) maleficent witches who simply do harm to children or kill them by bewitchment, 'Avenging the blood of children', in Ferreiro: *The Devil, Heresy, and Witchcraft in the Middle Ages*, 94–108.

11 All kinds of caveats are required here, of course. The essential point is to recognise that even during the sixteenth century the understanding of 'witch' and 'witchcraft' was fluid and that when panels accused of this crime appeared before the courts, there could be a multiplicity of definitions at work, which might well lead to misapprehension by everyone involved of what was the actual crime for which the panel was standing trial.

12 *JC* 2/1. folio 18. *APS* 2.539. Cf. the cases of Violet Mar in 1577 (*JC2/1*, folio 70) and of Alison Pearson in 1588 (*JC2/2*. folio 104).

13 *JC2/10*, folio 21v. Almost all seventeenth-century witchcraft dittays follow this pattern of wording.

recognisable in law as well as recognised by the community, between Type 2 (the sorcerer-witch) and Types 1 and 3 (the social and night witches)? Should this turn out to be the case, we shall have to examine very closely the offences alleged against the panel in any trial for witchcraft in order to see whether they give any indication that the assize was aware of this possible distinction, or whether 'official' demonological theory (which was very specific about those activities which constituted 'witchcraft') was regulating the basis for and conduct of the judicial proceedings.[14]

But to return to the notion of witchcraft as an exercise of preternatural power: let us note first the intensely personal nature of this kind of magic. An act of magic is triggered by a strong emotional response to what is seen as an adverse situation, and the responder feels, for some reason, that he or she can best react to it by having recourse to preternatural means rather than or as well as natural. Preternatural action in such a situation is therefore merely the alternative to natural. It is the strong emotion of those involved which impels them to choose the former over or in addition to the latter. Nevertheless, to approach a practitioner of magic for some kind of answer or response to one's problem is to admit that one is inferior to him or her in power, and the subsequent obligation therefore involves a gain of some kind to one party and a loss of some kind to the other. It may be status or 'face'; but more importantly, it may be a gain or loss of power itself. For perceived ability to work magic is increased with every magical act requested or performed, while the request for such an act weakens the person who asks by exposing his or her weakness and thus exposing him or her to the possibility of future bewitchment and thus domination. As Favret-Saada observes, "Any kind of contact between the strong and the weak . . . whether it operates through speech, sight, or touch, provides a loss of force or wealth in the bewitched".[15] Hence, perhaps, the unwillingness of people to respond favourably to a witch's request for bread, milk, soup, money, and so forth. It is not so much a refusal of charity as an unwillingness to create the means whereby the witch may establish some kind of physical contact with the person she means to bewitch.[16]

---

14 It may be useful here to note that the frequent distinction between witchcraft as a preternatural power inherent in an individual, often inherited, and activated by that person's malicious thoughts, and sorcery as a set of magical skills which can be learned, is not applicable to Scottish witchcraft. Nor, indeed, is it universally true of witches and sorcerers, anyway. See the warning reservations made by Sanders: *A Deed Without A Name*, 18–19.
15 *Op.cit.*, 112.
16 Since most of those accused of witchcraft were indeed women, from now on I shall tend to identify the witch as a female, merely in order to avoid having to qualify the gender each time the word 'witch' is mentioned. Men, however, were also tried for witchcraft or the operation of various types of magic in Scotland throughout the sixteenth and seventeenth centuries.

Now, no one will attract the hostile epithet 'witch' as the result of a single occurrence of misfortune. A single illness, whether of human beings or of animals, a single loss of crops, a single unfortunate death, a single injury or storm or failure in business, constitutes no more than a piece of bad luck and is commented upon as such. What indicates the presence of a magical attack is the observation that such events are falling into a pattern which is repeated over and over again during a long period of time, and is "always unexpected, always inexplicable".[17] Indeed, it is a constant feature of witchcraft dittays that the accusations frequently stretch back over many years – ten, twenty, even thirty. The panel has not suddenly acquired a reputation. It is something which has been growing in her community during an extended period sometimes amounting to what may have been a third or perhaps even a half of the witch's lifetime.[18]

After a while, then, someone in the local community decides to attach the label 'witch' to this operator of preternatural or magical power. This explains why a previous set of determinant indicators fails to provide a satisfactory definition for the word 'witch'. 'Witch' is a designation attached to a particular individual by some person or persons in a particular community at a time of the sufferer's choosing and for reasons peculiar to that sufferer's circumstances; and these may or may equally not coincide with learned expectations of what it is a witch is supposed to be and do. The word 'witch', however, satisfies what the designator sees as the requirements of the situation and describes the operator in accordance with the designator's newly acquired point of view.[19] Two consequences follow. First, the witch acquires a reputation which is now openly expressed, whether the label 'witch' is given derisively in flyting (as frequently happened), or deliberately by someone who has decided that her/his sequence of misfortunes is no longer explicable by unhappy coincidence but is due to an individual's malefice. Secondly, upon attachment of the label 'witch', the power the witch exercises ceases to be undifferentiated 'magic' and becomes, specifically, 'witchcraft'. The exercise of this newly designated magical power, however, and the receipt of its consequences are likely still to remain a private matter since bewitchment represents dominance of the weak-but-good by the strong-but-wicked, and the weak will not be willing to challenge the strong until there has

17 Favret-Saada, 6, 67–8.
18 Cf. Favret-Saada, 59–60.
19 Cf. Larner: 'Witchcraft is the labelling theorist's dream. It would not have been possible to commit secret acts of witchcraft without prior public recognition of the witch's powers. There was no such thing as a single act of witchcraft committed by a person not recognised as having special powers, and recognition came with multiple acts of witchcraft *socially identified as such*. The crime was that of being a witch. *Being a witch was entirely a matter of social recognition*', *Witchcraft and Religion*, 29–30. [My italics.]

been sufficient of a psychological shift in their appreciation of their relationship with the strong to make them think that they have reached a point at which they, or someone else on their behalf, can exercise a counter-power strong enough to overcome that of the person oppressing them magically.

This moment is likely to come when the witch has gone too far, has challenged the individual's or community's patience once too often, presumed too much on her control of the situation. *Hybris*, therefore, precipitates the witch's downfall.[20] The counter-power may be that of another witch, asked by an individual to remove a particular bewitchment. It may be that of the Church in the person of the priest who can offer a variety of counter remedies: saying Mass, giving a blessing, performing an exorcism, sprinkling holy water, touching with a relic, and so on; or it may be the power of the Kirk exercised through prayer and exhortation to suffer in silence and trust to the goodness of God. One may observe of this last, principally passive option, however, that if all the Kirk offers by way of suggestion or help is such prayer and exhortation, it is more likely that the sufferer will want to take the initiative and do something he/she sees as positive to prosecute his/her own active counter-magical steps against the witch while at the same time being prepared to make an official complaint to the minister and apparently accepting his non-magical solutions.

Once the complainant resorts to Church or State, however, the witch will pass from the relative safety of the silence and fear of her local community into a realm she may not understand and which does not operate according to the conventions which have hitherto worked in her favour. The major difference is that a kirk session or a court of law requires a legal definition of her offences. Now, exercising preternatural power cannot of itself be deemed a crime, for if God has created laws in nature, it is possible quite legitimately to discover what those laws are and how they operate, even if the result may seem extraordinary to those who do not understand how the *mirum* is done. Consequently, if one wishes to prosecute a witch one must provide a definition of her exercise of preternatural power, which does not consist of features present in other types of the exercise of preternatural power: and this is what the lawyers and demonologists sought to do. One may compare the necessity to distinguish between 'killing' and 'murder'. Not all killing is murder. What is more, killing of one kind or another is an everyday occurrence. Swatting a fly, destroying a wasp or moth with insecticide or rats with poison, slaughtering animals for food, putting down terminally sick

---

20 Cf., *mutatis mutandis*, Gentilcore: 'The fact that a group of people charge a
    certain priest with drinking, gambling, and womanising does not necessarily mean
    that such behaviour was not tolerated in ecclesiastics. There are occasions when
    an accumulation of misdeeds breaks the tolerance of the parish or community
    concerned', *From Bishop to Witch*, 45.

or injured animals, abortion, suicide, turning off life-support machines, injuring someone fatally in traffic accidents – all these are types of killing. All are socially accepted, even if some are not socially approved: but none of them is illegal.

But a legal definition of witchcraft, whether that definition be ecclesiastical or civil, may not – indeed often does not – coincide with the perception of witchcraft by the witch herself or by the community in which she has been living. Now the Church or State will always define witchcraft as the aggressive exercise of malevolent magic (hence the attribute 'diabolical'), because the Church or State is seeking to define a *crime*. In the context of a tacit complicity between the witch and her community, however, such a definition is limited and partial, for in such a case, because the witch is someone who has the ability to exercise preternatural power, use of this power may be sought by those who do not have it for a variety of purposes, beneficent as well as malign. Therefore, when the witch comes to court and faces her accusers and her judges, she is looking not at people who do not understand what she has been doing, but at people who have, for reasons connected with fear and perhaps intellectual disapproval, decided to shut their eyes and ears to all but the narrowest legal interpretation of both her conduct and her motives, although her assize may not be so prejudiced that its members are unable to find her innocent of some or all of the charges brought against her. Indeed, it was often the case they declared the panel 'clengit'.

Finally, it must be remembered that in every European society of this period there existed a constant level of magical activity, whether learned or traditional, which everyone took for granted. Their *mentalité* was attuned to an expectation that preternatural power both could and would manifest itself in a thousand different ways, from the influence of the planets upon herbs and stones and metals, to the heavenly warnings conveyed by ghosts and comets, and the alarming appearance of unforeseen sickness or inexplicable death. Therefore when the kirk session or the magistrate's court was presented with a witch and multiple evidences of her witchcraft, its members may have been disconcerted or fearful or filled with righteous anger: but they would not have been surprised.

Sìthean

Belief in a preternatural race of beings commonly known as *sìthean* in Gaelic and as *fairies* in English was widespread in Scotland, as indeed elsewhere, during the sixteenth century and contributed significant details to certain trials for witchcraft. The word 'fairy', however, is nowadays more or less inseparable from certain visual images seen most vividly in the pictures of Richard Dadd and the forged photographs from Cottingham, so unhappily authenticated by Conan Doyle; and variants upon the theme, such as elves, goblins, brownies, wee folk, and so on are equally freighted. To avoid these associations, therefore, I shall choose to employ the Gaelic word except in quotations where the English word must, of necessity, remain.[21]

A useful summary of beliefs about the *sithean* was compiled, probably during the winter of 1691, by the minister of Aberfoyle, Robert Kirk, who seems to have been stimulated by the sceptical views of an English bishop to record those details he had absorbed from his Highland parishioners. The relevant passages are as follows:

[The *sithean*] are said to be of a midle stature betwixt man and Angell (as were daemons thought to be of old); of intelligent Studious Spirits, and light changable bodies (like those called Astrall) somewhat of the nature of a condens'd cloud, and best seen in twilight . . . They are distributed in Tribes and Orders; and have children, Nurses, mareiages, deaths and burials, in appearance even as wee . . . Their houses are called large and fair, and (unless at som odd occasions) unperceivable by vulgar eyes . . . women are yet alive who tell they were taken away when in Child-bed to nurse ffayrie Children, a lingring voracious image of theirs being left in their place[22] . . . The Tramontanes,[23] to this day, put bread, the Bible, or a piece of iron, in womens bed when travelling[24] to save them from being thus stolen . . . Their apparell and speech is like that of the people and countrey under which they live . . . They are said to have Aristocratical Rulers and Laws, but no discernible Religion, Love or Devotione towards God the Blessed Maker of all. They disappear whenever they hear his name invoked, or the name of Jesus . . . There be manie places called Fayrie hills, which the mountain-people think impious and dangerous to peel or discover, by taking

21 There are several different terms in Gaelic to describe these and other supernatural beings. A useful summary is given in Thomson: *The Supernatural Highlands*, 101–33. In Lewis, the *sithean* are known as 'Finlay's people' (*muinntir Fhionlaigh*). Cf. the traditional name 'Finn' for witches in Orkney and Shetland, Marwick: *The Folklore of Orkney and Shetland*, 48.

22 Cf. T. Pennant, writing of Banff in 1769: 'children are watched till the christening is over, least they should be stole, or changed', *A Tour In Scotland*, 101. Buchan: *Folk Tradition*, 83–5.

23 Kirk's term for Highlanders.

24 I.e. during childbirth. The custom of leaving a piece of iron in the bed lasted well into the nineteenth century, as James Napier records. 'When writing of fairies I noticed a practice common in some localities of placing in the bed where lay an expectant mother, a piece of cold iron to scare the fairies, and prevent them from spiriting away mother and child to elf-land. An instant of this spiriting away at the time of child-bearing is said to have occurred in Arran within these fifty years', *Folk Lore*, 29.

earth or wood from them; superstitiously beleiving the souls of their predecessors to dwell there.[25]

In several essential details, then, *sithean* were not so very different, at first glance, from human beings. They were of human height – not very tall and certainly not 'wee'[26] – wore the same kind of clothes as were worn by those they encountered, and spoke not in a strange or untoward tongue, but in the language of the area in which they appeared. Therefore a meeting between a human and a *sith* might not produce any immediate feelings of fear or sensation of displacement such as one might expect between two people of different orders of creation; and the encounter might well be described by the human participant in terms similar to those he or she would employ for speaking about a meeting with a stranger or slight acquaintance. So it is interesting to note that exactly the same matter-of-fact tone can be heard in the evidence given by several witches of their first encounter with Satan.

But belief in, or at least acceptance of, the notion of *sithean*, like the acceptance of magic and the apparent powers of witches, was not confined to the commons. William Dunbar, for example, wrote a poem, 'The Tretis of the Tua Mariit Wemen and the Wedow', for recitation at the court of James IV at

25 *The Secret Commonwealth*, 2–3, 5–7, 12. Kirk, it should be added, was well able to understand what his parishioners were telling him, since he had the Gaelic and indeed produced a metrical Gaelic version of the Psalms in 1684, the first work for which he became famous. See also Sutherland: *Ravens and Black Rain*, 53. The word *sith* comes from Irish *sidh* meaning 'fairy hill', and is cognate with the Latin *sedes* = 'seat' or 'dwelling-place'. *Sithean* are therefore spirits to be found within hills, and are a form of *dei terreni*, 'divinities of the earth'. Cf. Martin: 'They had a Universal Custom, of powring a Cows Milk upon a little Hill, or big Stone where the Spirit call'd *Browny* was believed to lodge', *A Description of the Western Isles of Scotland*, 110. Cf. Sutherland: *op.cit.*, 20. Belief in *sithean*, however, was not limited to the Highlands and Islands. Bessie Dunlop, for example, who was tried for witchcraft in 1576, came from Ayrshire, Alison Pearson, who was tried in 1588, came from Fife, and Andrew Man, who was tried in 1597, came from Aberdeenshire.

26 Martin on the brownie: 'This Spirit always appeared in the shape of a Tall Man having very long brown Hair', *loc. cit. supra*. The particular tasks associated with the brownie (Gaelic *gruanach*) include guarding the herds and flocks and performing various household chores. D. Monro, who was High Dean of the Isles, and travelled through most of them in 1549, records an intriguing piece of archaeology: 'At the north poynt of Lewis there is a little ile, callit the Pigmies ile, with ane little kirk in it of ther awn handey wark, within this kirk the ancients of that countrey of the Lewis says, that the saids Pigmies has been eirdit thair, maney men of divers countreys has delvit dieplie the flure of the litle kirk, and I myselve amanges the leave, and hes found in it, deepe under the erthe, certain baines and round heads of wonderfull little quantity, allegit to be the baines of the said Pigmies', *Description of the Western Isles of Scotland*, 37. Monro does not suggest that these bones were in any way those of preternatural beings, but it is always possible that something of the kind gave rise at some point to the notion of 'wee folk' in connection with *sithean*.

the end of the fifteenth century, and it is clear from his description of these three women that the audience is to recognise them as *sithean*.

I saw thre grat ladeis sit in ane grene arbeir,
All grathit in to garlandis of fresche gudlie flouris;
So glitterit as the gold wert thair glorius gilt tressis,
Quhill all the gressis did gleme of the glaid hewis;
Kemmit was thair cleir hair, and curiouslie sched
Attour thair schulderis doun schyre, schyning full bricht;
With curches, cassin thair abone, of kirsp cleir and thin:
Thair mantillis grein war as the gress that grew in May sessoun.

The green clothing immediately suggests *sithean*, since green is their especial colour, and the ladies are depicted sitting within a green arbour enclosed by hawthorn trees, a significant detail, for the hawthorn would have indicated that the arbour was a magical spot, the hawthorn being the *sithean*'s own tree with something of their double-edged powers of curing and killing.[27]

More explicit is a verse by Alexander Montgomery in his *Flyting*, part of a poetic quarrel with Sir Patrick Hume of Polwarth, a gentleman of the bedchamber to James VI, intended again as entertainment for the Court. The poem was produced c.1580 and proved popular with the young King who quoted from it twice in later years in his essay on versification. The verse in question is well known:

Into the hinderend of harvest, on ane alhallow evin,
When our goode nichtbouris ryddis, if I reid richt,
Sum buklit on ane bunwyd and sum on ane bene,
Ay trippand in trowpis fra the twie-licht;
Sum saidlit ane scho aip all grathit into grene,
Sum hobling on hempstaikis, hovand on hicht.
The king of pharie, with the court of the elph quene
With mony alrege incubus, ryddand that nicht.
Thair ane elph, and ane aip ane unsell begate,
    In ane peitpot by Powmathorne;
That brachart in ane buss wes borne;
They fand ane monstour on the morne,
    War facit nor ane cat.[28]

27 See Hope: *A Midsummer Eve's Dream*, 14, 18, 20–1. Hope prints both the text and an English translation of the poem, 270–299. The verses quoted here are 17–25. The poem belongs to a genre known as 'elrich'. See Bawcutt: 'Elrich fantasyis in Dunbar and other poets', 163–78.

28 For the text, see Bawcutt & Riddy: *Longer Scottish Poems*, 282. See also Simpson: 'The weird sisters wandering', 9.

Evidence from flytings, of course, must be treated with care. They were carefully crafted poetic exercises intended to be full of coarse invective while at the same time demonstrating the author's sophisticated command of alliteration and rhyme, not historical or sociological records of cultural phenomena. But what gives both Montgomery's *Flyting* and Dunbar's *Tretis* (similarly bawdy in tone and brilliant in execution) their peculiar tone is the presence in both of *sithean* – and of witches, too, in Montgomery – which were intended to engender in their audience a frisson of recognition; for, in spite of the courtly laughter, there can have been few, if any, present who did not accept the reality of the preternatural world, even if they did not approve of or feel comfortable with some of the ways in which that world was likely to manifest its existence;[29] and Simpson makes an observation which applies equally to Dunbar's poem and to Montgomery's *Flyting*: "There is no undertone of mockery, patronage, or blame directed against the beliefs themselves and those who might hold them. The poem thus operates within a shared culture which appears to override any distinction between 'elite' and 'folk'".[30]

James VI himself, however, did not remain insouciant on the subject of *sithean*. After he had been frightened by the magical attempts on his life in 1590, he seems to have come to the conclusion that *sithean* were actually evil spirits whose purpose was to deceive and ruin those human beings with whom they came into contact:

> Although in my discourseing of them, I devyde them in divers kindes, yee must notwithstanding there of note my Phrase of speaking in that: For doubtleslie they are in effect, but all one kinde of spirites, who for abusing the more of mankinde, takes on these sundrie shapes, and uses diverse formes of out-ward actiones, as if some were of nature better then other . . . That fourth kinde of spirites, which by the Gentiles was called *Diana*, and her wandring court, and amongst us was called the Phairie . . . or our good neighboures, was one of the sortes of *illusiones* that was rifest in the time of *Papistrie*: for although it was holden odious to Prophesie by the devill, yet whome these kinde of Spirites carried awaie, and informed, they were thought to be sonsiest and of best life.[31]

---

29 Cf. the censorious view, recorded by Gavin Douglas in the prologue to his translation of the sixth Book of Vergil's *Aeneid*:
   All is bot gaistis and elrich fantasyis,
   Of browneis and of bogillis ful this buke:
   Owt on thir wandrand speritis, wow! thou cryis;
   It semys a man war mangit, tharon list luke,
   Lyke dremys or dotage in the monys cruke,
   Vayn superstitionys agaynst our richt beleve, 17–22.
30 *Art. cit. supra*, 18.
31 *Daemonologie*, 57, 73–4.

There are themes here which we shall examine in more detail later; but James's evident hostility to the notion of the existence of *sìthean* is not necessarily evidence of non-belief on his part. It may be, rather, a kind of defiant whistling to try to reassure himself that these things were not real, for the North Berwick episode of the winter of 1590 had a profound effect on the King's psychology, and although it was not permanent, it lasted long enough to colour the final years of his reign in Edinburgh. We must also bear in mind, of course, that James was a Lowlander and may simply not have understood, or even known, the Highland conception of *sìthean*. Moreover, his published views on fairies may have been influenced, and indeed anglicised, by his reading of those of Reginald Scot, since he claims to have read Scot's *Discoverie* in preparation for writing his own witchcraft tract.

If James, then, had not been too disturbed by the notion of *sìthean* before 1590, or even if he had been disinclined to believe in their existence or at least in the preternatural powers attributed to them, he seems to have changed his mind once evidence of a widespread magical plot against his life had come to light. For it is not so much the existence of the *sìthean* themselves which the King denies as the tales told about them by "sundry simple creatures" and "sundry witches" which the King cannot bring himself to accept, even though he had no difficulty in believing the other tales they told about trying to raise a storm at sea by magic with a view to causing him and his Queen to drown, or making a wax image of him which would kill him by sympathetic magic as it melted before a fire. Under the circumstances, then, James's dismissal of what he was told about the *sìthean* seems to contain an element of racial prejudice. James, in common with many Lowlanders, tended to regard the Highlands and Islands as an impoverished area much in need of civilisation, and the linguistic divide between the Gaidhealtachd and the Lowlands emphasised all kinds of differences, making it a part of the kingdom with which James and his Lowland courtiers preferred not to become better acquainted if they could help it. The King's attitude towards the Highlands and Highlanders may be gauged from remarks he later addressed to Prince Charles: "As for the heelandes, I shortleie comprehende thaime all in tua sortis of peopill the ane that duellis in our maine land that are barbarouse and yett mixed with sum shaw of civilitie . . . I have begunne in plaunting colonies amongst thame [the islands] of aunserable inlandis subjects, that within shorte tyme maye roote thaime out and plaunte civilitie in thair roumes".[32] The prejudice against Highlanders and Islanders was not new, however, nor was it peculiar to James, as is evident from at least as early as the fourteenth century.[33] But both it, and

32 *Basilikon Doron* 1.70–1.
33 See Whyte: *Scotland's Society*, 94–6.

James's lack of Gaelic, may help to account for the tone of *de haut en bas* he adopts when discussing popular beliefs about the *sìthean*.

Most Scots, however, did not adopt James's nervous repudiation of fairy belief and thought it best to treat the *sìthean* with some degree of caution. Evidences of this can be found right up to the twentieth century. *Sìthean* might lurk in coalmines for, as one miner in Whitehaven told Thomas Pennant, although he himself had never met any of them, "his grandfather had found the little implements and tools belonging to this diminutive race of subterraneous spirits".[34] Old women on Jura kept sticks of the wicken tree or mountain ash to protect themselves against *sìthean*,[35] and in 1664 it was recorded that an Orcadian was in possession of a girdle called an 'elf-belt' whose purpose seems to have been to protect the wearer against such supernatural beings, and the presbytery which had uncovered the case wanted the belt destroyed because it was an object of superstition.[36] *Sìthean* were known to carry off newborn human babies and leave changelings in their place; a cradle song well-known throughout the Highlands and Islands records the lament of a mother whose child the *sìthean* have stolen: "O I searched the hill from end to end, from side to side, to the edge of the streams . . . [but] I did not find my Cùbhrachan".[37] Small wonder, then, if Gaels were heard to utter the prayer, "Crìosd eadar mi 's na sìdh" [Christ be between me and the fairies.] and begged God to "preserve the old and the young, our wives and our children, our sheep and our cattle, from the power and from the dominion of the fairies (*cheannas nan sithichean*), and from the malice of every evil eye".[38]

Some of this nervousness may have been connected with the belief that there was a close link between the *sìthean* and witches. David Rorie in the early years of the twentieth century noted in 1909 that "In Aberdeenshire of old days red worsted would be tied round a child's wrist to keep away the 'witches'. The chief thing, however, for the latter purpose was the little heart-shaped silver 'witch-brooch'. It was pinned to the child's underclothing at its first dressing. The shape was probably derived from its being originally the mounting of an 'elf shot' or 'fairy dart', i.e. flint arrow head. An old man in Kincardinshire some thirty years ago had such a 'fairy dart' which he kept as a safeguard against warlocks and witches. It would lose all efficacy if allowed to touch the ground, and in showing it he always held his hands below those of the person looking at it, in great anxiety lest it should fall".[39] This connection

34 *Tour of Scotland*, 49.
35 Pennant: *op.cit.*, 215.
36 *CH* 2/1081/3.
37 Shaw: *Folksongs and Folklore of South Uist*, 166–7.
38 Carmichael: *Carmina Gadelica* 5.250–1. Beith: *Healing Threads*, 126.
39 See Buchan: *Folk Tradition*, 45.

between *sithean* and witches was important, as several early accounts of witchcraft trials describe meetings of humans with what the records describe as 'evil spirits' or 'the Devil' but which sound much more like encounters with *sithean*. It is a point to which we shall return in due course.

Charming and Curing

"Charms, casting nativities, curing diseases by inchantments, Fortune-telling", observed Shaw in 1775, "were common practised and firmly believed"; and in the previous year, the Reverend George Low went on a tour of the Shetland islands, which clearly demonstrated that Shaw's past tense was unwarranted, for there was plenty of evidence that such beliefs were still alive and active.

"The people of Hoy", he wrote, "are very much given to superstition, and an universal belief of witchcraft prevails among them, which by no arguments can be rooted out even from among people otherwise not a little sagacious. They put a great deal of trust in the cure of diseases by spells and enchantments, also they give great power to witches to inflict these by the same means; and this is not confined to themselves, but extended to their goods and cattle, which they imagine witches have power to hurt, or at least to take away their milk, butter, or cheese, etc., by their magical incantations. They are afraid of hurt either in person or goods from the evil eye,[40] and have particular ceremonies to avert the malignity of it, but pretend to make a mighty mystery of their rites. They also fear an evil tongue, and there are not a few instances of poor creatures falling ill thro' mere imagination upon being cursed by an enemy. Nobody must praise a child or anything they set a value on, for if anything evil afterwards befals it, these poor ignorant creatures will be sure to attribute to the tongue that spoke of it, and very probably quarrel on that account. This they call forespeaking, and pretend to cure persons so forespoken by washing them with a water compounded with great ceremony, the recipe of which our female sages, the only administrators, make an impenetrable secret; however these superstitious notions are not confined to Hoy alone, but are spread up and down the whole country, and to be found more or less in every corner of it".[41]

Low was quite right in thinking that such beliefs were very widespread. They occur over and over again in accusations of witchcraft produced against women and men during the sixteenth and seventeenth centuries, and were clearly common throughout the whole of Lowland Scotland. His observation about the tendency of people forespoken to quarrel is particularly interesting,

---

40 There are many traditional charms intended to counteract the effects of the evil eye. See Carmichael: *Carmina Gadelica* 4.150–83; 5.42–71.
41 Shaw: *History of the Province of Moray*, 307. Low: *Tour*, 6–7.

since one of the most noticeable features of witchcraft dittays is the amount of quarrelling which appears to have occurred, over what was often a very long period of time, between the panel and those who turned up to witness against her. It may, of course, be an indication of a society whose relationships were particularly aggressive; but it may also indicate the constant tension under-lying intercourse between neighbours where one had preternatural powers attributed to her by the other, and the other felt under constant threat from such a neighbour's slightest word or glance, were these good or ill.

One may notice, too, that the counter-charm against forespeaking seemed to be in the hands of women with specialist knowledge.[42] Charming and curing were frequently seen as the preserve of just such individuals. In 1695, Martin Martin noted that the Northern Islanders "have a charm for stopping excessive bleeding, either in man or beast, whether the cause be internal or external; which is performed by sending the name of the patient to the charmer, who adds some more words to it, and after repeating those words the cure is performed, though the charmer be several miles distant from the patient. They have likewise other charms which they use frequently at a distance, and that also with success".[43]

Similarly, Samuel Hibbert noted that "when people are afflicted with consumptive complaints on Zetland, they imagine that the heart of the person so affected has been wasted away by the enchantment of the fairies, or witchcraft of some other evil beings. Old women, and sometimes men, profess to cure this disease. The patient must undergo the following curious and very ridiculous operation: He is directed to sit upon the bottom of a large cooking pot, turned upon its mouth; a large pewter dish is placed, or held upon his head; upon the dish a bason or bowl is set nearly full of cold water; into this water the operator pours some melted lead through the teeth of a common dressing comb. A large key is also employed in this operation. All this is performed with many strange incantations and gesticulations. If the lead falls into a shapeless lump, they declare that the heart and the lungs of the patient are completely wasted away, that they will have infinite trouble, and perhaps, after all, will not be able to bring back the heart and lungs to their natural and healthful form. The lead is again melted, and run into the water through the teeth of the comb; it most likely assumes some shape, which the operator assures the spectators is the exact form of the patient's heart in its diseased

---

42 Such knowledge may or may not be extensive, and possession of such knowledge does not necessarily render its possessor a witch. Cf. Favret-Saada: 'To touch or to encircle the ill is a traditional method of magic healing which theoretically bears no relation to witchcraft . . . Usually the *toucheur* is a simple peasant who has inherited one and only one 'secret' (for example he can cure scurf, but not warts)', *Deadly Words*, 45.
43 *Description of the Western Islands*, 368.

state. The lead is repeatedly melted, and poured through the comb into the water; every time it is asserted to be more and more like the natural heart and lungs, and the bewitchment, of course, is rendered weaker and weaker".[44]

These kinds of unofficial healing along with curses and magic for love and counter-charms were not, of course, confined to the Northern Isles but were in general use all over Scotland[45] (as, indeed, elsewhere), and constitute overwhelmingly the kind of magic which was being practised by specialists and non-specialists alike. On Jura, for example, Pennant noted that "a present was made me of a *clach clun ceilach*, or cock-knee stone, believed to be obtained out of that part of the bird; but I have unluckily forgotten its virtues. Not so with the *clach crubain*, which is to cure all pain in the joints. It is to be presumed that both these amulets have been enchanted".[46] In many places the sick were passed through circles made of a variety of materials. Thus, in November 1597, Janet Stewart from Edinburgh, standing trial with three other women, all four delated of various acts of witchcraft, was charged among other offences that she had cured several women of 'wednonynpha', puerperal fever, "by taking of ane garland of grene wodbynd, and causing of the patient to pass thryise throw it, quhilk thairafter scho cuttit in nyne peices and cast it in the fyre".[47] *Tinneas an rìgh*, scrofula, could be cured by the seventh child of a line of boys or girls, the charm therefor being handed down from one person to another under the greatest secrecy, a magical remedy which was still being used as late as 1932;[48] and in the early nineteenth century pregnant women were still climbing a hill on the east side of Glenavon to sit in the hollow of a huge granite rock, *Clach na bhan*, the woman's stone, in the belief that this would ensure them an easy delivery.[49]

There seems, then, to have been a charm for almost every condition and eventuality, and a counter-charm against almost every type of malefice, and if the records of jaundiced eighteenth- and nineteenth-century travellers in Scotland are filled with so many examples of still extant, still vigorous belief in and practice of exercises in magical power, they are a vivid testimony to that tenacious hold the preternatural world had upon Scottish society, high or low, during the preceding two centuries and beyond.

Very often the charms were accompanied by phrases or petitions clearly

44 *Description of the Shetland Islands*, 603.
45 See, for example, MacKenzie: 'Gaelic incantations', 108–16, 137–47, 151–77. Larner: *Enemies of God*, 139–43.
46 *Tour*, 232. Cf. Martin: 'There is a sort of stone in this island [Berneray], with which the natives frequently rub their breasts by way of prevention, and say it is a good preservative for health', *Description*, 94–5.
47 Pitcairn: *Criminal Trials* 2.27. See also Buchan: *Folk Tradition*, 127–31.
48 Shaw: *Folksongs and Folklore of South Uist*, 49. Cf. Carmichael: *Carmina Gadelica* 4.272–3.
49 MacPherson: *Primitive Beliefs*, 79.

religious in content and origin. Agnes Sampson, for example, was accused of witchcraft and treason in January 1591, and during her trial it was alleged she was accustomed to use the following prayer to heal the sick:

> I trow in Almychtie God that wrocht, Baith heavin and erth and all
>   of nocht,
> In to his deare sone Chryst Jesu, In to that anaplie lord, I trow,
> Wes gottin of the Haly Gaist, Borne of the Virgin Marie,
> Stoppit to heavin, that all weill thane, And sittis att his faderis rycht
>   hand;
> He baid ws cum, and thair to dome Baith quick and deid, as he thocht
>   convene.
> I trow als in the Haly Gaist. In Haly Kirk my hope is maist,
> That halyschip quhair hallowaris winnis, To ask forgevenes of my
>   sinnis,
> And syne to ryis in flesch and bane, The lyffe that newir mair hes gane.
> Thow sayis Lord lovit mocht ye be, That formed and maid mankynd
>   of me.
> Thow cost me on the haly croce, And lent me body, saull and voce,
> And ordanit me to heavinnis bliss; Quhairfore I thank ye Lord of this;
> And all your hallowaris lovit be, To pray to thame to pray to me,
> And keep me fra that sellon sea, And from the syn that saull wald slay.
> Thow Lord for thy bytter passioun in, To keip me frome syn and
>   wardlie schame,
> And endles damnatioune. Grant me the joy newir wilbe gane.
> Sweit Jesus Christus. Amen.[50]

Clearly this is nothing less than a version of the Apostles' Creed, put to magical use in a manner by no means peculiar either to Agnes or to the period in which she lived. Indeed, Agnes appears to have been in possession of more than one such religious invocation, as it is recorded she used another:

> All kindis of illis that ewir may be,
> In Chrystis name I conjure ye,
> I conjure ye baith mair and les
> With all the vertewis of the mes;
> And rycht sa be the naillis sa,
> That haillit Jesus and na ma;
> And rycht sa be the samin blude,
> That raikit owir the ruithfull rude;
> Furth of the flesch and of the bane,

---

50 Pitcairn: *Criminal Trials* 1.2.234.

And in the eird and in the stane,
I conjure ye in Godis name.[51]

Appeals to the Trinity were also common. A conjuration for curing cattle, for example, runs: "I charme thee for arrow-schot, for dor-schot, for womb-schot, for ey-schot, for tung-schote, for lever-schote, for lung-schote, all the maist: in the name of the Father, the Sone, and Haly Gaist"; and in the middle of the seventeenth century we find an accused witch, Isobel Gowdie, confessing to using a charm in which an appeal is made not just to the Trinity, but to the saints as well:

> I forbid the quaking fevers, the sea fevers, the land fevers and all the fevers that ever God ordained, out of the head, out of the heart, out of the back, out of the sides, out of the knees, out of the thighs, from the points of the fingers to the tips of the toes: out shall the fevers go, some to the hill, some to the hap, some to the stone, some to the stock. In Saint Peter's name, Saint Paul's name, and all the saints of Heaven, in the name of the Father, the Son, and the Holy Ghost.[52]

None of this is unusual, even after the Reformation in Scotland, and traditional charms to cure various diseases in both human beings and animals continued regularly to employ the language of Christian prayer and supplication. It was this aspect of 'popular' magic which undoubtedly alarmed and irritated the Church, whether Catholic or reformed, and, as we shall see, most of the magical acts prosecuted before kirk sessions or in the criminal courts were actually acts of 'popular' rather than 'diabolical' magic, although the authorities tended to interpret the former as the latter. Whether they were more exercised by the intermingling of magic and Christianity or whether, after the Reformation, they were more disturbed by continuing evidence of Catholic terminology and

---

51 Pitcairn: *op.cit.* supra, 237.
52 Pitcairn: 2.536, the trial of Bartie Paterson, 16 December, 1607. Another of Paterson's cures recommended that the patient say, 'I lift this watter, in the name of the Father, Sone, and Haly Gaist, to do guid for thair helth for quhom it is liftit', *Ibid.* Cf. an English charm against toothache, from the revenue books of Sir Thomas Stanley and his wife, Margaret, Countess of Richmond (modernised): 'I conjure the tooth, after touching it three times in the name of the Father and the Son and the Holy Ghost together in the Trinity, three persons in one God, that the ache go away and never return, nor have power in the said tooth again', Westminster Abbey Muniments 32407, folio 19. Isobel Gowdie: *JC* 2/10. Cf. the charm of William Kerow from Elgin against various kinds of fever: 'The quaquand fever and the trembling fever, and the sea fever and the land fever, bot and the head fever and the hart fever, and all the feveris that God creatit. In Sanct Johnne's name, Sanct Peteris name, and all the sancts of heavin's name, our Lord Jesus Crystis name', Cramond: *Records of Elgin* 2.182. Cf. also Carmichael: *Carmina Gadelica* 4.194–279, 280–313; 5.2–21, 72–3. McKenzie: "Gaelic incantations', 131–47.

sentiment is perhaps a moot point, and examination of the details of dittays in trials for witchcraft may help to throw some light on this particular question.

Magical Wells

An example of the kind of belief and practice the authorities were keen to see diminish and disappear was the resort to wells whose water was credited with healing or preternatural powers. Martin noted that on Harris there was a well in the machair, which was reckoned to be efficacious against colics, stitches, and gravel; while several wells on Skye were believed to remove various kinds of illness.[53] Innis Maree had a holy well belonging to Saint Maelrubha, which could cure cases of lunacy (as did that of Saint Fillan in Strathfillan), and also of epilepsy; the holy pool of Loch Earn at the foot of Dùn Fhaolain was visited by barren women hoping to conceive, and by people suffering from rheumatism; and the Black Isle still has many healing wells, all decorated with strips of cloth left by grateful pilgrims.[54] Nor were such wells restricted to the Highlands and Islands. They were to be found, for example, in Canisbay, the isle of Eigg, Culloden, Speyside, Fyvie, Menteith, Falkirk, Inverness, and in many places in Fife.[55] In other words, visiting magical wells was a custom spread all over Scotland and one which the reformed Kirk especially found very distasteful: so much so, in fact, that on 29 November, 1581 Parliament passed an Act against "pilgramage to chappellis, wellis and croces, and the superstitious observing of divers uther papisticall rytes". Such pilgrimages were now forbidden as "the dregges of Idolatrie", under penalty of heavy fines for offenders, and a commission was issued especially to find out and arrest anyone who might continue to practise these customs.[56] The Catholic

53 *Description*, 33, 141. Cf. 'St. Andrew's Well in the Village *Shadar* [on Lewis] is by the vulgar Natives made a Test to know if a sick Person will die of the Distemper he labours under: they send one with a wooden Dish to bring some of the water to the Patient, and if the Dish which is then laid softly upon the surface of the Water turn round Sun-ways, they conclude that the Patient will recover of that Distemper; but if otherwise, that he will die', *Ibid.*, 7–8.

54 See Beith: *Healing Threads*, 138–42. Many more examples can be found in MacPherson: *Primitive Beliefs*, 37–60.

55 MacLeod Banks: *British Calendar Customs: Scotland* 1.125–70. Simpkins: *County Folk-Lore* 7.12–17. *Records of the Presbytery of Inverness*, 88.

56 *APS* 3.212. The Act had no lasting effect, for in 1629 the Privy Council had to issue a violent denunciation of the practice of resorting 'in pilgrimages to chappellis and wellis, which is so frequent and common in this kingdome', and again provided a commission to have diligent search made 'at all such pairts and places where this idolatrous superstition is used: and to take and apprehend all suche persons of whatsomever rank and qualitie, whom they sall deprehend going in pilgrimage to chappellis and wellis, or whome they sall know thameselffes to be guiltie of that cryme, and to commit thame to waird', *RPC* 2nd series, 3.241. Cf. *Ibid.*, 264, 324. On 27 May, 1643 the Synod of Argyll noted that inquiry was being made 'whether the presbytery of Dumbarton was advertised to ditt up and demolish the well at Longlochshead conforme to the act of the former meeting', *Minutes of the Synod of Argyll*, 67.

Church, on the other hand, sometimes took a different course, by consecrating with Christian ritual a place which had evidently long been regarded as a source of magical import. Thus, Martin records that on Eigg "in the Village on the South Coast of this Isle there is a Well, call'd St. *Kathrine's* Well. The Natives have it in great esteem and believe it to be a *Catholicon* for Diseases. They told me that it had been such ever since it was Consecrated by one Father *Hugh*, a Popish Priest, in the following manner. He obliged all the Inhabitants to come to this Well, and then imploy'd them to bring together a great heap of Stones at the head of the Spring, by way of Pennance; this being done, he said Mass at the Well, and then Consecrated it; he gave each of the Inhabitants a piece of wax Candle, which they lighted, and all of them made the *Dessil*, of going round the Well Sunways, the Priest leading them".[57]

Second Sight and Divination

Second sight was explained by Martin as "a single Faculty of Seeing an otherwise invisible Object, without any previous Means us'd by the Person that sees it for that end; the Vision makes such a lively impression upon the Seer, that they neither see nor think of any thing else, except the Vision, as long as it continues; and then they appear Pensive or Jovial, according to the object which was represented to them".[58] Dalyell puts it more rhetorically but with greater detail: "[Second sight is] an intus-susception of transient events, at a distance from the seer, not unlike a reverie occupying the mind in a moment of abstraction . . . In the stricter acceptation of this faculty, co-temporary objects and incidents are beheld at the time, however remote their locality, but neither those which have passed, nor those which have yet to come. If extending to futurity, the subject of the vision is about to be realised. Therefore the second sight only borders on prognostication".[59] A modern definition, given to someone with second sight, expresses it simply as "a premonition of a death that's going to occur".[60] This last gets to the heart of the faculty, for most of the anecdotes told to illustrate the working of the gift involve premonition of death,[61] and Dalyell's attempt to suggest that second sight can be dissected into several parts of which prognostication is not the principal is not altogether happy,

---

57 *Description*, 277.
58 *Description*, 300. This is followed by a very large number of illustrative examples referring principally to persons on Skye, 300–34.
59 *Darker Superstitions of Scotland*, 467.
60 MacDonald: *Island Voices*, 163.
61 Thus, to give only one example, Pennant records that 'my informant said that Lauchlan MacKerran of Cannay [Canna] had told a gentleman that he could not rest for the noise he heard of hammering of nails into his coffin: accordingly the gentleman died within fifteen days', *Tour*, 244. Cf. his example from Skye, 310–11.

because foreseeing and thus being able to foretell is precisely what someone with the gift is able to do.

Dalyell has, however, noted an important point about second sight in his comments on seeing co-temporary objects and incidents, for 'second sight' is actually a slight misnomer. In Gaelic it is called *dà shealladh* which means 'two sights', implying that the envisioner has the ability to see in two different worlds, either the one immediately present to his or her physical sight, or this physical world and another co-existent with it, the world of spirits and the dead.[62] This ability is not restricted to one sex or the other, nor to people of a certain age. Martin noted that the ability was possessed by children and animals, as well as by men and women of advanced years;[63] and a modern source says it can take the form of a smell as well as a sight: "When I was young I could smell death when I walked through the door of a house. I could smell it straight away. I'd feel sick until I came back out. Many's the time I went into a house and had difficulty in controlling myself".[64]

Sometimes it is difficult to know whether the action of a witch is the record of second sight or of sorcery. It was alleged of Beatrix Leslie in 1661, for example, that she came to the house of John Wathenstone at noon, urinated in front of the fire, and said, "There shall be fewer folk here ere long". A week later, the house caught fire and John was told what Beatrix had done when she visited; at which he became very distressed and said, "My well days are done", and fell very ill, during which time he attempted more than once to take his own life. His wife watched him carefully and five times prevented him from committing suicide, but a year later, when she left the house for only a short time, she found on her return that he had hanged himself.[65] Was the act of urination a maleficent ritual intended to set the house on fire? It seems very unlikely and there is no precedent for such a piece of magic's being employed for such a purpose. It is more probable that the urination was no more than an act of relief, here recorded because the witnesses have included it in their statements. But the fact that Beatrix stood before the fire and then made her prognostication, after which a fire broke out and the man of the house became

---

62 See further Thompson: *The Supernatural Highlands*, 45–6. Sutherland: *Ravens and Black Rain*, 33–4. Dalyell is also correct, although he does not express it very clearly, in identifying second sight as involving several paranormal phenomena such as clairvoyance, telepathy, pre- and retrocognition.

63 *Description*, 306. He goes on to give an example: 'I was present in a House where a Child cried out of a suddain, and being ask'd the reason of it, he answer'd that he had seen a great white thing lying on a Board which was in the Corner . . . and accordingly [the board] was made into a Coffin for one who was in perfect health at the time of the Vision'.

64 MacDonald: *Island Voices*, 164. Cf. E. Watt: 'Some personal experiences of the second sight', in Davidson: *The Seer*, 25–36.

65 *JC26/27/9/19*.

ill and subsequently died, suggests that she saw a fire and a death; and John's distress at her words may therefore have been caused by his knowledge that she had the gift of the two sights. If so, it will be worth while looking closely at witchcraft dittays to see if there are other possible examples of second sight.

Other forms of divination were equally common. One could read the marks on the shoulder-blade of a slaughtered animal (a divination practised on the night of the Massacre of Glencoe, for example); and one could measure a person's sleeve or waist to find out whether he or she was suffering from a fever. This divination also had the advantage of being part of a charm, since the patient on whom it was tried might well recover.[66] Turning the sieve and shears involved sticking scissors into the rim of a sieve and then suspending the sieve by crooking one's finger in the ring of the scissors. One could then ask a question and see which way the sieve would swing.[67] On 11 September, 1649 Margaret Munro was delated to the kirk session of Dingwall for using the sieve and shears, and confessed to so doing, adding that she had learned the technique from a woman called Shihag Urquhart.[68] Hot stones were also employed in a variety of ways, usually to discover the source or cause of illness. Three stones, for example, representing the head, heart, and body, were placed overnight in the hot ashes on the hearth. In the morning they were uplifted and dropped one by one into a bowl of water and the one which emitted the loudest noise as it came into contact with the water indicated that part of the body wherein the disease was located.[69] Suspected murderers might be fetched to touch the corpse of the person they were supposed to have killed, and if the corpse bled, this was taken to be a sign of the alleged murderer's guilt; and physiognomy and palmistry were common enough methods of divination to warrant mention in an Act of Parliament in 1574.[70]

We also come across forms of divination associated with specific times of the year, such as harvest. In one area, for example, we are told that after the

---

66 Shoulder-blade: Campbell: *Superstitions of the Scottish Highlands*, 263–6. Cf. Dalyell: *Darker Superstitions of Scotland*, 515. Thread: MacPherson: *Primitive Beliefs*, 267–71. One may compare an unusual variant on this. In 1650 Bessie Graham 'was desyrit to met the belt for ane chyld of Andro Arolls efter shoe had done so hir anssr wes for standing deid thair wes no remeid and the bairne died accordinglie', Truckell: 'Unpublished witchcraft trials', 53. Larner (*Enemies of God*, 142) alters 'met' to 'wet' and claims this was a common form of divination. In fact it was not, and it is hard to see what could have been achieved by wetting a belt. 'Mett' is a Scots verb meaning 'to measure', and measuring by one means or another was undoubtedly a widespread method of divination, especially in connection with illness.

67 MacPherson: *op.cit. supra*, 269. Cf. Black: *County Folk-Lore: Orkney and Shetland Islands*, 160; Simpkins: *County Folk-Lore: Fife*, 115.

68 *Records of the Presbytery of Dingwall*, 156.

69 MacPherson: *Primitive Beliefs*, 266.

70 Stones: MacPherson: *op.cit. supra*, 274–5. Physiognomy and palmistry. *APS* 3.87. These seem to have been associated especially with gipsies.

reaping the harvesters embarked on a trial called *Cur nan Corran* (casting the sickles), and *Deuchair Chorran* (trial of hooks). The sickles were thrown into the air and people noticed how they came back to earth and how they lay on the ground, and from these signs they were able to divine an individual's prospects for marriage or state of health during the next twelve months.[71] But there are also records of quite unusual methods of divination in the Highlands and Islands. Collectively they are known as *taghairm*, 'noise' or 'echo'. Pennant gives an account of one of them: "In this country is a vast cataract, whose waters falling from a high rock, jet so far as to form a dry hollow beneath, between them and the precipice. One of these imposters [i.e. diviners] was sowed up in the hide of an ox, and, to add terror to the ceremony, was placed in this concavity: the trembling enquirer was brought to the place, where the shade, and the roaring of the waters, encreased the dread of the occasion. The question is put, and the person in the hide delivers his answer".[72] Startling as this technique may seem, however, one must recall that it was taking place in a society which was still prepared to sacrifice bulls and other animals in an effort to sway ancient divinities in their guise as Christian saints to answer the questions of their devotees, as the presbytery of Dingwall had cause to complain more than once in 1656 and again in 1678.[73]

Magical activity, then, allied to beliefs in the existence of preternatural beings such as *sithean*, and in the power of certain people to see into the future, was common in all parts of sixteenth-century Scottish society, as indeed it was elsewhere. Its everyday presence in society, however, did not necessarily make it an activity as ordinary as, let us say, a household chore. The very fact that it involved, to however minor a degree, some contact with or aspiration to powers greater than human made it an operation, or series of operations, of which everyone, including the operator, needed to be wary. Certain magical activities, such as those which overtly or tacitly called upon spiritual beings to assist the operator with their superior power and knowledge, were more likely than others to arouse communal nervousness and evoke condemnation from the ecclesiastical and temporal authorities. Magic, therefore, no matter how common in society, was never and could never be a matter of indifference either to individuals or to communities. What witches and other magical operators were believed to do was as extraordinary to their contemporaries as

71 Thompson: *The Supernatural Highlands*, 93–4.
72 *Tour*, 311. Sutherland mentions a variant which involved roasting a number of cats. Presumably one was meant to divine from their demonic screeching, *Ravens and Black Rain*, 45–6. It is possible that something similar lay behind the French custom of burning live cats on the Place de Grève in Paris at midsummer. See J.G. Frazer: *The Golden Bough*, Vol. 11: *Balder the Beautiful*, Part 2 (London 1913), 37.
73 *Records of the Presbytery of Dingwall*, 279–82, 338.

it is to us, but contemporary strategies for dealing with it were not the same as ours.[74]

All magic, then, involves the exercise, or attempted exercise, of preternatural power. It may try to manipulate the hidden forces, sympathies, and antipathies of nature to produce extraordinary effects; or it may rely upon the evocation of spirits, good or evil, and subsequent command of them to achieve the same end. But witchcraft, as defined by early-modern demonologists and statute, always has a maleficent intention motivating its employment of magical operations, although in fact witchcraft was simply one form of magical activity among many others. What singled it out for special consideration was its links with idolatry and heresy, which suggested to ecclesiastical and temporal authorities that it should be made a criminal offence warranting punishment of a particularly severe kind.[75]

Witchcraft must also be distinguished from such magical operations as the use of charms, too, although the distinction cannot be made hard and fast. Charming involves the use of both words and actions[76] – without words, the actions are much less effective and indeed such an operation cannot be accounted as 'charming' – and the important fact for the operator's community is that he or she is believed by the members of that community to have effectual power and therefore to be in possession of a force greater than theirs, which works through the sound of words.[77] The content of, or intention underlying, the words is also important. Charming which includes an incantation is likely to be regarded as less serious an operation than charming which includes an invocation, since the latter is openly intent upon putting the operator in touch with spiritual powers. Add ritual actions to these and the effect may be even more disturbing and graduate into 'sorcery'. Such gradations of magical activity may be (and increasingly were) observed, and the point at which charming ceased, as it were, to be 'charming' and became 'witchcraft' was clearly a point to exercise the judgement of the assizes which were charged with trying people as witches.

---

74 This is not to say, however, that magical activities were necessarily seen as evil, or morally reprehensible, by everyone in society. Most people, after all, were perfectly prepared to make use of the magical powers they attributed to certain individuals. They were therefore content to remain neutral until some more urgent stimulus propelled them into taking steps to have the operator silenced or stopped or punished by legal authority. See Behringer: *Witchcraft Persecutions in Bavaria*, 84.

75 In Europe it had been a criminal offence well before the sixteenth century, of course, but it had not always attracted the penalties it incurred in early-modern legal codes.

76 Pennant noted that on Jura 'the old women, when they undertake any cure, mumble certain rhythmical incantations; and, like the antients, endeavour *decantare dolorem* [to disenchant the pain]', *Tour*, 215.

77 Favret-Saada: *Deadly Words*, 19.

In addition to these considerations, one must also bear in mind that there were different aspects of witchcraft. One of the most common stemmed from disputes in local communities. These disputes may have been disagreements arising from particular quarrels, or they may have belonged to a chain of hostile incidents which were actually part of a struggle for power and prestige in a group within a local community. In consequence, one must be wary how one reads the accounts of such local quarrels in witchcraft records, and also ask whether sometimes personal malice gave the name 'witchcraft' to acts which the gossip or ultimate accuser, and his or her audience, knew perfectly well were acts of magical healing.[78] Moreover, it is worth remembering that prosecution of witches might provide a local community with an opportunity to cut the Gordian knot of local dispute and return to, or freshly create, a kind of social cohesion, however temporary that might prove to be. Motives for prosecution cannot be taken as stemming from a single theory or intention. All kinds of extraneous factors, including perhaps discontent with a political or religious establishment, or the political or religious convictions or ambitions of individuals, may be seen to have played a part in stimulating a prosecution for witchcraft, or indeed a whole series of them.

But since those in authority (were they priests, ministers, advocates, or justices), as well as those who were members of the assize in a witch's trial, were as much a part of this community of magical beliefs as anyone else, one must ask what was their understanding of the charges brought against the panels in such trials; what made them interpret superstition and minor magic as 'witchcraft'; and indeed (since one can hardly suppose that many of the assizes, at least, would have read any of the standard demonologies of the period), what did they understand 'witchcraft' to be? The assizes in particular tended to be composed of members from both within and outwith the panel's local community, and so it is likely, one might say probable, that some of them would have known the background and detailed circumstances of the charges brought against the panel standing before them. Verdicts of not guilty are thus as interesting as those of guilty, if not more so; for why were panels found innocent of certain charges and not of others, and what was it that made members of the panel adjudge certain acts to be 'witchcraft' within the

---

78 See Favret-Saada: *op.cit. supra*, 21, 53. Willem de Blécourt has made the
     important point that the victims of bewitchment were able to distinguish between
     malevolent witchcraft and magical healing, 'Cunning women', 47. This underlines
     the difference between two modes of explaining what were seen as preternatural
     events or actions – literate demonological theory which was usually accompanied
     by implications of criminality, and oral tradition which could provide
     psychological consolation for the stress undergone by suffering individuals, ritual
     solution of a problem, and perhaps also enhancement (albeit through an increase
     of the community's trepidation) of the status of the magical performer.

meaning of the law, but not others which, as far as one can see from the record, are the same as those on which the verdict was 'guilty'?

Witchcraft, then, was not a monolithic system of belief and practice, tried and punished by people without discrimination. It was, rather, a complex set of nuanced affirmations that power greater than that normally available to humans existed and might be contacted and utilised for human purposes. In as much as its intentions were maleficent, it was disapproved, and in so far as it strayed into heresy and idolatry, it was prosecuted. Few people, however, if any doubted that magical operations could be made to work, and therefore society's disapproval and authority's prosecution must be attributed to something other than scepticism.[79]

---

79 One must not be misled by the peculiar case of Reginald Scot into thinking that his arguments were commonplace among intellectuals for, as Anglo has remarked, 'few were willing to subscribe to his thorough-going rejection of magic', *The Damn'd Art*, 135.

2

The Kirk's Offensive

It is often said that there is not a great deal of evidence relating to witchcraft in Scotland before the first major outbreak of prosecutions in 1590, but actually there is rather more than is sometimes thought. Frequent references to the activities, arrests, and execution of witches and a number of noteworthy trials, which surface in the records, like bubbles bursting upon a pool, give evidence of the omnipresent practices and beliefs which might otherwise be difficult to detect in the murk below. The earliest such sign in the sixteenth century comes from 1510 when, listed among the questions to be asked during a justice air at Jedburgh, is the query "if anyone knows anything about witchcraft or sorcery in the area", a formula similar to the questions laid down in 1586 for the visitation of kirks in the diocese of Dunblane by James Anderson, minister of Stirling, among which is the instruction that he should "inquire if there be any witches, sorcerers, passers in pilgrimage to chapels or wells, setters out of fires on saints' eves, or keepers of superstitious holy days".[1] *Mutatis mutandis*, the expectation of both seems to be that there may well exist witches and sorcerers to be discovered.

The first to be mentioned by name appears in a commission issued to William Lyon, bailiff of the Bishop of Aberdeen, on 1 June, 1536 empowering him to execute justice upon Agnes, alias Lanie Scot, who had been convicted of the magic act called "witchcraft" in the vernacular.[2] The *alias* is interesting. It has nothing to do with Agnes's renouncing her baptism, swearing fealty to Satan, and being given a new name by him, none of which she may have done, in any case. This series of charges is one which became an increasingly common part of every witchcraft dittay, to the point of being standardised during the seventeenth century; but it does not appear in the sixteenth. The formula for such a re-naming is almost always the same: "and received a new name", followed by whatever the new name was.[3] An *alias*, on the other hand, meant just what it does to us, an alternative name by which an individual may be known in his or her community. Aliases were very common among the Border

---

1 Pitcairn: *Criminal Trials* 1.1.66. Another document of the same year relating to Jedburgh suggests that the justice air was held there in November, Pitcairn: *op.cit.*, 67. Kirk: *Visitation of the Diocese of Dunblane*, 3.
2 *ERS* 16, Appendix: *Libri Responsionum*, 612. The record is in Latin. Hence the reference to the vernacular.
3 See, for example, *JC2/10*. folios 4r, 6r, 13v, 14r and v, 15r, and 60r. These names include William, Janet Clearkeys, Buntein, Crooked Paterson, The Trotter, Bold Leslie, and Nancy Luckyfoot.

reivers and tended to distinguish between people of the same surname, or commemorate particular exploits, or point to physical oddities. Sometimes they were obscene or simply obscure. [4] Most were attached to men and usually replaced surnames rather than Christian names, but not all were tinged with the faint odour of unrespectability. Patrick MacCalyean, for example, an Edinburgh advocate who was to feature in the witchcraft trials of 1590–93, is recorded as "Patrick MacCalyean alias Moscrop" in allusion to his being the son and heir-apparent of John Moscrop, another advocate; and John Fean "alias Cunningham", who died convicted as a witch during that same period of trials, was a schoolmaster, a respectable occupation which was often conjoined with the task of being reader in the local kirk.[5] Agnes, therefore, need not have been a disreputable woman merely because she had an alias. Her witchcraft rather than her alternative name would have tainted her reputation.[6]

It is difficult to know whether Agnes was executed or suffered a lesser penalty such as banishment. There is an example of a condemned witch's being sentenced to the latter in 1563, the very year the first Scottish Witchcraft Act was promulgated.[7] But the likelihood is that she was strangled and her body burned, the usual penalty for witchcraft in Scotland, and 1542 gives us the clearest indications that this indeed was probably her fate. In that year, Cardinal Beaton issued a commission to John Major, the Provost of St. Salvator's College in St. Andrews, Peter Chaplain and Martin Balfour, canons of the college, and John Wynram to try three suspected witches, who are recorded only by their initials: JS, ML, and JG alias S, and it is likely that these were the same *maleficae et sortilegae* (workers of harmful magic and practisers of divination) who were brought that same year by command of the vicars-general from Edinburgh and Dunfermline to St. Andrews Castle, at a cost of 33s. 4d.[8] Here they were put in close ward along with William, an

---

4 See Fraser: *The Steel Bonnets*, 74–5. Sixteenth-century examples from Pitcairn's *Criminal Trials* show a large number of Border names such as 'Armstrong', 'Johnston', 'Graham', and 'Elliot'. See 1.1.154 (1531); 1.1.171 (1535); 1.1.173 (1536); 1.1.393 (1556); 1.1.397–8 (1557); 1.1.405 (1558); 1.1.466 (1565); 1.2.93 (1581); 1.2.159 (1588). For the various ways in which nicknames are created, see Clark: 'Nickname creation', 91–2, and 'People and languages', 14–21.

5 Pitcairn: *Criminal Trials* 1.2.247 and 209.

6 'Lanie' appears to fall into the category of obscure aliases. There is a Scots word, *lanyied*, referring to cows or horses and meaning 'striped across the back', but it scarcely seems applicable in this case.

7 Pitcairn: *Criminal Trials* 1.1.432 = Agnes Mullikine alias Bessie Boswell from Dunfermline.

8 *St. Andrews Formulare* 2.175–7. The third person's initials are later corrected to MG. *Rentale Sancti Andree*, 139. The use of initials is not especially significant. The *Formulare* is what its title proclaims it to be, a collection of examples, based upon actual documents, of the appropriate ways to compose official letters, etc. Thus, the names of those to whom this commission is addressed also appear only as initials: JM, PC de K, MB de D, and JW.

Englishman, Sir John Wigtoun, curate of Ballumby, two priests, prebendaries of Dunglas, and a condemned thief.[9]

The commission speaks of Cardinal Beaton's duty to take every opportunity of reforming, canonically punishing, and extirpating those who have been arrested for the crimes of heresy, divination (*sortilegium*), the practice of harmful magic by women (*maleficae*),[10] and apostasy. It then goes on:

> Within the last few days it has given me great displeasure to be told by many trustworthy people that certain women, (viz. JS, ML, and JG alias S) who are not in the least concerned for the salvation of their souls and have put aside their fear of almighty God, have conspired to contrive on more than one occasion devilish illusions and apostasies such as malefice, divination, and the apostate act of working harmful magic. They have brought, and have threatened to bring, various other temporal injuries and physical harm upon the inhabitants of this kingdom and, (which is even worse), have taken the opportunity to abuse various faithful Christians of both sexes by means of their incantations, superstitions, illusions, and acts of malefice, striving to draw them away from true Christian piety and religion and so bring them, via the disgrace of heresy, apostasy, and works of harmful magic, whither they themselves are bent – to ruin and damnation. For many reasons, they have acquired a bad reputation, been strongly suspected, and denounced to me, and in consequence, by command of my vicar-general acting on my behalf while I was busy in France, they are now under close ward and imprisonment in my castle of St. Andrews.

Cardinal Beaton therefore instructs his procurator fiscal, together with the doctors, licentiates, and bachelors of theology in the university acting as assessors, to hear the case against them, examine and question them either together or separately, and carry out whatever sentence is passed by the court. All these must have presented a formidable tribunal before which the women had to appear, and it looks as though the court found them guilty because the Rental records expenses incurred by John Wigtoun (who, as we have seen, was also a prisoner in the castle) and by three condemned witches up to the day of their being burned. This proved to be 10 October, 1542 and the cost came to £3. 18s. 0d. It is rather difficult to appreciate what this cost meant in relation

---

9 *Rentale*, 130. John Wigtoun was tried on a charge of heresy in 1544, and in order to secure his liberty he agreed to act as an agent for Cardinal Beaton at whose behest, if we are to believe the partial testimony of John Knox, he attempted to murder the heretic George Wishart in Dundee. See Laing: *Works of John Knox* 1.130–1. Cowan: *The Scottish Reformation*, 101–2.

10 The Latin here suddenly deviates from abstract nouns to personal. *Maleficae* indicates not only people, but specifically females who work this kind of magic.

to other costs of the period but, expressed as 78 shillings, it may be compared with the 67 shillings paid as six months' wages to the Cardinal's master chef in 1542, or the 40 shillings annual wage paid in 1541 to his gardener in Edinburgh.[11] The execution of witches was therefore by no means cheap. Indeed, it might well have been more expensive than this, for in 1594–5 Ayr spent £4. 4s. 0d (or 84 shillings) on "coles, cordis, tar barrellis and uther graith [equipment] that burnit Mareoun Greiff witche", and the burgh could not rely on confiscation of the panel's goods and property to pay all the expenses involved. As Larner observed, "there were rarely many pickings to be had from the conviction and execution of a witch; more often the process was an expense to the local authority".[12]

In none of these cases are we given details of the charges against the accused, although we may note that the women tried in St. Andrews seem to have been engaged in divination (*sortilegium*) as well as acts of malefice (*maleficia*). To be sure, in the early-modern usage there may well have been some overlap, particularly by non-academics, between *maleficium* (an act of harmful magic), *sortilegium* (divination), and the general concepts of 'witch-craft' and 'sorcery'. Nevertheless, in commissions or dittays or trial records, the words are not used as synonyms; they appear either as separate acts of magical operation (implying that they were conceived as different types of magical working), or coupled – as in "dilatit of airt and pairt of the slaughter of umquhile Patrik Ruthvene be Wichcraft and Sorcerie" – with the implication that the two are related but separate. *Sortilegium*, therefore, cannot be translated simply as 'witchcraft' *tout court*, and thus it appears as though the St. Andrews witches may have been engaged in beneficent as well as maleficent forms of magic. We may note, too, the strong link with heresy made by the wording of the commission. This is not surprising, of course, since apart from any expected tendency to link magic with idolatry and heresy, the Scottish authorities of this period were much exercised by the activities of heretical individuals (of whom the priest, John Wigtoun, appears to have been

11 *Rentale Sancti Andree*, 141, 137, 109.
12 *Ayr Burgh Accounts*, 183. In 1586–7, the expenses for burning 'the witche of Barnweill' had been even greater = £7. 3s. 8d (nearly 144 shillings), but these had included the costs of her imprisonment as well, *Ibid.*, 156. In May, 1568 Agnes Fergus, accused of witchcraft, was ordered to be put in the pit 'and have but vd [five pence] ilk day', Hay: *Arbroath*, 129. Larner: *Enemies of God*, 132, cf. 197. We are told that in Elgin 'the comptar in 1560, Andro Edie, discharges him of 40 shillings debursed be him at the towns command, for the binner [rattling noise] to the wyffis that war wardit in the stepill for witches in summer last bypast', MacIntosh: *Elgin Past and Present*, 120. 'Binner' is presumably a reference to the technique of depriving accused witches of sleep in order to induce them the more willingly to make confession of their guilt. So Edie must have paid people to come in and make the noise, and then claimed back his expenses from the town council.

one), and were therefore keen to investigate and root out any manifestations of heresy which might be uncovered.[13]

Noteworthy, too, is the accusation of ill repute (*infamia*) which the commission says has been brought against the women on more than one occasion, or by more than one person (*multipliciter*). Reputation at this time was a woman's weakest point and the one where she might be attacked with greatest effectiveness. It was not, however, preponderantly men who used this weapon against them. Women slandered other women, and once kirk session records begin we find them full of such accusations and counter-accusations. The usual epithets thrown or exchanged were 'harlot' and 'thief', with variants upon both, especially the former; where the actual words are not recorded, we are told simply that an action of slander has taken place. Once the offence had been admitted or proved, offenders were usually made to beg pardon on their knees of the person they had slandered.[14]

Calling someone 'a witch', however, was not as common[15] and might obviously constitute a greater threat to the individual so called since it could be evidence either that ill repute was beginning to accrue to her, or that ill repute had already been established. Thus, on 16 June, 1545 Margaret Hay was tried before the burgh court of Elgin for calling Margaret Balfour a whore and a witch; on 26 November, 1563 the magistrates of Arbroath directed that "Richart Brown sall pass to the chappell the morne and ask Jonat Cary and John Ramsay, her son, forgyffness for calling her ane she witch and him ane he witch"; on 7 December, 1566 Oliver Smith in Edinburgh slandered Henry Mill and Marion Jack as witches; while in Inverness on 26 July, 1572 Christian Dingwell complained that Agnes Cuthbert had accused her of being a witch.[16] While none of these may have led further to an open accusation of witchcraft before a court (although one cannot be sure they did not), the reputation of being a witch was not one with which it could have been easy to live, and indeed it might well have led to action by the local community. In the case of the three women tried in St. Andrews, clearly their ill repute played an important role in their trial and almost certainly con-

---

13 See Laing: *Works of John Knox* 1.117. Sanderson: *Cardinal of Scotland*, 84–5.

14 For examples from the sixteenth century, see the entries for March, April, and July 1599 in the *Presbytery Buik of Aberdein*, CH2/1/1; and for the seventeenth, *St. Monance Kirk Session Records*, CH2.624/3, pp. 55, 104, 110, 118, 121, 124, 166, 188; *Anstruther Wester Kirk Session Records*, CH12/89/3, pp. 118, 153, 169, 192, 193, 195, 207.

15 See, for example, figures for England which indicate that between 1572 and 1594 of recorded slanderous words relating to women 29% were 'whore', 'jade' or 'quean'; 37% referred to other specific sexual acts; but only 4% were 'witch', Gowing: *Domestic Dangers*, 64.

16 *Records of Elgin* 1.84. Hay: *History of Arbroath*, 129. *Buik of the Kirk of the Canagait*, 59. *Records of Inverness* 1.216.

tributed to their being found guilty as charged, and there is a case from Stirling which tells us that the simple fact of bad reputation was enough to get two women exiled: "Jonet Lyndesay being sumtyme duelland in Cambus, and Isabell Keir, hir dochter, being brutit with wichecraft, and na man to persew thame thairfoir, oblist tham of thair awin confessioun that thai sall nocht be fundin in this toune agane, under the pane of deid".[17]

The Witchcraft Act of 1563

The session of Parliament which sat in Edinburgh on 4 June, 1563 passed twenty-seven acts into law. First and foremost was an Act of Perpetual Oblivion, intended to achieve "ane commoun peax, unioun, reconciliatioun, and quietnes" after the rebellions and discords of the recent past. There followed a gallimaufry of topics thought to require legislation: wicker salmon-traps in salt water must be destroyed and those in fresh constructed in accordance with existing regulations; previous laws relating to the removal of gold and silver furth of Scotland, and to false coining, were ratified; people were to be forbidden henceforth to manufacture salt according to a new-fangled process; there were instructions anent occupation of church lands, weights and measures, armed disturbances, the registration and competence of public notaries, and exportation of coal; monies intended to be used for education in St. Andrews and elsewhere must not be diverted to other purposes; and someone was to be sent to Denmark to see if recently imposed customs duties could not be lifted in regard to Scottish merchant ships.[18]

In the midst of all these – item 9 – stands the new law relating to witchcraft:

Item: forsamekeill as [in as much as] the Quenis Maiestie and thre Estatis in this present Parliament being informit that the havy, abominabill superstitioun usit be divers of the liegis of this Realme be using of Witchcraftis, Sorsarie, and Necromancie, and credence gevin thairto in

---

17 *Records of the Burgh of Stirling*, 80: 1 September, 1562. One wonders why no one was willing to prosecute them for witchcraft. Is this an example of the fear a witch's reputation might generate in his or her local community, or an indication that the majority of people there were content with the magical services the two women might be able to offer them? Someone, of course, must have brought pressure to bear on Janet and Isobel, otherwise presumably they would not have felt obliged to confess to being witches. Cf. Margaret Hutchinson who had fallen foul of people in the course of her scolding and flyting, and was therefore accused of being a witch, a point her husband makes in his petition on her behalf to the justices deput, *JC* 26/27. Other forms of accusation, potentially just as dangerous, might accuse someone of actually practising witchcraft. Thus, on 7 March, 1559 'Sande McIllmertin is jugit in admerciament [was sentenced to pay a fine] for the saing in oppyn mercat to Hendre Kar elder that his serwandis pot wychecraft in his net', *Records of Inverness* 1.28.

18 *APS* 2.535–45.

tymes bygane aganis the Law of God: and for avoyding and away
putting of all sic vane superstitioun in tymes tocum;

It is statute and ordanit be the Quenis Maiestie and thre Estatis
foirsaidis that na maner of persoun nor persounis of quhatsumever
estate, degre, or conditioun thay be of tak upone hand in ony tymes
heirefter to use ony maner of Wichcraftis, Sorsarie, or Necromacie: nor
gif thame selfis furth to have ony sic craft or knawlege thairof,
thairthrow abusand the pepill; Nor that na persoun seik ony help,
response, or consultatioun at ony sic usaris (or abusaris) foirsaidis of
Witchcraftis, Sorsareis, or Necromancie, under the pane of dead: asweill
to be execute aganis the user-abusar, as the seikar of the response or
consultatioun.

And this to be put to executioun be the Justice Schireffis, Stewartis,
Baillies, Lordis of Regaliteis and Rialteis, thair Deputis, and uthers
Ordinar Jugeis competent within this Realme with all rigour, having
powar to execute the samin.[19]

Three questions need to be asked in connection with this Act: (1) What is
the meaning of the Act? (2) At whom was it aimed? and (3) Why was it
passed at this particular juncture?

The wording of the Act is important. It records, as separate though related
magical operations, witchcraft, sorcery, and necromancy and labels all three
'superstition'. These terms emanate, of course, from a hostile and official
source and it is therefore somewhat difficult to be sure precisely what activities
the drafter had in mind. But we have already seen the extent and variety of
magical beliefs and operations throughout mainland Scotland and both the
Northern and Western Isles even long after the Reformation and its
disciplinary bodies had long had time to take and maintain the effects they
wished to have. So it seems likely that the legislation was intended to forbid
all acts of maleficent magic, charming and divination, especially those which
involved ritual working or visits to particular places, or which relied upon the
second sight as a means of looking into the future; and as *sithean* were
sometimes associated with the dead,[20] or regarded as actually being the dead,

---

19 *APS* 2.539. A sheriff's criminal jurisdiction was usually restricted to cases of
   premeditated murder and certain cases of theft, but he was also obliged to
   enforce statutes and impose penalties for their contravention. A regality was an
   area subject to certain officials known as 'lords of regality', who had the right to
   hold their own justice-airs, i.e. itinerant courts. A 'royalty' was a similar, though
   smaller, area. In a regality court, the lord of regality was always the judge, even if
   only in name, but his functions were often carried out by a baillie or steward.
   Walker: *A Legal History of Scotland* 3.419, 561–2. Prior to this Act, practitioners
   of magic and their clients were subject to general excommunication four times a
   year. See *Statutes of the Scottish Church*, 26, 40, 75.
20 Sutherland: *Ravens and Black Rain*, 33.

a belief in them, and the ritual acts associated with that belief, could also have fallen under the Act's general prohibition.

Now, designations such as 'witchcraft', 'sorcery', and 'necromancy' cannot be regarded as satisfactory if they are to embrace this enormous range of preternatural belief and practice, and it is also true that the legal pen may simply have run away with itself and repeated three times, with different terminology, what the legislator conceived as more or less one and the same activity. Nevertheless, given that the legislator is unlikely to have been entirely insulated from the *mentalité* of his period, and given that the three words actually do refer to different types of magical operation, it is more probable that he intended his phrasing to cover as wide a ground as possible; and unless he was going to list every variant form of magical activity and item of popular belief, he is likely to have assumed that these three categories could serve his purpose well enough and be sufficiently flexible in practice to be able to designate most of the forms of magic the criminal courts would meet.

Next in the wording comes a significant contrast: the credence given "heretofore" to this kind of heavy, abominable superstition, and the law designed to put an end to it "in times to come". In other words, people believed all kinds of superstitious things while Scotland was a Catholic country, but now that Protestants are in charge of it such empty nonsense will be made to cease. It seems to have been these phrases about superstition, along with the references to "abusing the people", which caused Larner to suggest that the Act was "extremely sceptical in its tone".[21] But here I would beg to differ. 'Superstition' was not a word always used in its modern sense. It is true, of course, that the several Inquisitions often waved aside accusations of magical activity as ignorant nonsense, provided they were satisfied that no heresy was involved; and while it is also true that dismissal of magic by authors both Catholic and Protestant as 'superstitious' certainly conveyed the notion that the writers had serious reservations about it, their reserve tended to be directed towards theological propriety with regard to magic rather than caused by doubts anent its reality.[22]

Saint Thomas Aquinas discusses superstition and defines it as a vice opposed to religion by excess because it offers divine worship to an object which ought not to receive such worship. He then goes on to develop this notion further by subdividing superstition into worship of God in a manner

21 *Enemies of God*, 177, 188.
22 Kamen: *The Spanish Inquisition*, 271–3. Monter: *Ritual, Myth and Magic*, 67. Clark: 'Protestant demonology', in Ankarloo and Henningsen: *Early Modern European Witchcraft*, 79. The seventeen tracts by Catholic and Protestant authors, contained in *Theatrum de Veneficiis* (Frankfurt 1586), exhibit a wide range of opinion on the reality or illusion of various aspects of witchcraft. But if the authors express doubts about their reality, they tend to explain them as illusions created by the Devil to deceive people and so lead them into sin.

which runs to excess, idolatry, divination, and 'other practices'.[23] Later theologians of the sixteenth and seventeenth centuries then extended this last to include all forms of magic and its operations, while Protestants regularly used 'superstition' in all these senses (save perhaps divination) to describe Catholicism itself. Thus the way was open to abuse a technical term. Popular magical practices could be demonised by arguing that belief in the efficacy of an association between causes and effects which do not belong together in nature was based on the tacit, or in some cases overt, acceptance of a pact between an evil spirit and the human individual, especially since *maleficium* (an act of harmful magic) had been included within the broadened definition of superstition; and the epithet 'superstitious' could be used by churchmen against the generality of popular beliefs and practices in an effort to suggest that they were both wrong and valueless. Since much that was regarded as superstition actually consisted of magical acts aimed at improving the material condition of people's lives, the clear object of the Church (Catholic or Protestant) in demeaning these operations was to leave people no choice but to turn to God alone (or at least to God and his saints) for the relief and comfort they sought.[24]

The references to superstition in the Scottish Witchcraft Act, then, are unlikely to represent scepticism in the modern sense.[25] It is more probable that what the drafter had in mind was a combination of theological disapproval of acts which were being interpreted by contemporary demonologists and others as tantamount to idolatry, and cultural dismissal of these particular manifestations of popular beliefs and practices; and it is instructive to compare the wording of the Act with that of Archbishop Hamilton's *Catechism*, published in St. Andrews on 19 August, 1552. There the Archbishop makes clear that anyone who uses magic sins against the first commandment, and that all magical operations are founded upon a pact with the Devil:

> Nother can thai excuse thame self fra transgression of the first command, that supersticiously observis ane day mair than ane other . . . quhilk is plane superstition . . . Siclike supersticion is amang thame, that will nocht berisch or erde [bury or inter] the bodis of thair freindis on the North part of the kirk yard . . . It is nocht unknawin to us, that

---

23 *Summa Theologiae*, pars secunda secundae, 92.3, responsio. Cf. the Jesuit, Martín Del Rio: 'All forbidden magic is tacit idolatry', *Disquisitiones Magicae*, Book 1, Chapter 1.

24 Clark: *Thinking With Demons*, 474–83. Cf. Muchembled: 'Ils n'avaient pas tort, eux qui comprirent qu'une christianisation en profondeur passait pour la lutte contre les *superstitions*, en un mot contre la vision du monde populaire', *Culture populaire*, 116.

25 Clark has issued a timely warning against the misapplication of retrospective freighting in relation to the concept of superstition. See *Thinking With Demons*, 474.

mony and sundry uther sinfull and damnable kindis of witchecraftis and superstitionis ar usit amang men and wemen.[26]

The assumptions and sentiments are very similar to those of the anonymous drafter.

The Act's reference to persons of "quhatsumever estate, degree, or condition" may have been a standard legal formula intended to close any loophole for the aristocracy, but there was a also a particular point in its being included here since, as we shall see later, magical practices were common among members of the Court. "Abusand the pepill" follows naturally from the notion that magic is both idolatrous and superstitious, and seems to be linked with a genuine note of scepticism. But appearances may be deceptive. No one, says the Act in reference to witchcraft, sorcery, and necromancy, must "gif thame selfis furth to have ony sic craft or knawlege thairof" and thereby abuse the people. *Abutor*, the Latin verb from which the Scots verb is derived, has several ranges of meaning (as the Latin-educated drafter would have been aware), but the one obviously intended here is "to use unscrupulously, take advantage of, exploit", and there can be no doubt that everyone knew perfectly well that there were tricksters who pretended to a knowledge they did not have of esoteric practices. Archbishop Hamilton, for example, makes this clear when he refers to "wichecraft, Nicromansie, Enchantment, [and] Juglarie",[27] and so does Canisius with his list of "vitches, southsayers, deceavers, and siklyke".

One type of deceiver the Act may have had in mind can be illustrated from a later Act, passed on 5 March, 1574 against vagabonds and idle beggars, in which there are mentioned by name gipsies "or ony uther that fenyeis thame to have knawlege in physnomie, palmestre, or utheris *abused sciencis* quhairby thay perswade the people that thay can tell thair weardis [fates], deathis, and fortunes, and sic uther fantasticall ymaginationis" [my italics].[28] These branches of knowledge are 'abused' because they are used by tricksters to deceive other people, and they are 'fantastical imaginings' either because the drafter of the Act wished to emphasise scepticism in relation to the sciences themselves, or because he wanted to cast doubt on the reliability of those who promoted and practised them. 'Abused' can also mean 'misused', and an abused science may therefore be one which is not necessarily invalid of itself, but is being misapplied by its practitioner.

---

26 *Catechism*, 51. Cf. another Catholic catechism of 1588, which says that 'to use wichecrafte, or to give credit to vitches, southsayers, deceavers, and siklyke' is a sin against the first commandment, Appendix to Canisius: *Ane Cathechisme*, 211.
27 *Catechism*, 49. Cf. Del Rio on what he calls "deceitful magic", *Disquisitiones Magicae*, Book 1, Chapter 4.
28 *APS* 3.87. The English Act anent gipsies, passed in 1563, merely calls them vagabonds and does not mention magic, *Statutes of the Realm* 4.448–9.

The notion of abusing is emphasised, too, when the 1563 Act depicts people seeking help from those who practise witchcraft, sorcery, and necromancy; but the phrases must be read in the context of the Act as a whole. This seeks to contrast earlier Catholic (and therefore, in the eyes of Protestants, superstitious) times with a Protestant future freed from exploitation of the people. Hence, anyone who goes to a witch, a sorcerer, or a necromancer to ask for help, or who consults an expert in divination ("seiks ony response or consultatioun")[29] is to be considered as guilty as the witch – something which does not make much sense (or justice) if one is arguing that the seeker is being exploited because he or she is ignorant or simple-minded, but which begins to make sense if the abuser is seen as a peddler of Catholicism and Catholic practices and the seeker as someone who willingly continues to adhere to and believe in them. Seen in this light, the references to abuse start to look less like scepticism and more like anti-Catholicism, a tone and usage which fit rather well the overall tenor of the Act.[30]

So the Act appears to be aiming at more than one might think at first. There are, in fact, two targets. One is the practice of magic of almost any kind; the other (a sub-text, so to speak) is Catholicism in its guise of 'idolatry' and 'superstition'.[31]

Now, Larner has suggested that the Act was passed because between 1560 and 1563 there was a power vacuum in the area of social control which had previously been covered by the ecclesiastical courts, and the General Assembly of the Kirk asked the Privy Council either to let the Kirk take over these former ecclesiastical jurisdictions, or to take them over itself. "The list of offences", she continues, "did not in fact include witchcraft, but when Parliament incorporated these offences into the criminal law, the drafter included a witchcraft act between those against adultery and bestiality."[32]

To test this hypothesis, it now becomes important to look at various events leading up to Parliament's passing a variety of Acts on 4 June, 1563. At the

---

29 The Latin *consultatio* means 'putting a question' as well as 'discussing a problem'.
30 Larner makes a somewhat different point: that since the Act is forbidding all superstition, it must cover all those who practise it in whatever manner, *Enemies of God*, 67. This is true as far as it goes, but Larner does not attempt to explain what is meant by 'superstition' in this context.
31 Elizabeth Tudor's Witchcraft Act, published in the same year, concentrates on the practitioners of magic and punishes with death only those who kill others by magical means. Other magical offences are to be visited with a term of imprisonment. There is no punishment for those who merely consult such people. *Statutes of the Realm* (London 1819), 4.446–7.
32 *Enemies of God*, 66. Larner is partly mistaken here. Item 8 of the Act deals with the housing problems of those appointed to assist kirk ministers, and item 10 says that notorious adulterers shall henceforth, if they ignore repeated warnings, be liable to the death penalty. There is no mention of bestiality anywhere in this Parliamentary session. Williamson suggests that the Act was passed in an attempt by the Earl of Moray to smooth relations between the secular powers and the Kirk, *Scottish National Consciousness*, 56. Circumstances surrounding the passage of the Act, however, as described below, do not really lend support to this notion.

sixth session of the General Assembly of the Kirk, held on 4 July, 1562, it was agreed that, "touching the removal of idolatrie, the kirk now as of befoir, concludes humble supplicatioun to be givin in to her Hienes; but the maner how, they have referrit to further consultatioun of the godly of her Majesties secreitt counsell". There follows a list of the "vyces commanded be the law of God to be punished, and yet not commandit to be punished be the law of the realme", namely blasphemy, contempt for God's word and sacraments, profanation of the sacraments by their celebration at the hands of those "not lawfullie callit to the ministration therof", perjury, taking God's name in vain, breaking the Sabbath, adultery, fornication, "filthie talking", and transgression of the last Act made against those who celebrated *or heard* Mass. (One notes the parallel between Catholic priests and their congregations, and magical practitioners and those who consulted them. Participants on both sides of the equation are to be regarded as equally guilty and deserving of punishment.) Jurisdiction over divorce should either be surrendered to the Kirk or handed over to "men of good lyves, knowledge and judgement, to take order thereof", in which the Privy Council should decide how the guilty parties should be punished.[33] This is not quite the same as the generalised "vacuum of social control" to which Larner refers.[34]

The Assembly then heard read the supplication which would be presented to Queen Mary and the Privy Council. For its opening theme, it fulminated against the Mass and then, after demanding the Mass's abolition, went on to list several other things the Kirk wanted the Queen and Privy Council to see done. Punishment of vices came next: adultery, fornication, open whoredom, blasphemy, and contempt of God, the death penalty being demanded for adultery and blasphemy. Then followed less severe requirements: provision to be made for the poor and for Protestant ministers, punishment of Catholics or Catholic sympathisers who refused to obey the Kirk's superintendants, and lastly a repetition of certain points already made, including the punishment of both sayers and hearers of Mass.[35]

---

33 *BUK*, 19. Cf. 'We farder desyre . . . that juges be appoynted to hear the causes of divorcement; for the kirk can no longer sustene that burthen, especialie becaus thair is no punischment for the offendars', *Ibid.*, 23.

34 I am not, of course, arguing that politics did not come into the Kirk's struggle to contain and extirpate magic. I am simply giving more weight than does Larner to the religious aspect of the Kirk's intentions by suggesting that much that was magical practice (whether interpreted by the Kirk as 'witchcraft' or 'superstition') was equated by the Kirk with Catholic custom, and that in consequence the fight against magic and witchcraft is better seen as part of the general war waged by the Kirk against Catholicism as a whole.

35 *BUK*, 23. The Assembly held in December, 1562 concerned itself principally with details of church discipline, although there was also talk of finance and of specific matters to be referred to the Privy Council, mainly those which had been touched on in the previous Assembly, *Ibid.*, 25–30.

The Privy Council certainly discussed, at least in part, provision for impoverished kirk ministers,[36] but the General Assembly's list was largely passed over when it came to the next available Parliament's formulating what it considered to be necessary legislation. Items 8 and 13 dealt with ministers' finances, and item 10 with adultery. Otherwise, the Assembly's programme is conspicuous by its absence.

Political events at this time are significant. During August and September, 1562 the Queen was in Aberdeen and Inverness, the first time she had ventured so far north in her kingdom. The north-east was dominated by George Gordon, 4th Earl of Huntly, a Catholic, but he and the Queen were not on good terms. A running feud between the Gordons and Ogilvies broke out again when the Earl's third son, John Gordon, was involved in a street brawl with Ogilvies. As a result of this, John was imprisoned but escaped and fled deep into the safety of Gordon territory. Rumours then circulated that Huntly had formed a treasonable plan to stage a Catholic coup and marry the Queen to his errant son; so when in September the Queen moved out of Gordon lands to Inverness, the Frasers there offered to support her against the Gordons, and the stage was set for an extremely perilous confrontation. On 22 September the Queen came back to Aberdeen, dogged all the way by Gordons, and the question of how to proceed effectively against Huntly now became acute. On 16 October, both he and his son were put to the horn,[37] and the Countess of Huntly, a frequent consulter of witches, so it was said, took note of their prophecy that it would not be long before the Earl's body was lying, without a wound, in the Aberdeen tolbooth. The Countess took this to mean that her husband would return to the city victorious in any conflict. Finally, on 28 October, the opposing forces of Queen and Earl met in battle at Corrichie, a marshy hollow on the border of Kincardine and Aberdeen; but the Earl suddenly and without warning fell dead from his horse, stricken by some kind of fatal seizure. His body was first taken to the tolbooth in Aberdeen, thus fulfilling the witches' prophecy, and then embalmed and transported to Edinburgh where, in May 1563, it was brought before a session of Parliament, propped up in a chair, and tried for the crime of treason.[38]

As far as Protestants were concerned, then, a major Catholic noble had been removed and Catholic power and influence in the north-east curtailed, if only for the moment; and the news that, on 15 March, 1563 the Queen's uncle, the Duc de Guise, had been murdered would also have come as a sign that the pillars of temporal Catholicism were being badly shaken. Nor was

36 *RPC* 1st series, 1.234–5: 11 February, 1563. Even so, Knox was not satisfied with the Act against adultery and protested that it had been modified far too much, *History of the Reformation* 2.383.
37 I.e. officially declared outlaws.
38 See Fraser: *Mary, Queen of Scots*, 192–207.

this all to stimulate Scottish Protestant hopes that the tide of history was beginning to flow their way. For on Easter Sunday, 11 April, 1563 a number of prominent Catholics, including the Archbishop of St. Andrews, John Hamilton, and the Prior of Whithorn who was the brother of Mary Fleming, one of the Queen's intimate circle of attendant ladies, publicly celebrated Mass in an act of defiance. The Government took no immediate action against these law-breakers (for by an Act of Parliament passed on 24 August, 1560 such celebration had been made illegal),[39] but Protestant lairds in Ayrshire arrested some Catholic priests and imprisoned them. These lairds then wrote to leading Catholics in the West and warned them that if they too broke the law and had Mass celebrated, they would be apprehended and put to death. The Queen summoned Knox to a conference at Loch Leven, at which he offensively reminded the Queen to do her duty and uphold the law. A second conversation the next day, however, was more amicable in tone and indeed the Queen said that, upon reflection (meaning, in fact, a conversation she had had with Lord James, her half-brother) she was willing to have the Catholics who had celebrated Mass punished for so doing; so on 19 May the Archbishop, the Prior, and twenty others were tried and sentenced to be imprisoned at the Queen's pleasure.[40]

This, then, is the context for the passing of the Witchcraft Act on 4 May. Scottish Catholicism suffered a number of reversals in the Spring of 1563. Huntly was dead; so was a baleful French influence on the Queen; and although the Protestants were scandalised by a public celebration of Mass in April, by the beginning of May it was clear that the Protestant authorities were going to have their way and see the Act of 1560 enforced against the Catholic offenders. Catholic defiance had alerted Knox yet again to the ever-present threat of 'idolatry' (a subject upon which he was especially exercised),[41] and one must bear in mind how very Catholic many magical practices and beliefs not only seemed but actually were, with Catholic prayers used as charms, and pilgrimages to holy wells and chapels still continuing. These manifestations of 'the enemy' appeared to be widespread and exceptionally difficult to uproot, particularly since (as the General Assembly in 1562 complained) obedience to the Kirk's officials was often flouted. It is the unfortunate habit of discussing witchcraft separately from magic, removing it from its necessary ambience, which has helped perhaps to give rise to the notion that witchcraft somehow slipped into the 1563 Parliamentary session almost as an afterthought – an impression which Knox's relative and apparent

---

39 *APS* 2.534–5.
40 Knox: *History of the Reformation* 2.370–4. Sanderson: *Ayrshire and the Reformation*, 122–3. See also Ridley: *John Knox*, 422–5 and the contemporary literature there cited; and Lynch: *Edinburgh and the Reformation*, 188–9.
41 See, for example, Kyle: *The Mind of John Knox*, 179.

indifference to the subject may have assisted in reinforcing.[42] But if one looks at the prevalence of magical beliefs and practices as a whole, at the commingling of these with Catholicism in the minds (or at least the mouths) of powerful Protestants, and the relative novelty of the reformation in Lowland Scotland – it can scarcely be said to have taken much effect elsewhere in the country at this time – one can see that a Witchcraft Act might serve two very useful and desirable purposes. It would reinforce the illegality of a wide range of activities related to magic and other occult operations, a proper end in itself; and it would, by endeavouring to stamp these out, remove a good many Catholic practices, or practices with a Catholic tinge, and begin to wean people away from thinking in Catholic terms. I suggest, therefore, that the Act was an integral part of the *religious* war against Catholicism then being waged by the Protestant establishment in Scotland, and was likely to have been viewed in religious terms, rather than an attempt by the Kirk to fill a power vacuum or have it filled by a secular authority it hoped it could trust.

There is one more point worth consideration. At the General Assembly held on 25 December, 1562, John Erskine , Laird of Dun and the Kirk's superintendent of Angus and the Mearns, complained that Robert Cunningham, a schoolmaster in Arbroath, was "infecting the youth committed to his charge with idolatrie".[43] In the language of the Kirk at this time, idolatry meant Catholicism. Since Erskine had just been appointed Superintendent, he would have been eager to give proof of his credentials which included making every effort to transform people's ways of thinking and to win their acceptance of the Kirk's priorities and discipline,[44] and this would certainly have included eradicating as many traces of Catholic practice as possible. Erskine also had a highly developed view of Satan as the principal enemy of the Kirk: "Thair is nothing sa odious to Sathan as is the ministerie of Christis ewangell, and the samin he labouris continewalie to put furth of the earthe, becaus it is the instrument of mennis salvatioun".[45] What makes these two points significant in Erskine's case is his later pursuit of witches in Angus and the Mearns in 1568 and

---

42 Knox made no special comment on the passing of the Act, observing merely that the members of Parliament 'began a new schift, to speak of the punishement of adulterye, of witchcraft, and to seik the restitutioun of the glebes and manses to the Ministeris of the Kirk, and of the reparatioun of churches', *History of the Reformation* 2.383. Larner may be right when she suggests that the time he spent in Geneva, where witchcraft was not regarded as a crime of the first seriousness, could have influenced his attitude towards it, *Enemies of God*, 66. The next meeting of the General Assembly, too, ignored the subject and dealt almost entirely with matters of church discipline, scarcely glancing at the recent session of Parliament, *BUK*, 31–7.

43 *BUK*, 25.

44 These are the expressions of Bardgett: 'John Erskine of Dun', 72.

45 'Ane epistill wrettin to ane faythfull brother be Johne Erskyne of Dwne, 13th December, 1571', *SCM* 4.100.

again in 1588. The first of these especially is noteworthy because there were forty people involved as delated or suspect of witchcraft, a number which makes this the first apparent large-scale prosecution recorded in Scotland.

A combination of active anti-Catholicism and zeal to defend the Kirk against any assault of Satan, therefore, seem to be the principal motivating factors in his eagerness to extirpate witchcraft from the territory for which he had ecclesiastical responsibility. It is a question worth posing, then, even if it cannot be answered due to lack of evidence, whether Erskine may not have played some part in getting a Witchcraft Act included in the raft of legislation in 1563, and indeed, if that were so, whether he might not have had a hand in the wording of it, peculiarly anti-Catholic and inclusive of consulter as well as practitioner as it seems to be?[46]

After the Act

The Act, however, appeared to make little immediate difference. On 26 June, two women from Dunfermline were banished thence because of charges of witchcraft which had been brought against them, and in July, two witches were burned (it is not clear where), "the eldest . . . so blynded with the Devill, that sche affirmed, 'That na Judge had powir ower hir'"; and on 31 December four women were delated for witchcraft by the Superintendents of Fife and Galloway, their cases being referred to the Privy Council, after which we hear no more about them.[47] Then on 26 June, 1565 the General Assembly decided to send a petition yet again to the Queen, asking her to enforce the recent Acts of Parliament against "violaters of the Sabboth day, [and] committers of adulterie and fornicatioun", to request that Superintendents be given commissions to execute this legislation, and to see that Kirk ministers be paid their due stipends. Four members of the Assembly were deputed to draw up the

46 Erskine had suffered the indignity of a complaint against him at a meeting of the General Assembly on 25 December, 1563 to the effect that he was not doing his job of Superintendent properly, *BUK*, 39. But more or less the same complaints were made on the same occasion against the Superintendents of Lothian, Fife, and the West, and their defences seem to have amounted to the same thing, that they were overworked. In Erskine's case, it was added that the area he had to cover was too great to allow a proper discharge of his duties, and he was still making the same point on 25 December, 1565, *op.cit.*, 65. None of this need have affected his willingness to try to fulfil his duties, and indeed as he remained in his post for 28 years (the rest of his life, in fact), the Kirk could not have been displeased with the way he fulfilled his office.

47 *JC*1/12. Knox: *History of the Reformation* 2.391. Del Rio notes that some writers advised that witches appear before a judge with their backs turned towards him because judges were particularly susceptible to enchantment by such women, *Disquisitiones Magicae* Book 5, Section 7. Del Rio dismisses the idea as nonsense ("drivel" is what he calls it), and indeed it was generally believed that magistrates were immune from witches' spells. See Clark: *Thinking With Demons*, 572–81. Fife and Galloway: *BUK*, 44.

petition in suitable wording: John Erskine; John Willock, Superintendent of the West; Christopher Goodman, minister in St. Andrews; and John Row, minister of St. Johnstone. The petition they produced is interesting. It has six articles. The first demands suppression of the 'idolatrous' Mass; the second refers to payment of ministers; the third to the appointment of schoolmasters; the fourth to provision for the poor; the fifth to "sick horrible crymes as now abounds in the realme, without any correction, to the great contempt of God and his holie word, sick [such] as idolatrie, blasphemeing of Gods name, manifest breaking of the Sabboth day, witchcraft, sorcerie and inchantment, adulterie, incest, manifest whooredome, manteinance of bordellis, murther, slaughter, reife and spuilyie [plunder and robbery], with many other detestabill crymes"; and the sixth to the condition of poor labourers.[48]

One might argue from this that witchcraft does not appear to have been one of the Kirk's principal preoccupations. The Mass, ministers' pay, and the condition of the poor seemed to take precedence. But if we allow that witchcraft, sorcery and enchantment were seen as types of religious crime, this argument needs to be modified a little. The list of crimes requiring attention and punishment takes the order (a) religious, (b) sexual, and (c) violent, and unless one tries to maintain that magic is a fourth category, unconnected with the rest, a contention which runs contrary to everything we know about the mentality of the period, elimination of magical practices and beliefs is indeed here classed as a preoccupation of the Kirk, subordinate in interest, perhaps, to abolition of the Mass but an important part of the drive to establish a non-Catholic ambience in which the beliefs and practices of the reformed Church could take root and flourish.

So it is noteworthy that John Erskine had a hand in the drafting of this document, for none of the other three seems to have had any particular leaning towards witchcraft or sorcery. Indeed, Willock went to England in 1562 and was more or less a nominal Superintendent of the West – hence, perhaps, the complaints about him in the Assembly; Goodman, an Englishman, returned to his native country in the winter of 1565; and John Row devoted himself to scholarship and the doctrinal teachings of the Kirk.[49] So again it is worth asking whether perhaps Erskine might not have inserted, or suggested inserting, the reference to witchcraft, sorcery and enchantment in the fifth article. The Queen's reply was that she would refer the matter to Parliament. If she did so, it took no immediate action.

One of the provisions of the 1563 Witchcraft Act was, as we have seen, that its penalties should apply to everyone, regardless of his or her rank in society. That such a catch-all clause was necessary to prevent the aristocracy from

48 *BUK*, 58–60.
49 A summary of the careers of all these three may be found under their respective names in the *Dictionary of National Biography*.

escaping trial and punishment must have been clear to the General Assembly and Parliament, since it was well-known that members of the Court either practised magic, or consulted those who did, or at least were said to do so. Thus, during their conversation at Loch Leven in April 1563, Queen Mary told Knox that Lord Ruthven had offered her a ring, "whome", said she, "I can not love (for I know him to use enchantment)".[50] Such a saying would not have surprised Knox who recorded that the Countess of Huntly was a patron of witches and had been so for at least seven years. The Earl of Bothwell, too, was considered to be well-versed in magic, and even an Archbishop of St. Andrews could be lampooned for consulting not one but three female workers of magic when he was stressed and ill.[51]

All this, of course, might be dismissed as no more than evidence that an accusation of dealing in magic was a common stick with which to beat somebody one disliked, and there is plenty of evidence to show that this was so, with both Catholic and Protestant writers employing the same device. Knox, for example, had no reason to approve of the Countess of Huntly who was a Catholic, and the Earl of Bothwell collected many detractors during the course of his life. Indeed, Knox himself was the subject of similar ill-natured gossip, for when in Spring 1564 he married Margaret Stewart of Ochiltree, a woman much younger than himself, he was said to have been able to attract her because he had employed the appropriate magic; and a few years later, in 1572, Lady Hume and others maintained he had been banished from St. Andrews because he had called up the Devil, an operation which had so frightened Knox's servant, Richard, that the man had run mad and died.[52] (A

50 Knox: *History of the Reformation* 2.373. The Ruthvens had a history of interest in the occult sciences. Patrick's grandson, John, the second Earl of Gowrie, was credited with practising witchcraft and necromancy while he was at the University of Padua, and two of his relatives were known to be alchemists. Steuart: 'The Scottish 'Nation' at the University of Padua', *SHR* 3 (1906), 55–6.

51 *History of the Reformation* 2.357–8. Bothwell: Teulet, 'Comme il en sçait bien le mestier, n'ayant faict plus grande profession, du temps qu'il estoit aux escolles, que de lire et estudier en la négromancie et magie deffendue', *Correspondance diplomatique de la Mothe-Fénélon* 1.20. At his death, the Earl is supposed to have confessed, 'Poursuit après, comme par enchantement, auquel, dès sa jeunesse à Paris et ailleurs, il s'estoit beaucoup addoné, il avoit tiré la Reine à l'aymer', *Ibid.*, 244. Keith: *History of the Church and State in Scotland*, 144. On the Archbishop, see *infra*, p. 99–101.

52 Chambers: *De Scotorum fortitudine*, 276–7. Burne: *Disputation*, 143, 162. (It is interesting to note that Burne dedicated this work to James VI.) Bannatyne: *Memorials*, 216. These were not the only accusations of magic levelled at Knox. In 1561 he felt obliged to defend himself to the Queen, saying, 'whare they sclander me of magick, nycromancie, or of any other arte forbidden of God, I have witnesses . . . what I spake both against suche artis, and against those that use suche impietie', *History of the Reformation* 2.280. Such attacks were not, of course, confined to Scotland. Queen Mary, for example, was caricatured as the Circean enchantress Acrasia in Spenser's *Faerie Queene*. See Neill: 'Spenser's Acrasia and Mary Queen of Scots', *PMLA* 60 (1945), 682–8.

similar story was told of John Willock who was supposed to have raised Satan on Arthur's Seat.[53]) Satirical poems on both sides of the religious divide also used magic and sorcery as the basis of what were intended to be damaging accusations. The Protestant minister, John Craig, studied "practeces and propheceis of Nicromancie"; and the Earl of Moray's mother was described as a sorceress who seduced James V "by rings and witchcraft". Just so, it was said, Bothwell bewitched Queen Mary, while the Queen herself is likened more than once to Medea, the Classical enchantress.[54]

A rhetorical device, then: but this is not a sufficient explanation. Insults have no power if they are meaningless in the context of their delivery. The frequent cry of "whore" against women (frequently traded as an insult between women themselves) could cause offence only because chastity was accepted as a social value appropriate for women, and only if women accepted this value and measured their own worth and that of their female relatives and acquaintance by its standard; and the fact that it was employed often indicates a conscious awareness in the community of the importance with which that standard was endowed. If there is no such thing as chastity, and no general agreement that chastity is desirable and valuable, the insult "whore" is impotent. Similarly, the very fact that "witch" or "sorcerer" could be used so frequently by both Catholics and Protestants serves to indicate that there was an awareness in contemporary society of the active presence of magical practices and beliefs among the members of that society, and that these were regarded as sufficiently real to warrant the taking of offence or the feeling of guilt were they to be associated publicly with any individual. There is no point in accusing Knox of raising the Devil if nobody in one's audience, Catholic or Protestant, believes that raising the Devil is something which can be done; and it is of no consequence whether one believes the details of any given accusation. What matters is the truth of the general principle underlying it. Hence, we should not be surprised to find that when the Earl of Arran fell

---

53 Burne: *Disputation*, 143–4.
54 Craig. 'Ane complaint upon fortoun', vv. 131–2 = Cranstoun: *Satirical Poems* 1.338. Moray's mother. 'A rhime in defence of the Queen of Scots against the Earl of Moray, 11th December, 1568', vv. 209–12 = Cranstoun: 1.76. Bothwell. 'Ane declaratioun of the lordis just quarrell', vv. 113–19 = Cranstoun: 1.61. Mary. 'Ane ballat declaring the nobill and gude inclination of our King', v. 168 = Cranstoun: 1.36; 'The testament and tragedie of umquhile King Henrie Stewart of gude memorie', v. 117 = Cranstoun: 1.42. The same poem reproaches the Scots for being 'mantaneris of murther [and] witchecraft', v. 88. Mary's reign, indeed, attracted such rumours. Buchanan records that 'the predictions of wizardly women, in both kingdoms, did contribute much to hasten the marriage [of Mary and Henry Stewart]', *History*, 174; and anent Rizzio he noted that "there went a constant report, that one John Damiot, a French priest, *counted a conjuror*, told David once or twice, that now he had feather'd his nest, he should be gone", *op.cit.*, 182. [My italics.]

sick, for example, one of the explanations which occurred to him was that he had been bewitched; or that when the second Earl of Gowrie died, it was said that in his pocket there was found a folded paper on which were written magical words and characters. If at least some of the aristocracy practises magic, and if the aristocracy as a whole believes in its possibility, stories about such practices detrimental to their reputations can be written and published to some effect. Otherwise, the author is wasting his time and ink.[55]

Indeed if we require further indication that the aristocracy was perfectly prepared to turn to magic in moments of stress or need, we have only to consider the birth of James VI. The Queen's lying-in began on 3 June, 1566 and, after a false alarm on the 15th, her labour did begin on the 19th. But the labour was difficult and, in an effort to relieve the Queen of her pains, the Countess of Atholl at length resorted to magic, hoping thereby to transfer the Queen's dolours to Margaret, Lady Reres, who was also confined to bed at the time. There is no record of the Countess's efforts proving successful, but eventually the child emerged with a caul of membrane covering his head. Today one might look on this with suspicion as a possible cause of asphyxia and brain damage, and it has been suggested that the physical defects which contemporaries noticed and commented upon were the result of James's having been born with cerebral palsy. In 1566, however, the caul would have been regarded as a magical encasement which, if preserved, could give indications of the health and prosperity the child could expect to enjoy in his adult years, keep him from death by drowning, and make him invincible against attacks by fairies and sorcerers.[56] Now, the Countess of Atholl was a

55 Knox: *History of the Reformation* 2.328–9. Cowan: *The Ruthven Family Papers*, 163.
56 Bannatyne: *Memorials*, 174. Nau: *History of Mary Stewart*, 27. See also Fraser: *Mary, Queen of Scots*, 266–7. Lady Reres, who was appointed James's wet-nurse, was described in the most ungallant fashion by George Buchanan as 'a woman of maist vile unchastitie, wha had sometime been one of Bothwels harlots, and than was one of the chefe of the Quenis privie chamber', *Detectioun*, 9. On James's physical condition, see Beasley: 'The disability of James VI', *The Seventeenth Century* 10 (1995), 152–62. On the caul, see Dalyell: *Darker Supersititons*, 326. MacKenzie: 'Gaelic incantations', 142. Belief in the magical properties of the caul was still extant in the late nineteenth century. James Napier records, 'A child born with a caul – a thin membrane covering the head of some children at birth – would, if spared, prove a notable person. The carrying of a caul on board ship was believed to prevent shipwreck, and masters of vessels paid a high price for them. I have seen an advertisement for such in a local newspaper', *Folk Lore*, 32. Cf. Gifford, 'Not long ago we came across the following taken from the *Medical Adviser*. – 'Child's caul, to be sold for 30 guineas. A child's caul, that has already made 72 voyages, in which were encountered 38 hurricanes, besides sundry small storms, without a single drowning taking place. Application to be made to Mr. Underwoods, Fleet Street, where two old women attend daily. N.B. – This caul is particularly useful in steamboats and balloons' ', *An Ancient Seaport on the Shores of the Forth* (Dunfermline 1914), 76–7.

Catholic, and it might be argued that this account of her using magic is little more than another piece of Protestant propaganda, especially since the information was passed on to Bannatyne some time later, in 1571, by the Protestant Laird of Lundie. But it would be straining credulity too far to try to claim that every example of the aristocracy's involvement in magical operations was no more than adverse or lying comment, as though the aristocracy did not, somehow, partake of the same general magical outlook as the rest of the population. With reservation, therefore, we may accept at least some of the stories as likely to be true.

3

King James's Early Decades

Scotland passed through a crisis in 1567. Blamed as complicit in the murder of her husband, King Henry, and despised for marrying the Earl of Bothwell, widely regarded as one of the late King's assassins, Queen Mary had been confined to Loch Leven Castle where she miscarried of twins by the Earl and was then compelled to sign instruments of abdication. On 28 July that year, Parliament was told of the change of monarch, and on 29 July Prince James, only thirteen months old, was crowned King of Scots with Protestant rites in a Protestant church just outwith the gates of Stirling Castle. The Queen herself remained a prisoner until the beginning of May 1568 when she escaped and fled into England, leaving Scotland under the control of her half-brother, the Earl of Moray, regent for her son.[1] Moray intended to impose order and a Protestant régime upon the kingdom. Popular verses picked up the first of these and drew attention to it – "baith murtheraris, theifis, and Witches he did dant", said one lamenting his death: and "piracie [he] puneist, and devillishe sorcerie", recalled another.[2]

It is perhaps no accident that Moray was thus noted as a prosecutor of witches, and the following sequence of events is worth consideration. In December 1567, Parliament had an article laid before it for its approval: "how witchecraft salbe puneist and Inquisitioun takin therof and that the executioun of death may be usit alsweill aganis thame that consultis with the witche, seikis hir support, mantenis or defendis hir as aganis hir self".[3] This strong reminder of the 1563 Act may have been stimulated by half a sentence in a letter which was sent from the General Assembly to the Protestant nobility on 26 June, requesting them to attend a meeting of the Assembly on 20 July. The half-sentence asked, "that all superstition and idolatry, *and the monuments therof*, might be utterly removit and banishit out of this realme".[4] 'Monuments' here, of course, refers to more than buildings. Its early modern usage included the meanings 'indication, evidence, token; something serving

---

1 Nau: *History of Mary Stewart*, 60–3. Anon: *The Historie and Life of King James the Sext*, 17. Lindsay: *Cronicles of Scotland* 2.537. Fraser: *Mary, Queen of Scots*, 343–6. Messengers were sent out to proclaim Moray's regency on 14 August, *Accounts of the Treasurer of Scotland* 12.71.
2 'Ane tragedie, in forme of ane Diallog betwix Honour, Gude Fame, and the Authour heirof in a Trance', v. 376 = Cranstoun: *Satirical Poems* 1.93. 'The poysonit schot', v. 56 = Cranstoun 1.134.
3 *APS* 3.44: item 86.
4 *BUK*, 94. My italics.

to identify, a mark; something which gives warning, a portent", all of which hark back to its Latin root, *moneo* = 'I bring to the notice of, I serve as a reminder'. Under such a category, therefore, might well come magical beliefs and practices since they, in many of their manifestations, were indeed reminders of Catholicism as well as being unwanted instances of superstition.

When it came to the several sessions held by the Assembly in July, however, the subject most under discussion was finances. But then, on the 25th, appeared a list of ten articles which had been subscribed at Edinburgh on the 20th by several nobles and "uthers Commissioners present for the tyme", John Erskine included.[5] These articles contained two topics which might possibly encompass witchcraft and its attendant sorcery and enchantment: (a) a reiteration that "crymes, vyces, and offencis committit aganis Gods law" be punished in accordance with the secular law already passed (article 5), and an admonition that all subscribers to these articles "begin to ruit out, destroy and alluterlie subvert all monuments of idolatrie, and namely, the odious blasphemous messe, and therafter to goe fordwart throughout this whole realme, to all and sundrie places quhatsumevir idolatrie is fostred, hanted or maintained, and cheiflie quher messe is said, to execute the reformatioun forsaid, without exceptioun of place or persons" (article 10).[6]

Admittedly the link between all this and the Parliamentary article of December is tenuous, but a sharp note had been sounded in the December of 1566 by the General Assembly which had observed that "Satan, by all our negligences . . . hath so far prevailed within this realme of late dayes that we do stand in extream danger, not onely to losse our temporall possessions, but also to be deprived of the glorious Evangell of Jesus Christ, and so we and our posterity to be left in damnable darknesse".[7] So if the General Assembly's attention appeared to be directed to other priorities, its concern for the eradication of Catholicism and the punishment of crimes, vices, and offences committed against God's law was by no means blunted; and the articles promulgated during that Assembly may well have served to galvanise the Earl of Moray and those particularly sympathetic to his views on witches and sorcerers into seeking out that special manifestation of Satan's conspiracy against the Reformation. But whether or not this provided the motivation, a justiciary commission was issued from Glasgow in April, 1568 by Archibald Campbell, Earl of Argyll, naming James, Lord Ogilvy, James Erskine of Dun, Sir David Graham of Fintry, Sir John Ogilvy of Inverquharity, and James Haliburton, Provost of Dundee, together with David Pierson and John

---

5 Moray was probably in England at this point, having arrived in London on or
   soon after the 25th, *CSP Spanish* 1 (1558–1567). 662. He did not reach
   Edinburgh until 11 August, *CSPS* 2.380.
6 *Op. cit. supra*, 107–9.
7 Knox: *History of the Reformation* 1.539–40.

Hailes, baillies of Arbroath, as justices empowered to hold justiciary courts in Arbroath and bring to trial forty named persons "delatit or suspect of certane abhominable crymes of sorcerye and wychecraft laitlie committit be thame upoun divers our soverane lordis liegis".[8] Their commission referred to the sheriffdom of Forfar (i.e. Angus and the Mearns), and was to run for six months. A combination of three of them would be sufficient to provide a legal quorum, provided two of the three were Lord Ogilvy and John Erskine.

Several questions are raised by this commission. Who were the principals involved therein? What was the religious and political situation in Angus and the Mearns in 1568? What can be said of the forty people against whom the commission was directed? Why was the commission requested at that particular moment?

The political situation in 1567–8 was highly volatile.[9] Queen Mary's marriage to the Earl of Bothwell in 1567 had split the nobility, with the Earl of Moray taking his opposition as far as offering armed resistance to the Queen. He was supported in this by the Earl of Argyll and James Haliburton – the only figure from Angus to side with the Earl, for Angus and the Mearns on the whole remained loyal to the Crown. Lord Ogilvy, too, rallied to the Queen after her escape from Loch Leven Castle on 2 May, 1568; and in spite of the fact that he had played a prominent role in the infant King James's coronation, John Erskine also proved reluctant to enter the civil war on the King's side. His hesitation probably sprang from family connections. Katharine Campbell, widow of James, Master of Ogilvy, and second wife of the ninth Earl of Crawford, had married the daughter of her eldest son, Lord Ogilvy, to John Erskine's grandson. What is more, John Ogilvy of Inverquharity's son (also called John), had married Helen, one of Katharine Campbell's daughters from her marriage to the Master of Ogilvy, and through these same marriages John Erskine and Lord Ogilvy were allied to the Earl of Crawford who was considered to be one of the principal supporters of Queen Mary. Three out of the seven commissioners, including the two considered essential to any quorum, then, formed a fairly tight Protestant family group. Sir David Graham of Fintry's family, too, had been closely associated with the Earl of Crawford, and so of the titled or landed commissioners, it is interesting to see that it was only John Ogilvy of Inverquharity who chose openly to take the King's side in the war.[10]

8 *GD*16/25/4

9 The account which follows is based upon Bardgett: *Scotland Reformed*, 119–46.

10 The two baillies should not be regarded as insignificant. 'Pierson' was one of the leading families in Arbroath during the sixteenth century and later, and David Pierson represented Arbroath at a Convention held at Stirling in 1574. The Hailes family, too, was highly influential within the burgh. One may note that a George Hailes brought an accusation of witchcraft against Janet Lamb from Arbroath, one of the women who appear in the 1568 witchcraft commission. See Hay: *History of Arbroath*, 135, 128–9.

The Queen's battle, however, was fought over in the west, on the outskirts of Glasgow (which is why the witchcraft commission was issued thence). Angus and the Mearns, loyal as they may have been to the Marian cause, were not directly involved as a principal theatre of war.[11] Political considerations, therefore, are unlikely to have furnished a reason (certainly not the principal reason) for the issuing of a commission to investigate and try witchcraft, and one is thus drawn to the conclusion that religious rather than political motives lay behind the judicial proceedings. It is no more than one might have expected.

Angus and the Mearns by and large welcomed Protestant reform, although the welcome was by no means as warm in the former as it was in the latter. The Mearns lairds formed a more cohesive Protestant group than those from Angus who were somewhat ill-assorted. Apart from John Erskine, indeed, the Angus lairds seem to have lacked clear local leadership, and their shared history – forfeitures under James V, occupation by the English, economic changes attendant upon the need for the rich to buttress their status by ever-increasing expenditure – meant that they were inclined to be cautious rather than risk their estates in war or with over-bold political or religious gestures. If they had turned Protestant, it was for a variety of reasons. Some were anti-Catholic; some found the reformed religion provided satisfactory answers to their personal perceptions of the troubled times in which they were living; some relished the opportunities of patronage which religious change offered them; others took the chance to add to their estates.[12] Nevertheless, the Angus lairds in particular were conservative. Their political inclination, for example, was to support the monarchical status quo, even though in this case the monarch was a Catholic – and their conservatism, as we have seen, was mirrored in the witchcraft commissioners – and this cautious attitude may well have contributed to slowing down the acceptance of Protestantism, especially within Angus. For the state of the Kirk in the region was not altogether satisfactory, in spite of there being a good nucleus of reformed ministers in both Angus and the Mearns from as early as 1561. Many of these ministers were local men, serving parishes they knew well, and in consequence the region was among the first in which parochial reformation was implemented quickly.[13] But (and it is an important 'but') reaction to the imposition of reformed parochial discipline was not uniformly favourable. Several lairds failed to give it their support, and entrenched vested interests often delayed effective establishment of the reformed religion. The state of its local finances

---

11 This is not to say that there were no local conflicts. Several are recorded between Queen's men and King's men near Brechin at various times during James's minority. See Hay: *op.cit. supra*, 133.
12 See Bardgett: *op.cit.*, 82, 81, 3–18.
13 Bardgett: 88–90, 94–5, 101–2.

gives an indication of local attitudes. Money to keep the churches in repair was often not forthcoming and Erskine was criticised at the start of the General Assembly of March, 1575 because "the quires within his diocy were ruinous".[14]

So in spite of the initial impetus of 1559–60, by 1568 progress for the reformers had actually been slow and was being hampered by a variety of local considerations. Slow progress must have meant that eradication of Catholic beliefs and practices would not have proceeded at a pace congenial to the wishes of the Kirk, in spite of there being a nominal sufficiency of ministers in the region to see such eradication effected.[15] So Angus, rather more than the Mearns, would appear to present the greater challenge to anyone who wished to punish witchcraft and set an example of abolishing 'superstition'; and a review of the places whence came the forty individuals named in the commission confirms this impression. We can be sure of the origins of 31 out of the 40: of these, 12 came from Arbroath and 1 each from Carmylie, Coupar Angus, the Mains under Fintry, Panbride, Lundie, Brechin, Kirriemuir, Tealing, and Fowlis (= 10). Now, these places congregate within a relatively small geographical area, approximately 40 miles by 20, in the south of Forfarshire, (Angus) between Arbroath and Dunkeld, and Kirriemuir and Dundee. The other people came from villages and towns widely dispersed, a small number (6) from the north in Kincardineshire and Aberdeenshire, the rest from unconnected places south and west.[16]

This area was not one in which any of the landed commissioners had a particular political interest. The Ogilvies, for example, were much more directly concerned with Strathmore, from Alyth to Edzell. Moreover, it is difficult to see what political point could have been made by any of them requesting a witchcraft commission at this moment. Since all of them except Ogilvy of Inverquharity were supporters, or at least tolerators, of Queen Mary, only if one or more of the others had been at odds with Inverquharity would it have made some kind of political sense to embark on a concentrated prosecution of witches. But as all the commissioners concerned were fervent in the Protestant cause, a prosecution conducted for political reasons would have made no sense and, indeed, produced no special gain for anyone except,

---

14 *BUK*, 314. Cf. Bardgett: *op.cit.*, 104–7.
15 The Mearns actually fared better with ministers than did Angus, Cowan: *The Scottish Reformation*, 162.
16 From the north: 1 person from near Canny, a rivulet in Kincardineshire; 2 from Auchmill, a village in Newhills parish; 2 from Got beside Kelly, a rivulet in East Aberdeenshire; and 1 from Balgownie. These, however, are too scattered to form anything like a group. For the rest, one came from Kilgour in the south and one from 'St. Johnston' which may be connected with Laurencekirk. If so, it belongs in the north. One person is described as coming from 'Stormont' which is a district rather than a place.

perhaps, Erskine within whose superintendency the investigations and trials were to take place.[17]

If, then, it is unlikely that politics played a part in the request for the commission, what particular (as opposed to general) religious benefit might there be for any of the commissioners? Or does one have to look for a minister or group of ministers behind the commissioners, stimulating their interest in the project and working through their authority? South Forfarshire included parts of several presbyteries – Arbroath, Dundee, Brechin, and Forfar – and it is interesting to note that almost all the relevant parishes within this area had received fresh or renewed appointments of clergy and readers in 1567.[18] Within the Presbytery of Arbroath, for example, Arbirlot had a minister, whereas Arbroath, Barry, Inverkeilor, Kinnell, and Lunan all had readers. Only Guthrie and Carbuddo and St. Vigeans had been under the control of ministers since 1566 and 1564. In the Presbytery of Dundee, Lundie, Fowlis, and Tealing had ministers, but the first two lost theirs when they were transferred to other parishes in November, 1567, while the last had a fresh charge that same year. John Hepburn in the Presbytery of Brechin, after a period of sickness, had his charge renewed on 31 December, 1567 when Panbride was added to his cure; and in the Presbytery of Forfar, both minister and reader for Kirriemuir were appointed in 1567.[19]

Two points can be made about this. First, since most of the appointments were very recent, and because in the Presbytery of Arbroath the majority were readers and not ordained ministers, their lack of ministerial authority is likely to have meant that they would have found it somewhat more difficult than a minister to discipline their parishioners. One must not over-emphasise this point, of course, because it is equally true that the lack of such final authority and the newness of their appointments could equally well have made them the keener to prove themselves competent by trying to implement whatever parochial reformation the Kirk might require. But, as we have seen in Angus especially, the initial impetus of reform had slowed down quite noticeably since 1563, and the presence of readers rather than ministers in a number of

17 It is true that Argyll and Moray were on opposite sides in the current civil war, but a decision by Argyll to permit prosecution of witches would not have troubled Moray who would undoubtedly have agreed with its aims.

18 The reader who was often the local schoolmaster as well, conducted the first part of the Sunday service and sometimes read the daily services and took catechism. He often delivered formal summonses to kirk sessions, too, and kept the session minutes. See Foster: *The Church before the Covenants*, 192–4.

19 See *Fasti Ecclesiae Scoticanae* 5 under the appropriate presbyteries and parishes. One of the problems faced by Angus and the Mearns in finding suitable clergy was that most of their Catholic priests refused to assist the reformed Kirk. See Bargett: *Scotland Reformed*, 101.

parishes may have made some small contribution to this, merely because parishioners could have felt it was somewhat easier to resist the strictures of a reader (even when he was supported by the elders of their kirk) than those of a minister.[20] Secondly, Catholicism lingered on in many parts of the Lowlands in both towns and rural areas well into the 1570s and 1580s, even if this represented "a traditional conservative reaction against innovation rather than a positive preference for the old religion".[21] There is an interesting coincidence, then, in the lack of authoritative ministers, especially within the Presbytery of Arbroath which saw the largest number of suspect witches named in the witchcraft commission, the conservatism of the Angus lairds, the article laid before Parliament in December, 1567 seeking renewed investigation of witchcraft and punishment of witches, and a request by Erskine to the General Assembly in January, 1568 to resign his superintendency on the grounds of age and infirmity.[22] His application was refused and it looks as though one possible reason for the request for a witchcraft commission in or before April, 1568 could have been Erskine's wish to exert a renewed discipline and control over certain areas within his jurisdiction, relying perhaps on the willing co-operation of newly appointed officials in a particularly sensitive area.[23]

The results of the investigation and likely subsequent trials is not known. There is no reason to suppose that all those named as suspect or delated must have been found guilty and executed, since acquittals in witchcraft trials were not uncommon. One other person described as a witch, but not included among the forty named in the commission, Agnes Ferguson, is recorded as being sentenced in May, 1568 to 'the pit', probably the lowest cell in the Abbey tower of Arbroath, where she was to be maintained at the rate of 5d (c.13 new pence) per day. Presumably she was put there to await her trial or possible execution; while in August, Sir William Stewart, Lyon King of

20 Many of the ministers and readers in Angus and the Mearns were regarded by the Kirk as unsuitable either because (in a few cases) they had been Catholic priests – one may note, for example, that Thomas Lindsay in Arbroath was a former monk – or because they were too young and inexperienced, or because they set a poor example by less than righteous private lives, or because they were absent from their posts. Such, at any rate, were the complaints made against John Erskine in the General Assembly in December, 1562. *BUK*, 25. See also Bardgett: *op.cit. supra*, 91–4. Judging by the rash of new appointments in 1567, however, it looks as though the Presbytery of Arbroath in particular was trying to start afresh with a clean slate.

21 Whyte: *Scotland before the Industrial Revolution*, 105.

22 *BUK*, 120.

23 His concern for discipline may have been stimulated by complaints levied against the neighbouring Superintendent of Fife at the General Assembly of 25 December, 1567 that he was not visiting kirks, nor teaching in them, 'nor taking up crymes and offenses to be punished', *BUK*, 112.

Arms, was brought from Edinburgh Castle to Dumbarton "for conspyring to take the Regents lyffe by sorcerey and necromancey, for wich he was put to death".[24] Another account of the incident tells us that he was hanged,[25] but this was not the standard form of execution for witchcraft, even if the convicted party was a man, and his dittay makes it clear that treason accompanied much of his magical activity.[26]

He was accused of fifteen separate points, seven of which alleged he had tried to divine the immediate future by using the shears and riddle, three that he had invoked spirits, and two that he had consulted witches.[27] Two of these recorded invocations of spirits took place in Merchiston, one of them at least with the active assistance of Sir Archibald Napier in whose house and yard the sessions were held. Sir Archibald was one of the leading advocates in Edinburgh at the time and had been knighted at the wedding of Queen Mary and Henry Stuart.[28] Together he and William, it is said, invoked and worshipped the spirit Obirion whose picture Stewart had drawn upon a lead tablet along with the words *servitus pulcher* ['handsome slave'],[29] and who appeared to them in the form of a king or a good-looking youth, the object of this and of the other invoking session being to receive "consolatioun and knawlege of thingis to cum concerning the estait of this realm and utheris".[30] The name 'Obirion' is obviously reminiscent of

24 (Agnes Ferguson), Hay: *History of Arbroath*, 129. (William Stewart), Balfour: *Annales of Scotland* 1.345. It was quite a fall from grace. Only six months before, he had been paid £94 to cover his expenses while he was on the King's business in Denmark, *Accounts of the Treasurer of Scotland* 12.128–9. Perhaps one should also note that during 1568 there was widespread famine in Scotland, and in December that year the General Assembly remarked on sickness in Edinburgh and tempests and storms all over the country, *Historie and Life of King James the Sext*, 21. *BUK*, 133. These phenomena would not necessarily have caused accusations of witchcraft to be levelled against so many individuals, but they might well have heightened tension in many places.
25 *Historie and Life of King James the Sext*, 41.
26 The commission authorising his trial, indeed, specifies treason and witchcraft as the principal crimes of which he and his co-panel, Nicolas Haubert, were accused, *JC26/1/51*.
27 *JC40/2*.
28 An interest in practical magic seems to have run in the family, since his son, James Napier, the inventor of logarithms, was also rumoured to dabble in the magical arts.
29 Strictly speaking, *servitus* is an abstract noun meaning 'servitude' or 'bondage', but is here clearly being used as a form of *servus* = 'slave'.
30 We are told that on this other occasion the spirits were invoked 'in Italian', these words having been added above the line. Since it is unlikely any of the participants were Italian, the probability is that this was the language of the magical text they were using. Even so, it is very unusual. A complex ritual for summoning 'Oberion', accompanied by two rough drawings, appears in *GD188/ 25/1/3*, pp.146, 148–59. One of the drawings shows a man, fashionably dressed, with a moustache and a Van Dyke beard, and carrying a sceptre (p.158).

'Oberon', King of the Fairies, and it may well be that he and certain other entities invoked by Stewart were *sithean*, re-interpreted by the dittay as evil spirits. For the third such recorded occasion took place in Holyrood park beside Arthur's Seat, where Stewart was assisted by several men who together performed a magical ceremony taken from a book by the notorious magus, Cornelius Agrippa.[31] The area below Arthur's Seat was also used by Janet Boyman as a place suitable for invoking *sithean*, and it may be that the name 'Arthur's Seat' is a corruption of the Gaelic *Ard na Saighead*, 'high place of the arrows', a reference to Neolithic arrow-heads which could be picked up from the ground and were considered to be weapons belonging to the *sithean*.[32]

But Stewart also used the shears and riddle as a less disconcerting method of divining the future,[33] at which he was clearly believed to have some skill, for his dittay records that he employed them to answer questions posed by other people as well as himself. These questions tended to relate to the immediate concerns of a small group of men in the late 1560s. Stewart prophesied, for example, that the Regent (Moray) would die violently before 17 November, 1567 and that Queen Mary would win the battle of Langside [2 May, 1568]. It was also alleged that Stewart knew in advance by magical means of King Henry's murder, and that he prophesied the King would die before 26 March, 1567.[34] This last prediction was made in the house of Gilbert Balfour in about January, 1566. Balfour was an important man, Master of the Queen's Household since 1565, who seems to have encouraged Stewart to believe that when the shears and riddle revealed the Queen would escape from imprisonment in Loch Leven Castle and marry again, the man intended for such an honour was Stewart himself; and indeed, so keen was Stewart to ascertain or confirm the truth of this that he visited two witches on two separate occasions. The first woman, bearing the common 'witch name' Nicnevin, was simply asked about the future and in particular when the Queen would be free; but the second, known as 'Dame Steill", from Edinburgh, came to Stewart's house in answer to his summons and there gave specific replies to specific questions. These replies were (a) that the Queen would be furth of Loch Leven on the first Sunday in May, 1567; (b) that Stewart would be in very good standing with the Queen; and (c) that

---

31 Actually, if they took their directions from Agrippa, as the dittay claims, it is likely they used the *Fourth Book of Occult Philosophy* attributed to rather than written by him, since this contains details of how one may invoke spirits.
32 See Kirk: *Secret Commonwealth*, 58–9. On Janet Boyman, see *infra* pp. 62–6.
33 See *supra*, p. 25.
34 Moray was assassinated on 21 January, 1570. The Queen lost the battle of Langside. King Henry died in the grounds of Kirk o'Field on 10 February, 1567.

Mary would be mistress of Scotland, marry Stewart, and bear him children.[35]

In view of this mixture of magic and treason, therefore, it is not surprising that Stewart was found guilty and executed. Indeed, his dittay records "confessit and filit" beside each separate item. His case is interesting because it shows a group of important political and legal figures willingly taking part in both magical and divinatory operations, for not only Sir Archibald Napier and Gilbert Balfour involved themselves, but so also did Patrick Hepburn, Bishop of Moray and kinsman to Queen Mary's third husband, the Earl of Bothwell. All had reason to wish to know the outcome of the struggle for power which was going on in 1567–8, and it is notable that all turned to magic to satisfy their curiosity. The impulse was one they shared with a large number of other people of their rank and influence. Stewart's dittay also illustrates a kind of magic indistinguishable (except perhaps for the use of the book by Agrippa) from the kind of magic practised by female witches – invocation of *sithean* and use of the shears and riddle – although the dittay is unusual in that it accuses Stewart of witchcraft, sorcery, *and magic*.[36] This last phrase is never applied in such documents to females *accusées*, presumably because either they did not practise ceremonial magic in Agrippa's sense, or because they were not perceived by the courts as doing so.

Such, then, was the biggest scandal of 1568. In 1569 it was the turn of Fife to receive official attention. On 18 May, the Earl of Moray left Edinburgh in order to "dant the insolence of George erle Huntlie" who had gathered an army and was menacing the Mearns, Angus, and Fife. The two men met in St. Andrews before Moray proceeded further north to Aberdeen where he summoned Huntly's supporters to appear before him in the tolbooth.[37] It is not surprising, therefore, that on 16, 25, and 26 May we find messengers being paid 20 shillings to summon assizes within Fife for the purpose of trying witches.[38] Moray himself tried witches there on his way north, another called Katharine Cultis while he was in Aberdeen, and yet others on his return south through Dundee.[39]

---

35 The prophecy about Mary's escape was correct in as much as she left Loch Leven on Sunday, 2 May. Whether the dittay is mistaken in giving the year as 1567 or whether the question was put before that date and the year is correctly recorded, though wrong in fact, is not altogether clear.

36 The record is badly damaged at this point, but there is enough visible of the beginning of 'witchcraft' and the end of 'sorcery' to be sure that these words were there. The phrase 'and magik' is clear and undamaged.

37 *Diurnall of Occurrents*, 144. *Historie and Life of King James the Sext*, 39.

38 *Accounts of the Treasurer of Scotland* 12.161.

39 *Diurnall of Occurrents*, 144. *Accounts of the Treasurer of Scotland* 12.163. *Diurnall*, 145. *The Historie and Life of King James the Sext*, 40 refers to a sorceress called Nic Neville who was burned in St. Andrews at this time. Lord Herries calls the witch 'a fellow' but, in view of the *Nic* (Gaelic = 'daughter of'), he seems to have been mistaken, *Historical Memoirs*, 115. Another witch, Elspeth Graham, was to be tried by an assize summoned from Dunkeld in August, *Accounts of the Treasurer of Scotland* 12.167.

These two years seem to have opened the sluice-gates of prosecutions, for the succeeding decades saw what appears to be a big increase in the number of accused witches brought before the courts; and yet this appearance may be illusory, owing something to the records which had begun to note more frequently either the trials themselves or the concern of the Kirk and Parliament in the face of a problem which seemed to be incorrigible. Witches in plenty there were, but they are recorded as ones and twos from all over Scotland and thus cannot be counted as part of a general sweep of prosecution directed from the centre and thus amounting to some kind of hunt as might, though with reservations, be argued for the 1568 commission and its concentration on south Forfarshire. So, to give one or two examples, Bannatyne remarked that a present was sent in October, 1570 to Queen Mary, "we suppose from the witches of Atholl", a reasonable enough assumption as the Countess was known to have frequent dealings with such people, although the gift itself, a medallion made of horn and gold carrying the arms of Scotland, an enthroned woman, and a device to indicate Mary's regal claim over Scotland and England, has nothing overtly magical about it. In 1572, John Knox preached at a witch who was made to stand in front of him, on 28 April a witch was burned in St. Andrews, and on 29 December Janet Boyman, spouse to William Steill, was delated of various points of witchcraft, convicted, and burned.[40]

The witch burned in St. Andrews was relying on magic to help her resist strangulation or the flames. At first she was full of bravado. "Being desyred that she wold forgive a man that had done hir some offence, as scho alledged, refuised; then, when ane uther that stude by said, gif shoe did not forgive, that God wald nocht forgive hir, and so shoe suld be dampned; but sho, not cairing for heavin nor hell, said opinly, 'I pass not whidder I goe to hell or heavin!' with diverse utheris execrable wordis." Her hands were then bound and the Provost lifted up her clothes, perhaps to see her Devil's mark, as Bannatyne says (although in Scotland at least this was usually to be found on the shoulder or neck), or to check whether she was wearing any magical talisman. Sure enough, he found between her legs a white cloth like a neckerchief, with strings attached, each string carrying a large number of knots. When this device was removed, much to her distress, she cried out, "Now I have no hoip of my self!", evidently believing that the talisman would have preserved her from death.[41] This notion that witches were able to protect themselves magically, to resist the pains of torture, for example, was common. The Jesuit Del Rio observed that Satan "usually furnishes them with pieces of parchment and other instruments of magic, on which are written various

---

40 Bannatyne: *Memorials*, 61–2. Melville: *Diary*, 46. Pitcairn: *Criminal Trials* 1.2.38.
41 Bannatyne: *op.cit. supra*, 233.

characters. These are concealed in the most private parts of the body and, in accordance with the [diabolical] pact, remove the sense of pain". Hence, he says, those about to be tortured should be searched for such amulets.[42] It seems very likely, therefore, that this is why the Provost lifted the woman's clothing and conducted his search.

Janet Boyman is particularly interesting, partly because hers is one of the first surviving dittays to record any significant details, and partly because of the nature of those details.[43] There are six articles altogether. In the first we learn that she claimed she could help Alan Lauderstone, a smith in the Canongate, only if someone sent her his shirt, for "be the sight therof schoe could knaw quhat seiknes he had and gif schoe could mend him therof or not". The shirt was duly sent and Janet took it to a spring beneath Arthur's Seat in Edinburgh. Its water ran southwards – an important point in this type of magical operation – and Janet believed it to be "ane elreth well", that is, a well or spring belonging to or frequented by the *sithean*. There she called upon what the dittay calls 'evil spirits' to come and tell her what fate awaited her client, "and ther cam thereftir first ane grit blaste lyk a quhurlewind, and thereftir ther cam the schap [figure] of a man and stand on the uthir syd of the well foranent [opposite] hir". Janet then addressed him in the name of the Father and the Son, and of King Arthur and Queen Elspeth, to answer her questions regarding Alan Lauderstone, "and that ye owthir giff him his healthe or ells tak him to yow and releive him of this pain". Finally, she washed his shirt in the spring-water, and sent it back to him with instructions that it be laid on top of his bed as though he were wearing it, left arm to left arm, right to right, and so on. This, apparently, was a compromise. He should actually have it on, but his illness had made him so delirious that he could not bear to have it touch his body.[44]

Further instructions were sent to Alan's wife. Not only was she to see the shirt laid out in the manner Janet had specified, she was to make sure her husband was kept under close surveillance that night, "and that quhatevir schoe hard or saw, [she] sould not speik ane word out of hir mouth". Alan's wife, however, disregarded what she was told. She hung the shirt upon a door to dry and therefore paid the price for her neglect. For as she was sitting with Alan, "about midnyt cam lyk a grit wind about the hous and ane very grit dyn

---

42 *Disquisitiones Magicae* Book 5, Section 9.
43 JC40/1/1.
44 Cf. the case of William Craig whom Janet was called upon to cure. She said his shirt should be washed after sunset and dried during the hours of darkness, away from either sunlight or firelight. The shirt was then to be put on William before the sun rose, and 'he sould ayther mend of his seiknes within nyne dayis or incontinent depairt'. The procedure was carried out, with what result we do not know; but failures are often referred to in the records as 'the late X', and since this formula is not applied to William, it may be an indication that he recovered.

quhilk maid hir very affryed". A horse shoe next to the bed suddenly began to rattle, as though someone were dragging or shifting it about. From the smithy came the noise of a hammer striking the anvil very fast, although investigation showed there was no one there at the time. Everyone in the house, says the dittay, trembled. Next morning Janet scolded Alan's wife and told her that if she would do as she was told, her husband would get well; if not, "he wald be a cryple all his dayis". Fortunately this time the woman did as she was bid, and Alan duly recovered.[45]

Several features of this item are worth noting. First, Janet employed a well-known means of divination by going to a place frequented by the *sithean* and asking them to pronounce on the sick man's prospects. *Sithean* are prominent in the records of Scottish witchcraft during the sixteenth century, and although the clerk who drew up this rough version of Janet's dittay chose to re-interpret them as evil spirits, neither Janet nor her audience in court would necessarily have viewed them in that particular light. Everyone knew about *sithean*. A remarkable number of people had faith in the reality both of their existence and of their powers. But the criminal charge brought against Janet required such a re-interpretation. The Witchcraft Act said nothing about consulting *sithean*, but if *sithean* could be represented as spirits or illusions of the Devil, the implicit intention of the Act would be satisfied and the charge against Janet allowed to stand in court without challenge by her proloquitor who might otherwise claim it was 'not relevant', that is, that it should not be heard because it did not fulfil the requirement of the law.

Why did Janet choose to go to Arthur's Seat? Partly because it lay outwith the city and was thus symbolically beyond the pale of law and the civilised order, an extra-liminal space in which the forces of nature and praeter-nature exercised sway; partly because the spring with its south-running water was located there; and perhaps because, as we have seen earlier, Arthur's Seat was by definition a haunt of the *sithean*. Having made her incantation, Janet was presented with the sight of an apparition. The members of her assize would have debated his identity, some at least perhaps coming to the conclusion it was the Devil. There are problems with this. To be sure, Janet charges him to to give her information in the names of only two of the Trinity, with Arthur and Elspeth (King and Queen of the *sithean*, or perhaps here their substitutes) taking the place normally occupied by the Holy Ghost; and this mangling of

---

45 Using an item of clothing, very often a shirt, either to effect a sick person's cure or to kill someone against whom the magical operator entertained animosity, was a common practice among Scottish witches. When Agnes Sampson wanted to murder the King by magical means in 1589–90, for example, she tried to get hold of something he had worn or used – a shirt, a handkerchief, a napkin, anything of that nature – and witches were often alleged to be able to diagnose the cause of a sick person's illness by handling his or her shirt.

the Christian formula would not have passed unnoticed, nor is it likely to have been regarded with indifference. Nevertheless, the apparition is not described as 'black' or 'clad in black clothes' or even 'clad in green', which tend to be the standard phrases by which the Devil is identified in witchcraft evidence, and the possibility therefore lies open that he or it was a *sìth* or a ghost.

It is clear from the surviving brief, scribbled copy of Janet's dittay that this episode was going to be presented to the court as an invocation of and meeting with the Devil, but we lack the final draft of the dittay and have no record of the precise words in which this prosecutory version of the event was conveyed to Janet's assize. Nor do we know whether her proloquitor attempted to counter this hostile narrative by seeking, as proloquitors did, some failure in the drafting of the dittay or some other technical loophole whereby he might have this item declared irrelevant. Nor can we tell whether any or all of the members of her assize were prepared to interpret the apparition as a *sìth* rather than an evil spirit, and whether this would have had any effect on the way they viewed the incident. An evil spirit might be taken as evidence, for example, of trafficking with the Devil and of an implicit pact with him, as well as of blasphemy and idolatry – all seriously grave offences. A *sìth*, on the other hand, might be accepted as evidence of 'superstition' and therefore of minor, less harmful magic, and the latter rather than the former might thus make the difference between a vote for Janet's life or for her death.[46]

Three years after Janet had cured Alan Lauderstone of his illness, he fell sick of it again and so Janet was duly summoned. This time, however, she refused to come, on the grounds that All Hallows' Eve had passed. Had they come to her before that day, she said, she would have been able to help: "Ye being inquyrit quhairfoir on hallowevin nor [rather than] any uthir day, ye anserit because the good nichboris rest on that day, and ye had mair acquentance with thame that day nor ane uthir". Janet also revealed to her official interrogators that the *sìthean* rode out upon All Hallows' Eve, and that she saw them the last time she was in the park on Arthur's Seat. There were three people with her at the time, and one of them, Janet Henderson, was so frightened that she died eight days later, and even Janet Boyman herself lay sick for four or five days, the principal cause of their distress, seemingly, a blast of evil wind which had struck them while they watched the *sìthean* ride. Janet confessed in another item of her dittay that she had seen such a blast twenty times, and described it as "the wind with ane thing lyke ane hat in it quhurland about the skay".

46 We are told by the brief official record in the *Book of Adjournal* that Janet was convicted and burned, but the record says nothing about the voting of her assize upon the individual items contained in her dittay. She could have been acquitted on this point, for example, and found guilty on the others, and that would have been sufficient to cause the final verdict and sentence.

Evil winds of a similar kind were also responsible for other illnesses, and in the third article of her dittay Janet relates how Alan Lauderstone's wife was breast-feeding her child when Janet asked her why she bothered. The child, she said, had not 'heart' and could not live; and sure enough, soon afterwards, it died. Janet's interrogators asked her how she knew that would happen and she answered that "it had gottin ane blast of evill wind and the mother had not fund it weill aneughe [had not given it a good enough start in life]". In consequence, one day when it was lying quietly outwith the house, some witches had given it the blast and its life had begun to shrink away. How can children be saved from that particular danger? Janet's answer is slightly obscure: "Gif a dish had bene quhomlet [whummled] one the feit of the bairne, it suld bene saiff". The meaning of this seems to be supplied by her answer to the interrogators' next question. How did she know this? A woman called Megie, said Janet, had once helped her when she was ill from the same cause. First Megie heated water, together with some woodbine leaves, in a cooking-pot and then put Janet in the water, saying, "In the name of the Father and the Holy Gost, [may] King Arthor and Quene Elspet send this witches thing furwith [at once], or els tak furth yow aff this worald". So the remedy seems to be that the patient's feet be dipped into a warm, herbal infusion, and the dish or vessel turned rapidly round and round (whummled) while the spell was being recited.

Such, then, is the sum of the surviving charges brought against Janet. She appears to have been a healer who relied partly upon techniques learned from another healer, and partly upon communication with entities from another world.[47] She herself clearly identified these beings with the *sithean* local to Arthur's Seat, and used Christian terminology during her invocation of them. Her assize, however, was meant to view these *sithean* as evil spirits, and during her trial there may well have been tension created in the minds of her assizers between what could have been their strict religious views and their sense of public duty to uphold the law, and their knowledge of long-held popular beliefs and practices. But if the six items of Janet's dittay discussed here represent the whole of the case against her, it seems by her conviction and subsequent execution that the assize, either as a whole or by a majority of its members, was hostile to her intercourse with the *sithean* – a conclusion which does not necessarily mean they were sceptical of the reality of the *sitheans'* existence and power, merely that they were frightened or disconcerted or offended by the active demonstration of Janet's belief in such things and her

47 This last is the kind of activity which might nowadays be called 'channelling', defined by Hastings as 'a process in which a person transmits information . . . that he or she receives mentally or physically, and which appears to come from a personality source outside the conscious mind. The message is directed towards an audience and is purposeful', *With the Tongues of Men and Angels*, 4.

willingness to exercise that belief in practical ways in the face of the Kirk's and state's expressed disapproval.

It may be significant that Janet and the other witches we mentioned earlier were apprehended in 1572, for that and the succeeding year give indications of fresh (or perhaps continuing), alarm in the Kirk that its campaign against Catholicism and magic were not having that success for which the Protestant establishment was looking. Throughout 1572 there are records of people being brought before the criminal court for celebrating or being present at the celebration of Mass. They came from a wide band of southern Scotland, from near Edinburgh to the shires of Renfrew, Ayr, and Dumfries, and it must have been irritating for the authorities to note that at least one of those charged was a parson, clearly prepared to continue saying the old service for those who wished him to do so.[48] On 3 October, the General Assembly sent an address to the new Regent, James Douglas, Earl of Morton, which revealed another related concern: "the furious rage and lawlis creweltie of the bludy and tressonable papists, executouris of the decreis of the . . . devillishe and terrible Counsall of Trent".[49] It was necessary, said the Assembly, to alert the Protestants of Scotland to this foreign menace, and therefore the Kirk's commissioners should be granted full authority by the Government to carry this message throughout the kingdom without being stopped, searched, harassed, or impeded in any way. This was followed on 20 October by a list of recommendations whereby, in the light of "the tressonable crweltie of the papists", Kirk discipline was to be tightened and the Government asked to implement the existing Acts of Parliament against Catholics and to assist in making sure that "wickitnes and such hynous crymes that offendis the majestie of God may be purgit furth of this cuntrie".[50]

Part of the reason for this renewed action by the Kirk obviously springs from nervousness engendered by the massacre of Protestants in France on St. Bartholomew's Eve, the previous August. But the Kirk was also aware of shortcomings in its own officials, since some of its Superintendents and commissioners were still not carrying out their duties satisfactorily. On 6 March, 1571, for example, the Superintendent of Fife had to face complaints that he had either failed to visit certain parishes for at least a year (in one case

---

48 Pitcairn: *Criminal Trials* 1.2.29–30, 31, 32, 35, 38. The trials occurred at intervals throughout the year: March, May, June, July, and December. The parson was Archibald Crawford from Eaglesham. Cf. *Diurnall of Occurrents*, 301, 341.
    Historie and Life of King James the Sext, 40. *RPC* 2.40–1. Ross: 'Reformation and repression', 368–9.
49 *BUK*, 251. Cf. 'The grytt and crwll mwrther and messecar of Paris wes committit be Hendre, Kyng of France . . . with consent of the haill papithis of that religione, efter the decre of the Consall of Trentt', *Chronicle of Aberdeen* = *SCM* 2.37–8.
50 *BUK*, 252–3.

three years), and that even when he had inspected one of them, he had not consulted its ministers or elders; and apparently Moray was in need of an extra commissioner to visit ministers and establish Protestant churches, so one had to be appointed for that purpose.[51] In spite of this, however, matters clearly did not improve, for on 6 August, 1573 the Assembly was informed that one of the Moray commissioners was not resident in his area and had made no attempt to perform his function except in Inverness, Elgin, and Forres.[52]

How much of this might be excused by the difficulties attendant on contemporary travel? Movement between communities tended to be governed by strict necessity, and a day's walk or, in some cases, a day's ride represented the desired extent of anyone's intention to travel; and although there was certainly a network of roads in the east to afford greater ease of movement, impediments existed or could come into existence. For, as Barrow points out, "even a small burn in spate might be impassable and . . . a knowledge of the firmest crossing places was essential for everyone in the community".[53] The sketchiness of Pont's maps of the Highlands in the late sixteenth century suggests that he found travel therein more difficult than on the eastern side of the country; and one must bear in mind the large number of vagrants who were seen as a problem, divided into 'deserving' and 'idle' by legislation, and who sometimes formed gangs which could frighten or terrorise a neighbourhood, to the disapproval of successive Parliaments.[54] Problems, therefore, there were. Nevertheless, one cannot help wondering whether the enormity of the distances they were expected to cover and of the task laid on their shoulders by the Assembly did not simply prove too daunting for some of the Kirk's officials who made some attempt to fulfil their appointed duties, but often gave up in the face of the difficulties these entailed.[55]

More, however, was going to be required. The Assembly of 6 March, 1573,

51 *Ibid.*, 237, 239.
52 *Ibid.*, 270–1.
53 'Land routes', in Fenton and Stell: *Loads and Roads in Scotland*, 51–2, 54, 60. Houston: *Population History*, 48–9. See also Cowa: 'Church and Society', in Brown: *Scottish Society*, 133–4 for comments on travel in the fifteenth century, and Kelsall: *Scottish Lifestyle*, 107–8 for travel in the seventeenth.
54 Stone: *The Pont Manuscripts*, 5–6. Whyte: *Scotland Before the Industrial Revolution*, 168.
55 On 7 August, 1574 the Bishop of Dunkeld was in trouble with the Assembly for not visiting (he was still not resident in his district in August, 1575); and in mid-March that year the Assembly noted that the Diocese of Glasgow was so large that it was impossible for the Bishop to visit it properly, and in consequence the Assembly appointed two commissioners to render him assistance. *BUK*, 300, 332, 297. The Bishop was also in trouble for apparently winking at the presence of large numbers of Catholics in his area, who failed to communicate in a Protestant church, *Ibid.*, 315.

in the spirit of its own supplication of the previous October to the Regent and Privy Council, ordered all its Superintendents and commissioners to excommunicate all Catholics within their respective territories who refused to convert to the established Protestant faith, a command given extra force by the Assembly's awareness that a large number of heretical books was being brought into Scotland and that people were still making pilgrimages to wells: "Lett the discipline of the Kirk be used against the users of such superstition", says the record, "and the civill Magistrat shall also hold hard to the punishment".[56] One's natural inclination is to understand 'heretical' in this context to mean 'Lutheran', but the Jesuit Father Robert Abercrombie noted that he had brought some books into Scotland with him from the Continent and had sent in others via other hands; and in August, 1574 the General Assembly complained: "there is diverse books sett out be Jesuits and other hereticks and erroneous authors, containing manifest contumelies and blasphemies against God, and his revealed truth, and yet are dayly brought in this countrey be Poles, crammers [people who sell goods from a pack or stall] and others, to the heavy offence of the Kirk of God".[57] So what with the massacre of St. Bartholomew's Eve, the Council of Trent, the failure of Superintendents to sweep away Catholicism and magic, the increase in the number of undesirable, possibly Catholic, books coming into the country, and people's continuing resort to their old Catholic or magical habits, whether this involved their attending Mass or visiting special wells, the Kirk was presented in the early 1570s with a situation it was evidently failing to handle as well as it would have liked; and if, as I maintain, much that the Kirk designated as witchcraft was in fact either remnant Catholic belief and practice, or persistent popular magic, the Kirk's eagerness to deal with Catholicism on the one hand and her concern to sweep away magical behaviour on the other are likely to have been interconnected.

Thus it should come as no surprise that in mid-August, 1573 the Assembly recorded, "Anent them that consults with witches. The Kirk presentlie assemblit ordaines all Bishops, Superintendents, and Commissioners to plant kirks, to call all sick [such] persons as salbe suspect to consult with witches before them, at their awin particular visitatiouns, or utherwayes; and if they be found to have consulted with the saids witches, That they cause them make publick repentance with sackcloth upon ane Sunday in tyme of preaching, under the paine of excommunicatioun; and if they be disobedient, to proceid to excommunication, dew admonitions proceiding".[58] It is a noteworthy statement, in that establishing new Protestant churches and rooting out

---

56 *BUK*, 262, 279–80.
57 Anderson: 'Narratives of the Scottish Reformation I', 33. *BUK*, 306.
58 *BUK*, 283.

suspect consulters of witches are clearly linked together, suggesting that, at the very least, the Kirk saw the existence of a religious vacuum as an invitation to practise magic, or to continue to practise it unchastised. Once a kirk was set up, however, along with its disciplinary body of minister and elders, such divagations could be dealt with, and such divagations are likely, in view of the accumulated evidence we have seen already, to have included remnant (or even full-scale) Catholicism. But it is particularly interesting that the Assembly should now see fit to suggest that guilty consulters of witches undergo no greater punishment than public repentance in the body of their local kirk, in flat contradiction of the provisions of the 1563 Witchcraft Act which said that consulters as well as witches should suffer death. It is true, of course, that kirk sessions had no power of life and death over their parishioners. Nevertheless, it is remarkable that the Kirk's principal body, sitting in Edinburgh at this time, should openly and officially advocate winking at the law, especially when it frequently urged the Government to implement the law against Catholics.

Such a recommendation for guilty consulters of witches, however, is unlikely to have had anything to do with a more tolerant attitude on the part of the Kirk. Her main concern at this time was Catholicism, and if errant or ignorant adherents to the old ways could be persuaded to abandon them at the cost of a transient humiliation rather than death, the Kirk might well have considered its technically illegal provision for consulters of witches one which it was worthwhile to adopt. Moreover, the General Assembly here clearly makes a distinction between the witches themselves and their clients. It is only the latter who are offered the chance of admonition and repentance, so one must presume that when it came to actual practitioners of magic, the Kirk remained firmly on the side of the legislation.

Certainly her concern with witchcraft continued. In August the following year, the Assembly addressed an article to the Regent, which asked that "his Grace will give commission to certaine gentlemen in every countrey, that incest, adulterie, witchcraft and sick odious crymes, qherewith the countrey is replenishit, may be punisht".[59] But the Government seems to have failed to respond, at least directly, contenting itself with including provision to designate as idle vagabonds a long list of travelling people – actors, minstrels, forgers, scholars from St. Andrews and Aberdeen, mariners without a ship, those banished from their local communities after being found guilty of slaughter, and "the ydill people calling thame selffis egiptianis, or ony uther that fenyeis [pretends] thame to have knawledge in physnomie, palmestre, or utheris abused sciencis quhairby thay perswade the people that thay can tell thair weardis [fates], deathis, and fortunes, and sic uther fantasticall ymaginationis".[60] Again, it is important not to misunderstand the note of dismissal which sounds in this part of the text. Physiognomy and palmistry are sciences, that is to say, legitimate branches of knowledge. It is the abuse of these by people perceived as charlatans to which the Act takes exception, and the attempt to use these sciences to tell people's fortunes which is treated with contempt. A parallel can be seen in those many scholars of the period who criticised judicial astrology on the grounds that this use of the science was flawed and the ends to which it was put improper, but who did not necessarily reject all branches of astrology.[61] Moreover, the Privy Council showed that it took witchcraft seriously by excepting it (along with incest and theft) from amnesties it was prepared to offer to certain groups of wrongdoers, thus indicating that whatever may have been the opinion of legislators on gipsies and fortune-tellers, witches were not to be taken lightly.[62]

From the early 1570s one has to bear in mind that the Kirk was involved in a process which would turn into a serious tussle between herself and the secular government to decide exactly which matters should lie within whose jurisdiction; and the return of Andrew Melville from Geneva in 1574 coincided with a determination by the Kirk to take a close, new look at her administrative structure and the role (and therefore the powers) her superintendents, bishops, and commissioners should have.[63] It is therefore notable that during its August meeting of 1575, the Assembly took care to make clear that the Kirk had certain specific claims upon certain offences: "Question: Whither if the Kirk, be the law of God, hath power to cognosce and decern [investigate and pass judgement upon] heresies, witchcraft, blasphemation of the name of God, and violation of the Sabbath day,

60 *APS* 3.87: 5 March. Later that same month, the Assembly echoed the point by saying that the performance of secular plays ought to be regulated and that none should ever be presented on the Sabbath, *BUK*, 323.
61 Cf. Calvin: *Commentarii in Acta Apostolorum* chap.7, verse 22 = *Opera* 6.56, and *Admonitio adversus astrologiam* = *Opera* 8.500–9. Calvin was particularly hostile to judicial astrology because it seemed to restrict the absolute power of God. Tycho Brahe, on the other hand, maintained that 'to deny the power and influence of the stars is to detract from divine wisdom and influence', *De disciplinis mathematicis oratio* = *Opera* 1.153.
62 *RPC* 2.198, 318. Cf. Aberdeen's composition for the discharge of all crimes *except* treason, fishing for black fish, and magic, *Extracts of the Council Register* 2.19–20. Larner is being somewhat disingenuous when she claims that this is the first time the Privy Council treated witchcraft as a special case, 'the *crimen exceptum* principle already familiar on the Continent', *Enemies of God*, 68. The Privy Council here noted that perpetrators of incest, witchcraft, and theft were not to benefit from the proposed amnesty. This has nothing to do with 'crimen exceptum' which refers to the legal opinion that because witchcraft cannot be proved by the same means as can other crimes, the usual standards and methods of interrogation and court procedure will be insufficient in this particular case. (See Larner: 'Crimen exceptum?' in *Witchcraft and Religion*, 56.)
63 See MacDonald: *The Jacobean Kirk*, 12–14.

especially upon the quidditie thereof" – that is, particularly to pronounce upon the essential nature of these crimes, to give an opinion about what makes heresy heresy or witchcraft witchcraft – "or whither if the Criminall Judge shall give sentence of death for such crimes, before the Spiritual Judge decerne upon the quidditie thereof".[64]

This is actually a new note in the Kirk's official records relating to witchcraft. There is nothing surprising about her claim to take precedence over laymen when it came to defining what a spiritual crime was, of course, but it is interesting that she should have wished to make this point in 1575, and one should probably view it as one among many pieces of evidence that the Kirk was preparing herself to enter into a new relationship with the state, one in which the Kirk's right to exert spiritual, and therefore to a large extent also temporal, control over all members of the state was going to be urged and promoted. One thinks of Andrew Melville's famous utterance to King James in 1596, that in Scotland "thair is twa Kings and twa Kingdomes . . . Thair is Chryst Jesus the King, and his Kingdome the Kirk, whase subject King James the Saxt is, and of whase kingdome nocht a king, nor a lord, nor a heid, but a member".[65] Melville himself never gave any indication of personal interest in the magical practices of others, but it may be significant that, just over a year after his return to Scotland from Geneva, the General Assembly decided to inject into its deliberations upon witchcraft a note reminiscent of his theocratic mode of thinking.[66] At the August assembly Melville addressed the members at length on the subject of episcopacy and was appointed, along with five others, to read and answer bills and complaints, the committee being directed to meet at two in the afternoon, in the Over Tolbooth in Edinburgh, "and so forth to continue till the same be answered and resolved".[67]

There is no evidence, however, that the new note regarding witchcraft set off any fresh wave of investigation. Indeed, apart from the instances we have just been discussing, there are only one or two others relating to 1575 and 1576. In January, 1575 Marjory Smith in St. Andrews was delated of witchcraft and called to answer the charge before two meetings of the kirk session; in December, two unnamed witches were convicted and burned (we do not know where) at a cost of £10; and on 2 May, 1576 a messenger was sent

---

64 *BUK*, 343–4.

65 Melville: *Diary*, 369–71. This was not, of course, a notion peculiar to Melville. The Regent, Morton, had already attempted to impose the royal supremacy on the Kirk in 1572. See Mason: *Kingship and the Commonweal*, 204–5.

66 Melville had returned to Scotland in July, 1574 and stayed with his brother in Baldovie, not far from Dundee, until November when he was appointed Principal of the University of Glasgow. In March, 1575 he became a member of the General Assembly's committee for drafting a scheme for church government. M'Crie: *Life of Andrew Melville*, 56–9, 64, 109.

67 *BUK*, 337. M'Crie: *op.cit. supra*, 110–12.

to summon an assize in Linlithgow for the purpose of trying a witch.[68] If the Kirk had indeed refined and politicised its approach towards witchcraft, the results did not show themselves straight away.

The Trial of Elizabeth Dunlop

Nevertheless, it is in 1576 that we have another early witchcraft trial which has been recorded in some detail, that of Elizabeth Dunlop, the spouse of Andrew Jack, from Lyne in Ayrshire, which was held on 8 November.[69] Pitcairn's introduction to his transcription of this trial, however, contains more fantasy than useful comment when he infers from the record that Elizabeth must have been tortured and that a combination of physical pain, overheated imagination, superstition, and ignorance produced the account she gave to the court. In fact, the use of torture in Scottish witchcraft trials is, except for one or two undoubted instances, a highly debatable matter. What is more, the exact procedure followed in the sixteenth century from a person's being arrested to the point of her or his execution is not well understood. So perhaps it will be helpful before embarking on a discussion of Elizabeth's trial in particular, to describe, as far as one can, what happened after a suspect witch had been apprehended.[70]

After the Reformation, most accusations of witchcraft seem to have come before one or more meetings of the local kirk session. Discipline within the parish was overseen by the elders, each of whom was assigned a particular area, sometimes alone, sometimes in concert with another elder, and they reported parishioners' breaches of acceptable behaviour at the session held each week for just this purpose. Those guilty of wrongdoing which was also an offence against the state were often expected to pay whatever civic penalty was due to their crime before they were admitted (should this be considered appropriate) to public penitence in the kirk. Hence, co-operation between kirk session and the local civic authorities was expected and, on the whole, willingly rendered. Rural parishes without ready access to a burgh council could apply to their local landowner for assistance, or even directly to the Privy Council. In the latter case, their request was usually for a commission authorising the session to impose civic penalties without the need to remit guilty persons to the civil authorities. Presbyteries and synods, too, held similar sessions but these were not as efficient as those of the local kirks – parties summoned to them, for example, often did not appear until several

---

68 *Register of the Kirk Session of St. Andrews*, 414–16. *Accounts of the Treasurer of Scotland* 13.88, 126.

69 Pitcairn: *Criminal Trials* 1.2.49–58.

70 The following account is based upon seventeenth-century practice which, while possibly differing in certain details from that followed during the sixteenth, still appears to furnish a reasonably accurate guide to what happened in earlier courts.

summonses had been issued, one reason being that they involved travelling outwith the offender's parish on a working day – and so anyone accused of witchcraft would probably find herself arraigned first in front of members of her local community before the seriousness of her offence took her perhaps a long way off to stand trial in a superior, criminal court.[71]

Initial investigation of a suspect witch, then, was in the hands of her minister and elders, and if they decided there might be substance in the charge rather than personal spite or a mere insult thrown in the heat of a hostile exchange, she could be detained while the matter was investigated further. It was common, in the absence of local prisons, for those accused of crimes to be kept in a steeple-cell of the church, or in the local tolbooth. There she – for most people accused of witchcraft were women – could be kept in irons[72] and subjected to a series of visits from the minister and elders whose aim was to get the suspect witch to confess and repent. During the seventeenth century, several records refer to men who 'watched' the woman, a task usually interpreted as depriving her of sleep with the aim of reducing her to a condition in which she would be more amenable to confession and repentance, although it is possible (if not as likely) that the watch was set to prevent her from committing suicide before a confession had been obtained. Whether such watching took place during the sixteenth century is not clear, but there seems no reason to suppose that it either could not or did not.

Close confinement, watching, and frequent intimidation by men of consequence from the suspect's local community, together with the other hazards attendant upon imprisonment in hard, possibly harsh, conditions did not, however, constitute torture. Torture was a judicially approved process involving the use and application of instruments intended to inflict pain. Anything else amounted to maltreatment or ill-usage, but could not be defined legally as a process for extracting information, or confirming information already obtained. Under Roman law, modified and adapted by canon law, proof of a crime, sufficient to lead to judgement and passing sentence, depended either upon a minimum of two eye-witnesses to the gravamen of the crime, or upon the accused person's own voluntary confession. *Indicia*, separate pieces of circumstantial evidence, were not in themselves enough to provide a sufficient basis for conviction and senten-

---

71 See Foster: *The Church Before the Covenants*, 71–80.
72 As, for example, were Janet Wishart and her son in Aberdeen, *SCM* 1.101. On steeple-cells and tolbooth prisons, see further *Tolbooths and Town-houses*, 19–20. Elizabeth may not have had too long to remain in imprisonment. She was arrested some time after February, 1576 and a messenger was sent out on 25 October to summon an assize from Cunningham and Renfrew, her local district, to try her, *Accounts of the Treasurer of Scotland* 13.141.

cing, and examination under torture was not allowed except when a confession was lacking, there was only one eye-witness, or when very grave *indicia* suggested that the matter should be pursued with some rigour towards a confession. The aim of this Roman-canon law of proof was to obtain certainty so that any subsequent judgement might rest upon a solid and trustworthy foundation. Such a basis two eye-witnesses, it might be allowed, could indeed provide. But a voluntary confession was not always forthcoming, and therefore the convention whereby the presence of serious *indicia* – not valid in themselves to establish guilt or innocence – might furnish a technical justification for investigating the accused under torture was developed during the later Middle Ages.[73]

Now, it is true that Roman law formed the basis of Scots law in the sixteenth century, but after 1560 canon law was no longer authoritative and municipal law took its place in the legal studies pursued at Scottish universities.[74] Moreover, Scotland kept her criminal assize, and every panel had the right to have someone speak to the court on his or her behalf, quite literally a *proloquitor*. So the conditions obtaining in Scotland had certain features which further modified the Roman-canon process and were certainly considered by later legal commentators either to have reduced the application of torture in Scottish courts to a minimum, or to have obviated the need for it at all.[75] We are therefore left in a position of not quite knowing whether witchcraft was treated as a *crimen exceptum* in Scotland and torture, as legally defined, was applied except in cases of voluntary confession or the absence of two or more eye-witnesses, or whether the absence of references to torture in the records, except in rare and unusual cases such as one or two in the North Berwick episode of 1590, indicates that torture was not often used in witchcraft cases. Any *argumentum e silentio* is fraught with danger, but it is probably fair to say that the common assumption by nineteenth- and early twentieth-century writers on Scottish witchcraft that torture was routinely used against the panel in such cases is likely to be exaggerated and to rest upon shaky foundations, especially since there are no

---

73 See Langbein: *Torture and the Law of Proof*, 4–8.
74 Walker: *A Legal History of Scotland* 3.376.
75 Hume: 'Confession was sometimes extorted by violence, and torture as applied to the body also. This, however, chiefly by the orders and under the direction of the Privy Council; for I cannot find that torture had ever become an ordinary instrument of inquisition, or one which even the Court of Justiciary, and much less any of the inferior courts, could presume to employ without the warrant of a previous consultation with that supreme and superintending authority', *Commentaries* 2.117–18. Cf. MacKenzie: 'Confession, though extrajudicial, may be sufficient (if adminiculated) to subject the Confessor to the Torture; but this is rarely practised with us', *Laws and Customs of Scotland*, Title xxiv = *Works* 2.249. Cf. *Ibid.*, 261.

means of telling whether a confession which appears in the records was or was not voluntary.[76]

Having been arrested and questioned, the suspect was eventually brought before an assize. By the seventeenth century this usually consisted of fifteen men, many of whom would come from the panel's own town or district; but in the sixteenth there might be more. Elizabeth, as it happens, was tried before an assize of fifteen. The accused was fetched into court and her dittay was read aloud. She pleaded guilty or not guilty, and then the pursuer and proloquitor might begin a series of arguments about the details and, above all, the wording of each article of the dittay. This last was most important. It was the task of the prosecution to prove its case, not of the defence to provide an alternative version of events, and therefore the dittay had to be framed in such a way as to exclude all possible objections by the defence. The evidence the pursuer was offering the court was directly relevant to the items contained in the dittay, and the panel could not admit any defence to anything other than those same items. Consequently, as Walker says, "the defence really depended on the prosecution witnesses failing to substantiate what was libelled, not on proving any alternative explanation of the facts".[77] So if the proloquitor could show that the dittay's narration of the circumstances of the alleged criminal act was in some way deficient, he could argue that the item was 'irrelevant' (not acceptable) and should not be tried by the assize. His plea would be answered by the pursuer, and it was then the task of the presiding judge to rule whether the item was relevant or not.[78]

Witnesses were then admitted, sworn, and repeated the evidence they had given on an earlier occasion to investigators. There is no indication that this was cross-examined. Each item of the dittay had its own witnesses, some of whom might provide evidence relating to more than one item, and it was important that witnesses corroborate each other's version of the narrative since proof by witnesses was the only available

---

76 It should be noted that Walker's assertion that torture was common in witchcraft cases (*Legal History of Scotland* 3.434–5) is based entirely on Pitcairn: *Criminal Trials* 1.2.50, 213–22, and 375–7. The first merely refers to instruments of torture; the second to the trial of John Fian in 1590 and the pamphlet *Newes From Scotland* which gives an account of the use of torture in his case and in that of Agnes Sampson. But one must bear in mind that these two were involved in an episode of treason in which maleficent magic certainly played a large part, but in which it was not the principal crime on trial. The third reference is to the trial of the Master of Orkney in June, 1596, and here fratricide and poisoning are the principal crimes rather than any maleficent magic involved. The incidents are thus not typical of Scottish witchcraft trials and the use of torture against individuals involved in them therefore cannot be taken as typical of such trials, either.

77 *Legal History* 3.433.

78 Walker: *op.cit.* 3.431.

evidence. Not until 1594 – and then in a treason case – did common talk and public reputation become admissible as strong proof in crimes of a secret nature (*in criminalibus clandestinis*).[79] Once the witnesses had been heard, the assize chose its chancellor (there was no summing up by pursuer, proloquitor, or judge), and the assize retired to another room to consider its verdict. When it returned into court, it pronounced on each item of the dittay. So the panel could be found not guilty on certain points of her dittay, but guilty of others. The overall verdict seems to have been obtained by seeing whether there was a majority of guilty or not guilty verdicts after totting up the results from each charge. If the over-all verdict was 'guilty', sentence was then pronounced. In capital cases, such as witchcraft, sentence of death was pronounced by the dempster of court, whose peculiar function this was. Death in witchcraft cases in Scotland meant strangulation, followed by burning of the dead body to ashes. (Exactly how such strangulation was effected is never made clear in earlier texts, but a seventeenth-century trial indicates that the executioner garrotted the con-demned person with a cord.)[80] In addition, all moveable goods belonging to the convicted person were escheated to the Crown. She or he had been imprisoned entirely at personal expense but execution, as we have seen, was an expensive business, and so although the value of the escheated goods might not be very great, especially if the term of imprisonment had been lengthy, nevertheless the state found it worthwhile to recoup what it could from the executed person's remaining estate.

Some such process, then, awaited Elizabeth Dunlop. She was accused of "the using of Sorcerie, Witchcraft, and Incantatione, with invocation of spretis of the devill, continewand in familiaritie with thame, at all sic tymes as sche thocht expedient, deling with charmes, and abusing the pepill with devillisch craft of sorcerie foirsaid . . . usit thir diverse yeiris bypast". The reference to "divers years bypast" is important, since it is a common feature of almost all witchcraft trials that the panel had been acquiring the reputation of a witch over a long period of time, sometimes as long as twenty or thirty years;[81] and although in 1576 ill repute was apparently not admissible as evidence, there can scarcely be any doubt that it must have had an effect on the deliberations of the assize. Elizabeth's record is unusual in that it consists not so much of the final list of articles drawn up against her as of the questions she

79 Walker: *op.cit.* 3.435.
80 *JC26/27*: trial of Margaret Hutchison. The reference therein is to the execution of Janet Ker.
81 This also has relevance to the view of witches, several times enunciated by demonologists of the period, that witches were old women. If they were indeed elderly or middle-aged at the time of their trial, many had been been young or fairly young when they began to acquire ill repute two or even three decades before their arrest.

was asked and her fairly detailed answers during two separate interrogatory sessions, the second held in September, 1576 and the first undated but probably held in that same month as well.

The record is also unusual in that the whole of Elizabeth's magical working seems to have depended on her familiarity with what the nineteenth century would have called a 'spirit-guide', a person who had died at the Battle of Pinkie 29 years before the date of her trial. His name was Thomas Reid. He appeared to Elizabeth in the form of an elderly man dressed in grey with a black bonnet on his head and a white stick in his hand. Elizabeth had not known him while he was alive, but at his suggestion she tried to verify his claim to be Thomas Reid by visiting his son and some of his other relatives and friends, and conveying to them messages from Thomas, the details of which would serve to identify him.

Not surprisingly, therefore, most of the questions during Elizabeth's first interrogation concentrate upon Thomas Reid. He had appeared to her, she said, several times during the previous four years, his last visitation being on 3 February, 1576 when he predicted that the weather would turn severe. He usually came to her at noon, not always in the same place. She first saw him while she was driving her cows to pasture, then at a thorn bush, then in her own house; she had also seen him in the kirkyard of Dalry,[82] in Edinburgh, and at Restalrig Loch when she and her husband had come up to Leith on business. On the first occasion, he had given her a Catholic greeting – *Sancta Maria*! – and asked why she was looking so troubled. According to her answer, her husband and newborn child were ill and one of her cows had died. But Thomas offered her little comfort, saying that the child would die, as would another cow and two of her sheep; only her husband would recover. He then disappeared, seeming to make his way out "at ane narroware hoill of the dyke nor ony erdlie man culd haif gane throw", and Elizabeth had to confess she was somewhat afraid.

His meeting her next[83] at a thorn bush must be accounted significant since the thorn was often associated with the *sithean*. It was there that he asked her to renounce her faith in return for temporal goods – a standard offer made by Satan to those he wanted to entice into his service – but Elizabeth refused and Thomas became angry. This, however, was the only occasion on which he made such a request, and one must wonder whether this exchange represents the actual content of the conversation as Elizabeth reported it, or whether it was subject to some kind of nudging by her interrogators who would obviously be keen to establish, if possible, that Thomas was a diabolical figure rather than any other kind of spirit-visitant,

---

82 A town and parish in the Cunningham district of Ayrshire.
83 Actually the third time. The record, however, does not describe the second.

since this would be simpler to understand and would clarify to the assize the enormity of her wrongdoing. Otherwise there was a chance they might mistake him for a *sith* rather than a devil and fail to be as censorious as they might when it came to a verdict.

It is clear, however, that Thomas was not actually a *sith*, as the following episode shows. When he appeared to her in her own house while her husband and three of his friends were in company there, Thomas took hold of her apron and drew her to the far end of the kailyard where he warned her to remain silent regardless of what she might see. They moved a little further forward, and suddenly (so it seems) Thomas was surrounded by twelve other people, eight women and four men, all clothed like gentlefolk, the women wearing plaids. Apparently they could see Elizabeth because they told her to sit down and then asked if she would accompany them; but she, remembering what Thomas had told her, said nothing. They continued to talk, but Elizabeth heard no sound. She saw only the movement of their lips. Then, after a short while, they disappeared, followed by a strong blast of wind. Thomas disappeared with them and Elizabeth says "sche lay seik quhill [until] Thomas came agane bak fra thame". Who were those people? she asked. The good people ("gude wychtis") who live at the Fairy Court, he answered.[84] Again Thomas urged her to go with them, saying that she would gain all kinds of temporal benefits, but Elizabeth refused and once more Thomas was angry with her.

Several features of this episode are worth noting. It seems to have been a common experience that Scottish *sithean*, at least, wore everyday clothing rather than garments of a particular colour such as green. As Robert Kirk observed, "Their Apparell . . . is like that of the People and Countrey under which they live: so are they seen to wear Plaids and variegated Garments in the Highlands of Scotland, and Suanochs therefore in Ireland".[85] Their request that Elizabeth come away with them is also a common feature of *sithean* behaviour. But it is the nature of the experience from Elizabeth's point of view which is particularly interesting. It was partly visual, partly auditory, and the visual experience seems to have begun and ended suddenly without any prior warning. Elizabeth's environment remained unaltered throughout. She was perfectly well aware of where she was, and there are no indications that she had entered a dream-state. Two of her senses were involved; the others were not affected. There was, apparently, no change in temperature. Essentially, therefore, one might say that Elizabeth experienced a visual

---

84 Pitcairn explains the phrase as meaning 'the good neighbours or brounies' (p.58, note 3), but he is being far too specific. A *wicht* is not a neighbour, but a supernatural being, and there is nothing in the context of Elizabeth's record to relate these *wichts* to brownies.

85 *Secret Commonwealth*, 55.

hallucination with attendant auditory phenomena.[86] That she may have felt faint or unwell after it is an indication that she was not used to encounters of this kind, in spite of the fact that she knew her meetings with Thomas Reid were those between a human and a supernatural being.[87]

Now, visual hallucinations may occur when the subject's normal environment is temporarily replaced by the hallucinatory alternative, or the hallucination may seem to be superimposed on the normal environment; and the same may be said of auditory hallucinations. Either the subject's normal sequence of auditory perceptions is suspended while the auditory hallucination replaces it, or the subject experiences both normality and hallucination simultaneously.[88] In Elizabeth's case, if we allow she was experiencing an hallucination, the indications appear to be that both the visual and auditory phenomena were superimposed on her normal environment. During part of the experience she was standing but then, at the *wichtis'* command, she sat down and when the experience was over and before Thomas returned, she "lay sick". This does not necessarily mean she was lying down. It could mean she stayed sitting where she was. Moreover, 'sick' could mean 'deeply affected by some strong feeling ' or even just 'pale', rather than 'ill'. So beyond the fact that she altered her physical position at some point during the experience and was left feeling shaken by what she had seen and heard, we cannot be quite sure of her exact posture and condition throughout. But still there is not sufficient evidence to allow us to suggest that Elizabeth may have been having an ecsomatic experience, since the majority of these take place while the subject is lying down, and Elizabeth was certainly not doing that when the phenomenon started.[89]

86 Such an experience involving more than one sense is relatively uncommon. See Green & McCreery: *Apparitions*, 81. One must be careful of the word 'hallucination' here. It is not used in any pejorative or sceptical sense, but with the pathological and psychological meaning of 'an apparent perception of an external object when no such object is actually present'. Cf. the example given by Green & McCreery: *op.cit.*, 1.

87 She says she felt rather afraid after he first met her, but this seems to have been occasioned by the novelty of his mode of disappearing and her realisation that he was not human. Thereafter, she gives no indication that she was in the least disconcerted by his appearances, even when he was angry with her. This is quite different from her feeling ill after the meeting with the *gude wychtis*.

88 Green & McCreery: *Apparitions*, 89–90.

89 Green & McCreery: *op.cit.*, 124–6. It is also common to subjects who experience an apparition that it happens without warning, *Ibid.*, 135. Was Elizabeth experiencing some kind of subjective fantasy, or is there any reason to suppose that objective reality came into it? A recent laboratory experiment has come to the following tentative conclusions: '(a) Certain altered states of consciousness may cause powerful, objective, physical effects in the environment; and (b) certain fluctuations in the environment may cause dramatic shifts in consciousness. The former suggests that apparitions may be objectively caused by mind-matter interaction phenomena; the latter suggests that apparitions may be subjective effects caused by external energies', Radin & Rebman: 'Are phantasms fact or fantasy?', 65.

But the incident in the kailyard was not the only occasion on which she saw the *gude wichtis*. There was a second when she and her husband were up in Leith; for while she was tethering her horse near the side of Restalrig Loch, just south of Leith, "thair come ane cumpanye of rydaris by, that maid sic ane dynn as heavin and erd had gane togidder". They did not pause, however, but plunged straight into the loch, and Thomas explained (although we do not know on which occasion) that these were the *gude wichtis* riding into 'Middle Earth', i.e. the land of the *sithean*. Obviously this, like the other experience, involved auditory as well as visual phenomena.

Sithean appear twice more in Elizabeth's account. Once, she says, while she was lying in childbed, she received a visit from a well-built, robust-looking woman who sat down on a bench beside her and asked for a drink. This Elizabeth gave her, only to be told that the child would die but that her husband would recover from his illness. So this incident may have happened soon after her first meeting with Thomas because he told her (so the two of them had already met) that the woman was his mistress, the Queen of Fairyland, and that he had told her to visit Elizabeth and "do hir gude". Is it possible that Elizabeth had been visited by a human woman (a passing traveller or 'Egyptian'), who commented upon the health of the child and the man, but that this encounter was explained in a somewhat different way by Elizabeth's spirit-guide? The interweaving of real incidents or people with preternatural explanations may well be a feature of some witchcraft confessions, especially in their accounts of meetings with the Devil, so we cannot discount this as one which may help to clarify this particular encounter with a *sith*, although the inclination to rationalise every event in the confessions must clearly be resisted.

The final appearance of *sithean* in Elizabeth's narrative involves the Laird of Auchenskeigh. Auchenskeigh is not far from Dalry in the Cunningham district of Ayrshire, in whose kirkyard Elizabeth had once seen Thomas "gangand amangis the people". The Laird of Auchenskeigh to whom Elizabeth refers had been dead the past nine years or so, but Elizabeth reported that she had seen him "rydand with the ffair-folk", that is to say, riding in company with *sithean*. Her account is a little confused because the details come in two parts given on at least two different occasions;[90] but we are told further that Elizabeth saw him by a thorn-bush beyond Monkcastle and that later, at Lady Auchenskeigh's request, Elizabeth asked Thomas to confirm what she had seen and that the man in the vision actually was the Laird. Thomas said it was.

---

90 The second took place at Dalkeith on 20 September, 1576 when it is said that the Laird died 'mair nor fyve yeir syne', not quite the same as the earlier specific 'ix yeir syne'.

One notices that the Laird's widow seems to have had no hesitation in believing that Elizabeth had the ability to see either *sithean* or the dead – she was asking for confirmation that the dead man was her husband, not questioning the vision itself. Did the two women know each other? Dalry is a geographical link between them; clearly they lived in the same area. The Laird's family name, too, was 'Dunlop' and this obviously raises the possibility that he and Elizabeth were in some way related. Now, while it is true that 'Dunlop' was a very common name in Ayrshire,[91] it is also noticeable that Elizabeth's clientèle seem to have included a number of local gentry. She was consulted several times, for example, about stolen goods. Lady Thridpart in the barony of Renfrewshire sent someone to ask who had stolen some items out of her purse,[92] and within twenty days, once she had spoken to Thomas, Elizabeth was able to tell her the name of the thief. Lady Blair asked her more than once about some stolen clothes, and again Thomas revealed the identity of the thief. Elizabeth had some kind of entrée to Lady Blair, of course, through Thomas Reid's son (also called Thomas), who worked for the Laird of Blair, for at Thomas the elder's suggestion Elizabeth had checked with him the identity of her spirit-guide. Indeed, there seems to have been more than one connection with the Blair family, because when Elizabeth was asked whether Thomas had revealed the future to anyone other than herself, she answered that he had sent her to William Blair of the Strand whose oldest daughter was about to marry the young Laird of Baidland, with the message that if the proposed marriage took place, it would be a disaster for the girl.[93] Far from being ungrateful for the warning, the Blairs came to Elizabeth's rescue when she told William Kyle, one of the burgesses of Irvine, who had stolen his cloak and Kyle, in spite of promising she would not get into trouble if she performed this piece of divination for him, had her arrested and beaten. It was James Blair, brother of William Blair, who had her released from the tolbooth.

This was not the only time Elizabeth had found herself in trouble with the civil authorities because of her gift for divination, especially anent lost or stolen goods. The very first recorded question of her interrogation is, "Be quhat art and knaulege sche culd tell diverse persounes of thingis thai tynt [lost] or wer stollin away?", and later we learn that Henry Jameson and James

---

91 For which see the *International Genealogical Index*.
92 'Twa hornis of gold', probably tags or tips usually affixed to a lace or thong, and 'ane croune of the sone', a coin.
93 In consequence of this warning, the marriage was broken off and the Laird married the youngest sister instead. A note in the record says that this claim of Elizabeth's was investigated to see if it were true or not. There is also a slightly strange reference to *sithean*. Elizabeth says that Thomas 'send hir to na creatour in middil-yerd' but to William Blair. Clearly the person who recorded the interrogation left out some salient points here.

Baird from the Mains of Waterstone had come to her to find out what had happened to their coulter and share. Her answer, as usual, was that she would have to consult Thomas, and when she did so he 'showed her' that John and George Black, father and son, both smiths, had stolen the items and hidden them in their father's house; and they were able to continue to conceal their crime because they had bribed one of the sheriff's officers, James Dougal, to look the other way. Elizabeth was thus running a risk in revealing what she knew, for the Blacks obviously had a corrupt officer of the law in their pocket, and Thomas warned her that she would find herself arrested and brought to Glasgow where she would be put in the custody of the Archbishop. However, Thomas further prophesied that she would be well treated and sent home again, and so indeed it seems to have turned out.

This kind treatment may have owed something to the fact that James Boyd, who had been appointed to the Archbishopric late in 1573, was known not to prosecute Catholics with that diligence the Kirk expected – he was in trouble for that reason in March, 1575[94] – and Elizabeth was probably a Catholic, as we shall see later on. Moreover, the Archbishop had difficulties in administering his diocese which, he complained to the General Assembly, was far too large, and he evidently did not find himself attuned to certain important aspects of his office, such as preaching, for which he explained he had little talent.[95] As late as April, 1576 the Assembly was trying to answer his difficulties by assigning him a limited flock and area of visitation, an offer he accepted on 24 October that same year.[96] So it is likely that Elizabeth's legal brush with him anent the incident of the plough-irons took place in 1574–5, the period of the Archbishop's apparent relative leniency.[97]

Finding stolen or missing articles, then, was one of the skills for which Elizabeth was known in the district, and that district appears to have been Cunningham in particular, an extensive region in the north of Ayrshire including one or two fair-sized townships such as Kilwinning and Irvine from which two of her clients came,[98] Dalry with which Elizabeth herself was

---

94 *BUK*, 315.
95 *BUK*, 297, 317–18, 331, 348. It was also complained of him that he did not insist against adulterers as he should have done, *Ibid.*, 348.
96 *BUK*, 359–40, 378–9.
97 As always, one wonders whether the panel was able to call upon a family connection to help her, and it is interesting that there was a George Boyd who was reader at Dalry and Kilbirnie in 1573 who was the subject of a complaint to the General Assembly for administering communion when he should not have done so, *BUK*, 276. He could have come across Elizabeth who seems to have been resident in or near Dalry, but whether the two Boyds were, in fact, related is not known.
98 James Cunningham, chamberlain of Kilwinning, and William Kyle, a burgess of Irvine. The population of Kilwinning in 1755 was recorded as 2,541 and of Irvine in the same year as 4,025: Sinclair, *Statistical Account of Scotland* 6.354–5, 246.

associated, and Kilbirnie which furnished three members of her assize. But she also cured, or attempted to cure, illness in humans and animals. When people came to her because their cow or ewe was sick, or a child "was tane away with ane evill blast of wind" or "elf-grippit",[99] Elizabeth would ask Thomas what to do and he would pull up a herb and give it to her. In the case of an animal, this was then mixed with other herbs, placed in its mouth, and in due time the animal would recover. On another occasion, Thomas gave her something which looked like the root of a beet and told her either to boil it and make a salve from it, or to dry it and make a powder of it. How did she know this would heal people? she was asked. Because, she replied, "sa son as sche rubbit the saw [salve] upoun the patient, man or woman, or chyld, and it drank in, the chyld wald mend; bot gif it swat out, the persoun wald die". There follows a list of individuals to whom she applied this particular medicine: John Jack's child, "Wilsounes of the toun",[100] and her sister-in-law's cow.

These three were, apparently, those who had received the herb. The powdered root had been given in drink to Lady Johnston's daughter.[101] Elizabeth asked Thomas what was wrong with the girl and he told her that the problem was cold blood round the heart, which was causing her to faint without warning. His remedy consisted of a drink including ginger, cloves, aniseed, liquorice, and strong ale boiled together and then strained. A small quantity of this, sweetened with white sugar, was to be taken twice a day, in the morning and before dinner. (The powdered root is not mentioned, but the start of Elizabeth's answer implies it was one of the ingredients.) For this, Elizabeth received payment of oatmeal and some cheese. The dowager Lady Kilbowie also sought her assistance. Could Elizabeth give her any help with her crooked leg? Elizabeth promised to ask Thomas, but he said nothing could be done because the bone marrow was used up and the blood was rotten;[102] and he warned that if Lady Kilbowie sought help elsewhere, her

---

99 Cf. 'elf-shot' as a description of certain diseases in cattle, Kirk: *Secret Commonwealth*, 60. On the evil blast of wind, cf. Janet Boyman, *supra* pp. 64–5.

100 Elizabeth was married to an Andrew Jack, so the child may have been her niece or nephew. "Wilsons of the toun" is a slightly odd phrase. The *toun* here is likely to refer to a ferm toun, perhaps six or a dozen households working jointly upon a farm, or a kirk toun, a somewhat larger unit with a kirk or a chapel as its focal point. 'Wilson of the toun' would thus be a nickname, well-known in the immediate district, and 'Wilsounes' a form of the genitive; so the phrase may be understood as referring to a child of this person, cured by Elizabeth's herbal salve.

101 At the time of Elizabeth's interrogation, the young woman was married to the Laird of Stanely. She had a sister, also married into the gentry, Lady Blackhall. The request for help had come via Lady Johnston's servant, Catherine Dunlop, and again one wonders whether there may not have been some kind of family connection here with Elizabeth.

102 'Consumit' and 'dosinit'. The latter I take to be 'dozed in it'. The verb *doze* means 'to stupefy, stun', and the past participle, 'rotten'. Running words together is a common feature of sixteenth-century legal records.

condition would only become worse. Pregnant women, too, it seems, bene-
fited from Elizabeth's magical assistance; for Thomas would give her a green
silk thread, with instructions that the woman sew it to her undergarment or
tie it round her left arm. This done, the birth would happen quickly. On one
occasion, however, Thomas put the thread down somewhere and Elizabeth
could not find it, no matter how hard she looked.

These two magical operations, curing and finding lost or stolen goods,
appear to have been Elizabeth's specialities. Her interrogators concentrated
on them, and especially, for some reason, on the episode of the stolen coulter
and plough-share. She was questioned again about this on 20 September in
Dalkeith in the presence of the Laird of Whittingham and George Auchinleck of Balmanno. From this we learn that Gabriel Black, presumably George
Black's brother, was also involved in the theft, that the crime took place on a
Saturday night, and that the two men carried the stolen articles to John
Black's house on the back of a grey gelding. These further details (or at least
some further details) Elizabeth must have reported to the articles' owners,
Henry Jameson and James Baird, at a second meeting, for the record says she
told them "agane". It is an interesting indication that either Elizabeth held
back information the first time (which is unlikely) or that she received or
remembered these extra details later on. Either way, it may serve as a glimpse
into the way Elizabeth worked with her spirit-guide, and may suggest that she
had more than one consultation with him about a single problem. Her
interrogators also pressed her to say how often Thomas came to her before she
asked who he was. She said three times and that during this early period of
their relationship she was unable to speak about him to anyone else. She
added that on several occasions he asked her to accompany him but that she
refused, whereupon "he schuke his heid and said that he suld caus hir forthink
it".

Her interrogations over, Elizabeth came to trial on 8 November. The assize
of fifteen which tried her contained a number of men from Ayrshire, so it is
possible, in view of her evident reputation, that she was not unknown to at
least some of them.[103] Her dittay was read and the witnesses were heard. The
assize then retired, considered the evidence, and returned to court with a
verdict of guilty on every point. The record notes that Elizabeth had confessed
to many of the articles of her dittay,[104] a series of admissions which may have
helped to sway their judgements, although we do not know whether the

---

103 Indeed, Elizabeth may have had reason to suppose that they would be favourably
     inclined towards her, for Thomas had prophesied to her that she would get into
     trouble because of her association with him, 'bot baid hir seik ane assyis of hir
     nychtbouris, and no thing suld aill hir'.
104 Principally those anent her meetings with Thomas and the cures she had worked
     with his help.

verdict was unanimous or dependent on a plurality of voices. But, having been found guilty, Elizabeth was sentenced and, according to the record, burned: that is to say, she would have been strangled and her corpse consumed by fire.

Why did the assize find her guilty? One reason may have been her confession. Another may be the complexity of the charges laid against her. It was usual for witches to be accused of witchcraft and sorcery. Elizabeth, however, was charged with witchcraft, sorcery, incantation, invocation of spirits, using them to make her charms work, and abusing the people. It is remarkably comprehensive – one might almost say 'catch-all' – and almost seems to have been designed to ensure that Elizabeth would not escape a guilty verdict. Nevertheless, the question still remains: why did the assize convict her? It cannot be said, for example, that Elizabeth's spirit-guide was a concept too difficult for her interrogators and the assize to grasp except in terms of the spirits of the Devil appearing in her delation. Neither the minister, nor the elders, nor the members of the assize would have been unfamiliar with the notions of *sithean* and ghosts, and it would be asking too much to suggest that not a single one of them afforded some credence to these preternatural beings. It can scarcely have been Elizabeth's own belief in the reality of Thomas and the *sithean*, then, which troubled her accusers and assizers. The record makes it clear she was not using the *sithean* in order to work magic; Thomas alone was her mentor and guide therein. So a crucial point in the assizers' deliberations must have been the question, who or what was Thomas? A ghost, the Devil, or a man in masquerade?

One question Elizabeth was asked has a bearing on this point. Had she ever been in a suspect place with him, or had carnal dealing with him? It is difficult to interpret accurately the thrust of this query since if she were to answer yes, it would be possible to argue (a) that Thomas could therefore not have been a ghost because ghosts are not capable of sexual congress; (b) that Thomas was an evil spirit, because these were known to have sex with women, especially those they had seduced into making a diabolical pact; or (c) that Elizabeth was merely an ignorant, foolish woman who had been drawn into committing adultery with a charlatan and was offering the court a whimsical interpretation of the relationship in an effort to disguise and explain her commonplace, though sinful, behaviour. This last, although something of the kind appealed to Pitcairn,[105] cannot be taken seriously in view of the mentality of the period, the tenor of the rest of the questioning, and the verdict of the assize, not to

---

105 'She was certainly the dupe of her own overheated imagination, already well stored with such fantasies, before her first interview with Thom Reid; who (if not entirely the phantom of a disordered brain) may not unlikely have been some heartless wag, acquainted with the virtues and use of herbs, and who possibly may have played off this too fatal joke on his unhappy victim', Pitcairn:*Criminal Trials* 1.2.50.

mention the initial set of charges brought against her. Kirk sessions frequently dealt with cases of adultery. Had there been any reasonable doubt about Elizabeth's story or behaviour suggestive of sexual misconduct, the session would certainly have picked it up. The apparent absence of any such evidence points to the strong contemporary assumption that magic was involved, and in consequence we must presume that the question about carnal dealing was designed to show either that Thomas was not a ghost (in which case the interrogators would be left to ask who he was) or that he was an evil spirit or Satan himself. This latter explanation would then open the way to show that Elizabeth was a witch and was therefore guilty of at least one of the charges against her – a conclusion to which the eventual verdict might seem to point.

But all that depends on Elizabeth's answering yes. In fact she answered no, "upoun hir salvatioun and condemnatioun", adding that Thomas had once taken her by the apron and would have had her go with him to the land of the *sithean* (a reference to the episode in her house and kailyard), an invitation which she clearly viewed with some distrust and unease. So in fact her interrogators do not seem to have made further progress on this point. But there was one other question, the answer to which may have been a crucial factor in Elizabeth's guilty verdict. She was asked what she thought of the new law, that is to say, of the reformed or Protestant faith. Elizabeth answered that she had spoken to Thomas about this and he said "that this new law was nocht gude; and that the auld ffayth suld cum hame agane, bot nocht sic as it was befoir". This answer, and Thomas's exclamation of "Sancta Maria" to her at their first meeting, indicate clearly enough that Thomas was a Catholic, and since Elizabeth had thought to question him about the new dispensation (why should she do that unless she had doubts of some kind about it which she wanted resolved?), and since Thomas acted constantly as her spirit-guide, we may take it that either Elizabeth herself was a Catholic or at least not unfriendly to the thought that a reformed version of the Catholic faith might one day be restored.[106]

Now, it may be significant that the marginal note against this article is different from those beside all the others. Whereas they say "confessit and fylit" or simply "fylit", here the clerk has chosen to write "fylit be the assyis heirof". Why did he take the trouble to differentiate this verdict from the others? The implications are that Elizabeth denied the article in court but that the assize homed in on it and was strongly convinced that she was guilty of it. But guilty of what? Neither witchcraft, nor sorcery, nor incantation is involved here. Consultation with an evil spirit, possibly; an implied abusing

---

106 This would be even more likely if 'Thomas' were to be viewed as an apparition emanating from Elizabeth herself, a subjective entity projected into a personal, audible vision, reflecting Elizabeth's own internal debate and decision-making.

of the people, also possible. The essence of the question, however, is religious. Does Elizabeth support the reformed faith or not? No, she does not, and one is left with the nagging doubt that here, if one had all the relevant trial papers and background information, may lie at least one cause of the final guilty verdict. For the Archbishop of Glasgow, one should recall, however lenient he may have been towards Catholics in the past, was in serious difficulties with the General Assembly by April, 1576, and during the late October Assembly he agreed to accept a restricted area for supervision, having had time during the summer to consider his position. Moreover, he had already been assigned commissioners to help him do his job properly. So there is reason to think that unorthodox behaviour and some measure of adherence to Catholic belief or practice (or belief and practice considered to be Catholic remnants) may have become targets for increased stringent discipline during the very time Elizabeth was arrested and found herself under interrogation.[107]

Finally, who or what was Thomas? The relationship between him and Elizabeth seems to have been highly personal, for there is no evidence that he could be seen by anyone other than her. When he appeared to her in her own home, for example, and led her out by the apron into the kailyard, neither her husband nor the other men present are recorded as having noticed his presence at all. Elizabeth consistently maintains that she can do nothing unless she consults him first. She can both see and hear him, receive material objects at his hand, and perhaps see events in a vision which Thomas has created. Such, at any rate, is a possible interpretation of the phrase in the legal record anent John and George Black and their theft of the coulter and plough-share. Elizabeth spoke to Thomas "quha schew hir" who were the thieves. "Schew" could mean simply that he explained or told her their identities, but it may also indicate that he revealed them to her by letting her see who they were. Thomas, then, seems to have been accepted by both Elizabeth and her community as a guide she saw and heard during a number of clairvoyant experiences, and as an apparition which first initiated Elizabeth into the alternative world of *sithean* and divinatory visions, and continued to operate as her contact throughout the four years of their association.[108]

---

107 Indications are that the imposition of kirk discipline in Ayrshire parishes at this time was an uphill task, but the loss of early kirk session records from there makes it difficult to judge precisely how that task was progressing at any given moment. See Sanderson: *Ayrshire and the Reformation*, 136.

108 There is a similar figure in the case of Elspeth Reoch, tried for witchcraft in 1617. She met a black man calling himself 'ane fairie man' (which, of course, Thomas Reid never did), who turned out to be John Stewart, killed at sunset, 'and thairfoir nather deid nor leiving, bot wold ever go betwix the heaven and the earth'. See Dalyell: *Darker Superstitions*, 536. Cf. also the parallels cited in Cassirer: 'ESP in post-Mediaeval witchcraft', 354.

4

Spirit–Guides and Attempted Murder

The late 1570s and early 1580s saw increasing struggles between the Kirk and the state for dominance over the hearts and minds of the realm, the particular (as opposed to the general) *casus belli* being episcopal authority. The then Regent, the Earl of Morton, encouraged bishops to disregard the General Assembly, while the *Second Book of Discipline*, which appeared in 1578, emphasised the independence of the Kirk from state control and the concept of a congregational ministry responsible for seeing to its own regulation and discipline; and in July, 1579 a start was made on the erection of presbyteries to embody and enforce this style of ecclesiastical governance.[1] In September, 1580, however, Morton's ascendancy was challenged by the arrival in Scotland of Esmé Stewart, sieur d'Aubigny, a scion of the house of Lennox, who rapidly entered the King's affections and was rewarded with many honours, ultimately including the title 'Duke of Lennox'.[2] So far did he advance with the King, indeed, that by the end of 1580 he succeeded in having Morton ousted from the regency on a charge of being complicit in the murder of King Henry, and on this charge Morton was imprisoned, tried, and executed.

The Kirk was uncomfortable with the new régime. Although Lennox avowed himself a Protestant, there spread abroad an allegation that Catholics had been granted a dispensation by Rome to feign conversion to Protestantism, provided they secretly kept their old faith and did everything they could to advance its cause.[3] True or not, the possibility coloured the Kirk's attitude to Lennox and helped to rehabilitate Morton in ministers' eyes as a champion of the Protestant cause. Inevitably, Lennox's domination, with its suspected sympathy towards Catholics,[4] was quickly undermined by a party led by William Ruthven, Earl of Gowrie, who used anti-Catholicism as a lever to dislodge the Duke; and on 22 August, 1582 the Earls of Mar and Gowrie

---

1 Cowan: *The Scottish Reformation*, 123, 132. MacDonald: *The Jacobean Kirk*, 14–18. Hewitt: *Scotland Under Morton*, 107–16.
2 Melville: *Memoirs*, 265. Bingham: *James VI*, 50–2.
3 M'Crie: *Life of Andrew Melville* 1.173–4.
4 On the Duke's Protestantism, see *BUK*, 466. Note, too, the wording of one of the grievances addressed to the King by the General Assembly during the seventh session of its convention in June, 1582: 'That your Majesie, be advyce of some Counsellours, is causit to take upon your Grace that spirituall power and authoritie quhilk properly belongs to Christ as only King and heid of the Kirk . . . swa that in your Graces person, some men preases to erect a new Paipdome', *Ibid.*, 582.

seized the King's person, thereby staging a coup, much to the applause and approval of the Kirk. Not that their collective triumph lasted long, for in July, 1583 King James succeeded in escaping from what was virtually his imprisonment, and the see-saw of Scottish politics tipped again in favour of the Crown. As a result, the Kirk lost ground in its fight for ecclesiastical supremacy and on 20 May, 1584 Parliament passed a series of laws known as the 'Black Acts', the first of which declared:

> Forsamekle as syndrie personis being laitlie callit befoir the kingis majestie and his secrete counsell to ansuer upoun certane pointis to have bene inquirit of thame concerning sum treasounable, seditious and contumelious spechis utterit be thame in pulpet, scolis, and utherwayis to the disdae and reproche of his hienes . . . contumptuouslie declinit the jugement of his hienes and his said counsell in that behalf . . . Thairfoir our soverane lord and his thrie estatis assemblit in this present Parliament ratefeis and apprevis and perpetuallie confirmis the royall power and auctoritie over all statis, asweill spirituall as temporall within this realme in the persoun of the kingis majestie.[5]

Such, then, is the political and religious background to those witchcraft trials which took place during the late 1570s and the succeeding decade; and while the Kirk was exercised over financial settlements for its ministers, the enforcement of discipline among its officers as well as the general populace, and especially its struggle with James and his ministers, success in curbing Catholicism, diminishing the number of Catholics, and stamping out magical and superstitious beliefs and practices still seemed to be elusive.[6] People were being arrested and punished for saying or hearing Mass, of course, and the General Assembly had begun to demand that those who sent their children abroad to be educated as Catholics should fetch them back; that anyone who had gone abroad, converted to Catholicism there, and returned to Scotland should repent or be excommunicated; and that something should be done about Catholics in the royal household; and all this went hand in hand with complaints about 'superstition', whether that referred to the trappings of the Earl of Atholl's funeral or continued pilgrimages to wells and chapels.[7] But the very fact that the Assembly saw the need to make such efforts is an

---

5 *APS* 3.292. MacDonald: *The Jacobean Kirk*, 21–6. The 'sundry persons' most notably included Andrew Melville who was obstreperous and rude when brought before the Privy Council in February, and chose to take refuge in England when ordered by the Council to ward himself in Blackness Castle.
6 See MacDonald: *The Jacobean Kirk*, 14–17.
7 *Diurnal of Occurrents*, 300–1. JC26/1/28. *BUK*, 407, 425–6, 429, 431, 432–3 (the case of Ninian Dalyell, schoolmaster in Dumfries), 458, 431, 462, 464, 528.

indication that Catholicism on the one hand, and 'superstition' on the other, were not so easily eradicated.

The King was petitioned in 1579 to assist the Kirk's attempts – "because some Jesuites are presently within this countrey, that ordour may be takin with them, as effeirs [as appropriate], seeing they are the pestilent dregs of most detestable idolatrie"[8] – and his attention was drawn to the sad moral state of the realm in an acknowledgement that so far, at least, the Kirk was far from achieving its reformative goal: "The manifest corruption of our lives in all Estates, and licentious and godless living of the multitude, the impunity of some, and wickedness, the cruell and unnatural murthers, hainous and detestable incests, adulteries, *sorceries*, and many such like enormities, with the oppression and contempt of the poor, almost universal corruption of justice and judgment, and many other evils which overflow this common wealth, bear evident witness how slender and small success hitherto followed the reformation of religion within this realm".[9] We need not take this jeremiad too much *ad litteram*, of course, but its general sentiments are clear and their context (that is to say, the reiterated concerns of the General Assembly during the late 1570s and early 1580s) suggests that the Kirk's apparent failure to roll back Catholic beliefs and practices in Scotland as a whole, and the Lowlands in particular, where her influence should have been greater, was beginning to fray the nerves of her principal officers.

The mention of 'sorceries' in this list of complaints, and Parliament's re-issue on 10 November, 1579 of its 1574 legislation anent vagabonds and sturdy beggars, gipsies, physiognomists, cheiromancers, and other diviners and fortune-tellers,[10] therefore makes one ask what kind of magical operations were being investigated and tried before the courts during the second half of the decade. There are perhaps fewer than the Kirk's concern might lead one to think (although this relative paucity may well owe more to the survival rate of the records than to lack of actual incidents), but one or two of those about which we know any details involved some remarkably important people.

Noteworthy, for example, is a trial which took place on 24 October, 1577. Violat Mar from Perthshire appeared on a charge "of the using of Sorcerie, Witchcraft, and Incantatioune, with Invocatioune of spreittis", an assize having been summoned to hear her case a fortnight before.[11] Five of the fifteen assizers were men of some standing, described as "of" a particular place, which indicates that they were landowners rather than renters (a distinction which may lend a little weight to Pitcairn's suggestion that Violat could have been a woman "of superior rank"). As seems to have been customary, some of

---

8 *BUK*, 437.
9 *Op.cit. supra*, 446–7. My italics.
10 *APS* 3.140.
11 Pitcairn: *Criminal Trials* 1.2.76–7. *Accounts of the Treasurer of Scotland* 13.182.

these men came from the same district as the panel, and in as much as one can tell the origins of the assizers, it is possible to say that three came from Perthshire and two from neighbouring Forfarshire. The one recorded item of Violat's dittay says that she was "ane commoune usare of sorcerie, libbis [magical incantations], and charmes, and abusare of the pepill, aganis the lawis of God and manne". 'Abuser of the people' is clearly a direct reference to one of the provisions of the 1563 Witchcraft Act and need not detain us further. But an earlier reference certainly catches the eye; for this says she confessed that the aim of her witchcraft had been to kill the present Regent, the Earl of Morton, by magical means. Now, we know of three attempts against the Regent's life: one in November, 1561, one in the middle of 1572, and a third in June, 1577. None, however, had involved magic.[12] Violat's undertaking, therefore, must be seen as a fourth, and it was taken seriously enough at the time for the Countess of Mar to comment on Violat's trial in a letter to her brother-in-law.[13] Apparently Violat was found guilty and convicted by her assize. Her sentence, however, is not recorded and Pitcairn may have been right when he suggested that "it had likely been referred to the Lord Regent and Privy Council; and when pronounced, omitted to be inserted in the record".[14] It is indeed only too probable that Morton would have been keen to learn the details of any attempt upon his life, however unusual or unexpected its circumstances.[15] Still, Violat's case was either successfully buried, or its more interesting details and ramifications still remain to be discovered.

Meanwhile, as tension between Kirk and state increased, evidences of witchcraft continued to plague the authorities. In 1580, John Erskine received a letter from the Laird of Dunipace, from which he learned that Master

12 See Hewitt: *Scotland Under Morton*, 4–5, 14, 141–3.
13 This letter was discovered by Michael Wasser and will be discussed by him in a forthcoming article. I am grateful to Dr. Wasser for drawing it to my attention.
14 *Criminal Trials* 1.2.77.
15 Violat's was not the only witchcraft trial in 1577. On 4 May, Edward Kyninmont *alias* Lowrie was accused of having sought out and then used enchantments and witchcraft in October, 1574 with a view to curing several of his cattle which had contracted some form of sickness. He was to come before a justice-air in Forfar to answer these 'and other crimes' which are not specified in the legal record, and John Adie and James Stirling pledged themselves to answer for his appearance there. But what happened at that later hearing, we do not know. See Pitcairn: *Criminal Trials* 1.2.70. The long interval between commission of the alleged offence and the date of Kyninmont's initial arraignment need not necessarily point to a lengthy term of imprisonment. It is usual in witchcraft dittays to find references to magical operations dating back one, two, or even three decades. In October, a commission was issued anent 31 named individuals delated or suspect of magic, incantation, and other crimes, *Exchequer Rolls* 20.525. *Calendar of Munro Writs*, no. 92; and in September, 1578 nine unnamed witches were tried and burned in Ross, *Calendar of Fearn*, 135.

Livingstone had been summoned before the presbytery of Montrose where Anne Gib and others were to be accused of witchcraft. Livingstone explained that although Anne Gib did not actually come within his jurisdiction, since he came from Stirling and she from the Mearns, he had expressed himself nevertheless perfectly willing to come and judge her, although he would not hear the cases against the others. The hearing had taken place and Anne Gib had been set free.[16] It is an interesting indication (and one which would later be mirrored in the mid-seventeenth century at the height of Scotland's prosecution of witches) that even when circumstances might appear to be particularly hostile to someone accused of witchcraft, the authorities were willing to acknowledge a person's innocence, or that the evidence presented to them was insufficient. On 20 December, 1580 a witch was banished from Perth, and in September, 1581 Catherine Keith was banished from Inverness for being a deceiver of the common people.[17] Witchcraft is not specifically mentioned in her case, but the phrase 'deceiver of the common people' is so strongly reminiscent of the 1563 Witchcraft Act and the intention of the 1574 and 1579 Acts anent Vagabonds that it seems likely, at any rate, that fortune-telling or some similar operation constituted the burden of her offence. On 26 October, 1581 Bessie Robertson was delated for witchcraft before the kirk session of St. Andrews; on 12 February, 1582, we learn, a woman suspected of being a witch and imprisoned therefore in the Meal Vennel in Perth was to be told that her trial was coming up in eight days' time; and on 1 April the kirk session of Perth authorised James Syme, box-master (treasurer), "to give the witch in the tolbuith eight doits in the day".[18] In Ayr on 14 June, 1582 William Gilmour, delated of using witchcraft, had his trial referred to a later justice-air, and one notes that two years later, on 4 March, 1584, a commission was issued to William Campbell in Ayr, giving him authority to arrest nine named men, including a certain "William Gilmour the younger" on charges of magic, sorcery, and other, unspecified crimes.[19] Whether the two men were one and the same is not altogether clear, since the absence of the qualifying phrase 'junior' in the earlier legal record need not be significant.

These traces of witchcraft in the official records of the time may seem sparse, but they clearly indicate that magical operations of one kind and another were still as common as they had ever been, and the fact that they appear all over the country, from Ayrshire to Fife to Inverness, serves merely

16 *SCM* 4.65–6.
17 Lawson: *Book of Perth*, 135. MacKay & Boyd: *Records of Inverness* 1.289.
18 *St. Andrews Kirk Session Register* 1.455. Lawson: *Book of Perth*, 141, 144. *Chronicle of Perth*, 54. A vennel is a narrow lane between houses, or a covered drain. Here the phrase seems to refer to a small cellar originally constructed for the storage of oatmeal. A doit was a small copper coin, worth very little.
19 *JC2/2*. p.20. *Exchequer Rolls* 21.499.

to underline continuing reasons for the Kirk's agitation over the prevalence of 'superstition'.[20] Indeed, to add to her concern it appeared that not only were Catholics flourishing at Court, but that members of the nobility very close to the King had no hesitation in associating themselves with witches. For it was noted that the wife of Mark Ker, Master of Requests to James VI, kept company with witches (one is reminded of the similar gossip directed earlier against the Countess of Atholl), and that the Earl of Arran hired Kate, an Edinburgh witch and common scold, to rail against the ministry and others in various royal palaces;[21] and it is this double concern over Catholics and witches which rings like a *leitmotiv* through the records of the period.

In the April Assembly of 1582, for example, it was noted that Catholics were still coming back to Scotland from abroad, to such an extent that the Kirk decreed observance of a general fast, forwarded a request to the King that people be warned about the "universall conspiracies of the Papists, and enemies of God, in all countreys, against Christians, for executioun of the bloody Counsel of Trent" and "the flocking home of Jesuites and of Papists", and sent a commission of its own to the North with authority "to call before them, where they shall think most expedient, such as be suspect of papistrie".[22] Similar concerns were voiced again in April, 1583 when it was hoped that a union of Protestants of different countries could be made to counter the threat posed by Trent; and the Kirk lamented the fact that there were some Scots, brought up as Protestants, who had converted to Catholicism and were being received at Court, and that a Catholic sent into Scotland for the purpose of making converts, and imprisoned by order of the King, had nevertheless been allowed to escape.[23] To all this, the Kirk added "that there is no punischment for incests, adulteries, *witchcrafts*, murthers, abominable oathes, uther horrible oathes, in such sort that daylie sin increases, and provokes the wrath of God against the haill countrey", and that the young Laird of Fintrie was a notorious supporter of Catholics.[24] The King replied, somewhat tartly, in October that if there was a lack of punishment it was

---

20 In October, 1581 the Synod of Lothian sent articles which were heard during the eleventh session of the General Assembly. These asked the Assembly to request that Parliament pass an Act 'aganis them that passes in pilgrimages, and uses superstitioun at wells, croces, images, or uther papisticall idolatrie, or observes feasts and dayes dedicat to Santes, or setts out beanfyres for superstitioun', *BUK*, 535–6. The thrust may have been principally anti-Catholic, but there can be little doubt that any other form of behaviour deemed superstitious was equally aimed at, for, as we have seen, there existed in the Kirk's mind a grey area between certain aspects and usages of Catholicism, and many magical beliefs and practices.
21 Scot: *Staggering State*, 104–6. Calderwood: *History of the Kirk of Scotland* 4.442. *RPC* 5. Introduction lxxiv and the references cited there.
22 *BUK*, 550, 569–70.
23 *Op.cit. supra*, 613, 631.
24 *Ibid.*, 632, 633. (My italics.)

scarcely his fault, since he had always been willing to issue the commissions necessary to deal with those problems.[25]

The Trial of Tibbie Smart

The King's point can be illustrated by a warrant issued under his signet on 9 May, 1586.[26] James Findlaw, his sisters Agnes and Elizabeth, Janet Will his wife, and John his son, all residents of Ardo in Kincardineshire, were engaged in a feud with William Reid, Richard Reid, Christian Mawder, and David Reid, her son. It may have begun when Richard Reid hit John Findlaw, although of course it is possible that relations had been poor or inimical before that. A second blow, however – one of the Reids struck a young shepherd belonging to the Findlaw household[27] – turned enmity to active hatred and the Findlaws looked for a way to take their revenge. In Mickle Coull, a village of South Aberdeenshire, some thirty miles or so to the north-west of Ardo, lived Tibbie Smart, "ane commoun and notorious witch", according to the warrant. Throughout January, February, and March in 1585[28] the Findlaws had been trying to persuade her to help them destroy the Reids, but when the Reids struck their provocative blow in March, James Findlaw vowed to have an end to them and therefore sent his sister Agnes to bring Tibbie back to Ardo, "secreitlie under sylence of nyt", and kept her in his house, without the neighbours knowing, for three whole nights while he and the rest of his family set about persuading Tibbie to murder the Reids "maist ungodlie and unnaturallie be sorsareis and witchcraftis".[29]

At last they succeeded and the magic was set in motion. It did not take long to produce its effect, for "in the samin moneth of march and yeir of god foirsaid [the Reids] contractit ane deidlie, terrible, and crewall sewerand seiknes and swalling at thair hairtis". David Reid died of his illness in May, Richard in September, Christian in December,[30] while William lingered until 30 April the following year. But the authorities quickly became alert to this concatenation of apparently magical deaths. Suspicions, indeed, must surely have been aroused by the time of Christian's decease, if not before. A warrant

---

25 *Ibid.*, 644.
26 *JC26/2*. The details which follow are taken from this and other surviving pre-trial papers.
27 He is described as a 'boy', a term which can refer to any unmarried male living under another person's roof.
28 The text gives '1584', but in view of the way the narrative develops, this must be a mistake.
29 Her coming to Ardo 'afoir the breking of day', however, had been noted by one Thomas Davidson.
30 The text has 'Apryll' written over 'December', but the latter must be correct since we are told that Christian remained ill for nine months and William for fourteen. Arithmetic thus dictates a date in 1585 for Christian's death.

for the arrest of Tibbie and the Findlaws, and the summoning of an assize to try them, was issued on 9 May, 1586. Its provisions were carried out on the 14th and the 19th, and members of the assize were summoned during the first week of June. The trial itself took place on 10 June.

According to Tibbie's dittay,[31] she was already a convicted witch of long standing. Originally from Caraldston in Forfarshire,[32] she was so notorious for her magical activities, which seem to have tended quite frequently to acts of malefice, that the local laird had her arrested and brought to trial at which, having been found guilty, she was sentenced to perpetual banishment and branded upon the cheek. The operations for which she had gained her reputation included healing a sick cow, boasting to Alexander Gray that she could find lost goods by means of the shears and riddle, and accurately prophesying to Robert Allan, her neighbour in Caraldston, who had asked her why all his lambs and sheep died, that he would be left with not a single animal that year.

But Tibbie could also be dangerous. John Davidson, described as "ane puir man", found a purse allegedly belonging to Tibbie Smart, and when this was opened it was found to contain white barley seeds, lumps of salt, some pieces of coal, threads of different colours, and "certane jont banes of men and women commonlie usit be sorceraris and witches". John Davidson burned the purse, and when Tibbie found out she came to him in a fury and told him that this day would be his best (that is, the last on which he would enjoy good health); "and he incontinent thaireftir tuik seiknes and dwynit on [wasted away] be the space of aught dayis and deceissit". John Dacre, too, made the mistake of sowing grass on land which Tibbie had intended to use for her own purposes, and was told by her that the sheep he was hoping to graze thereon would all die; "lyk as the samin be your inchantment and malice cam to pas". Two men, Robert Allan with whom she had had dealings before, and William Galloway, were involved with Tibbie in an extraordinary incident. They saw her standing beside an open gate, her hair hanging over her face, on St. Martin's Eve, described as being "ane of the nichtis of the conventione of witches" when people might find themselves bewitched. Sure enough, something seemed to go amiss, for when the men returned home "thair wyiffis wald not luik upone thame be the space of thrie dayis thaireftir", a reaction which, according to Tibbie's dittay, "wes notourlie knawin to haif bein done be yow".

But perhaps the most extraordinary episode of all is described in the very first article of the dittay. Tibbie had run away into the depths of the countryside for fear of some of her neighbours. A group of people (not

---

31 *JC*26/1/13.
32 Also appearing as 'Careston'.

her neighbours) was out hunting, and in an effort to avoid them Tibbie changed herself into a badger, but was caught by the hunters' dogs and badly bitten. Thinking their hounds were worrying a real badger, the hunters struck the supposed animal with their staves and cudgels, hurting its mouth and hindquarters to such an effect that Tibbie feared for her life and changed herself back into human shape, crying out, "Alas, alas, it is I, Tibbie Smart!" She explained that she had simply been trying to evade her enemies who were out to do her harm, an explanation which appears to have satisfied the hunters, for they did nothing further and continued on their way, leaving Tibbie alone in possession of her life. Shape-shifting of this kind is part of a long European tradition which holds that witches are able to turn themselves into any of a wide variety of animal-figures,[33] although examples of the belief are not particularly common in Scottish witchcraft. Tibbie Smart, indeed, is the first and best example we have of it.

If the reaction of the hunters to the startling transformation is unexpected – and here it makes no difference whether we regard the episode as entirely fictional or founded upon reality with fictional modifications and embellishments – the result of Tibbie's trial is even more so. For on an indictment of eleven articles, three of which are concerned with conspiracy to murder and attempted murder by magical means, and another of which describes a previous conviction for witchcraft, made manifest to the whole court by the brand upon her cheek, the assize still brought in a verdict of acquittal.[34] In the text which records this result, her offence appears as 'slaughter' rather than 'witchcraft'; but even if one tried to argue that the assize simply rejected those charges relating to the deaths of the various Reids, that would still leave eight articles concerned entirely with episodes involving magic, some of them clearly incidents of malefice, and one is therefore left with the remarkable situation of an acquittal in the face of all or some of these, and in the face of her previous conviction by an earlier court. It seems to be a demonstration (repeated often during witchcraft-trials of the mid-seventeenth century) of the willingness of assizes to exercise an independent judgement, since there is no indication whatever that Tibbie Smart (unlike the later Lady Foulis or Earl of Bothwell), had important or powerful connections able to sway an assize into bringing in a verdict contrary to the thrust and tenor of the available evidence.

But Tibbie Smart was not the only witch to come to notice that year. Visitations in the diocese of Dunblane during September and October discovered a Catholic priest, John Henderson, who charmed cattle, and a

---

33 See Pócs: *Between the Living and the Dead*, 44–8.
34 *JC*49/7. The notice dates her trial to 6 July, but as the case listed one line above
   is dated 10 June, it is probable that the clerk has simply made a mistake.

woman called Donaldson who was suspected of being a witch; while the Ayr Burgh Accounts record expenses sustained in burning the witch of Barnweill: to candles, to meat and drink, to pitch barrels, to coals, 'roset, hedir, treis', and other necessaries, £7. 3s. 8d.[35] In 1587, Helen Elliot "called the witch" absented herself from court in Jedburgh; Marjorie Robertson in Stirling was accused of bewitching a cow; the General Assembly railed that Satan in the form of Catholics and Jesuits in particular was at work, deceiving the ignorant, and the Privy Council, stirred by such "ydolatrie and mantenance thairof", issued a proclamation announcing a high court of justiciary, to be held in presence of the King himself on 27 November, to try all manner of great offences including "heiring and saying of messis, ressaving and mantening of Jesuitis . . . witchcraft or seikaris of responssis or help at witcheis".[36]

Jesuits, perhaps not surprisingly in 1587–8, continued to prey on the Kirk's mind. On 29 July, 1587 Parliament passed two Acts anent Jesuits and seminary priests, and the introduction of Catholic books into Scotland. The first provided that "quhatsoevir professit and avowit Jesuitis or seminary preistis salbe fund in ony pairt of this realme within the space of ane moneth efter the publicatioun of the actis of this present parliament Salbe takin, apprehendit, callit, and persewit, and incur the pane of death and confiscatioun of all thair guidis movable", with further penalties listed against those who sheltered such priests, heard Mass, or distributed Catholic books; and in a separate Act, the legislators decided that because "sindrie personis bringis hame furth of utheris realmes diverss buikis and writtis contening erroneous doctrine aganis the trew word of god and religioun professit and be the lawes establissit in this realme Or contening superstitious rites and ceremonies papisticall quhairby the people ar greitly abusit", the burgh authorities should have power given them to search for such books and destroy them whenever they were found, and to punish those who had brought them into Scotland "in thair personis and guidis at our soverane lordis will".[37]

This was followed up by the fourteenth session of the General Assembly in February, 1588 whence articles were sent to the King asking that two Jesuits, James Gordon and William Crichton, at present in Edinburgh itself, be called before James and the Privy Council to learn "how thair lyves are in your Majesties hand, for contraveining of your Hienes lawes", with a recommendation that if the King should choose to spare their lives, they be put on the first available ship and sent away with the warning that if they returned they would be put to death. The Lairds of Fintrie and Glenbarvie and other Catholics excommunicated by the Kirk should be warned likewise, and summons issued "aganis all receipters of

35 *Visitation of the Diocese of Dunblane*, 13–14, 56. *Ayr Burgh Accounts*, 156. Roset = resin, *hedir* = heather, and *treis* = stakes.
36 *RPC* 4.147. *Stirling Presbytery Records*, 247, 249–50. *BUK*, 694. *RPC* 4.217–18.
37 *APS* 3.430.

Papists, Jesuites, Seminarie Priests, and traffiquers aganis true religioun".[38] This
was followed by a list of grievances, handed in by the Kirk to the King on 20
February, 1588. It began: "First, *and above all other things*, It is ane exceiding
great greife to all such as have any spunck of the love of God and his Kirk, to sie
Jesuites, Seminarie Priests, and other teachers of Papistrie and errour, so long to
be sufferit to pollute this land with idolatrie, corrupt and seduce the people, and
spread abroad their pusyionable doctrine", and went on to give examples of
named individuals who maintained and favoured Jesuits in every part of the
country, especially Dumfries, Aberdeen, Ross, Angus, and Dunfermline, and
general censure of those who observed "superstitious days" such as Christmas
and Easter, and "superstitious ceremonies, pilgrimages to Chrysts well, fasting
[feasting], festives, benfyres, girdles, carrells, and such lyke". The final session
then decided to debate these matters again when it met once more in August.[39]

That next Assembly started on 6 August, just as the Spanish Armada arrived
in Calais, and the ministers duly noted the possible danger to Scotland, their
nervousness in the face of the Armada's progress breaking through in several of
their later sessions.[40] But in the main, they concentrated on problems of Kirk
discipline and the continued threat to Protestantism within Scotland from
Catholics active and unrepentant within the country. Hence the authority
delegated by the Assembly to the presbytery of Edinburgh "to call before them
papists and apostates quho sall happin to resort to Court, or to the said towne;
and in speciall to summond my Lord Seatoun, the Earl of Huntlie, William
Schaw,[41] John Chisholme, and Collonell Stewart, and proceed against them,
and every one, according to the acts of the Assembly".[42]

The Trial of Alison Pearson

Increasingly, then, during the later 1580s the Kirk was showing signs of
impatient frustration that her efforts not only to roll back the tide of
Catholicism but also to stem its returning flow were proving less than

38 *BUK*, 713–14. *JC26/2.*
39 *Op.cit. supra*, 715–24, 727. (My italics.) 'Girdles' looks like a reference to a post-
    marriage custom. On the day after the marriage, a creel was tied to the
    bridegroom's back and he then started running, to be followed by friends who
    tried to throw stones into the creel as they ran, the aim being to make him fall
    over with the weight of his burden. This continued until the bridegroom
    managed to free himself from the creel or his bride caught up with him and cut
    the cords which bound it to his back.
40 'Ther is ane ship latelie arriveit in the Firth from Dunkirk, suspect to be ane spy',
    BUK, 732. 'Report . . . of the Kings Majesty his good mind and earnest affection
    to the defence of the true religioun, and of his commonwealth against the
    forraigne enemies', *Ibid.*, 734.
41 Master of the King's Works and founder of Freemasonry in the late 1590s. See
    Stevenson: *The Origins of Freemasonry*, 117–24.
42 *BUK*, 738.

successful; and in the midst of what she perceived as religious or confessional superstition, there appeared to be an equal advance (or failure to retreat) of magical superstition, the two undesirable phenomena overlapping at certain points. What is more, the King attained his majority in 1586 and therefore began to play a larger personal role in the political direction of the state, and two of his ministers gave the Kirk particular alarm – Lord Seton, a Catholic who conformed outwardly to Protestantism from 1588, but whose previous adherence to the old faith struck the Kirk as sufficient warrant to regard him with very grave suspicion, and John Maitland of Thirlestane, James's Chancellor from 1586 to 1595, whose policy, effective if not quite openly declared, was to curb or at least modify the political pretensions of the Kirk.[43]

It is against this background that we must examine the trial of Alison Pearson from Boarhill in Fife, which took place on 28 May, 1588. Like Tibbie Smart, she had been in trouble before. On 28 August, 1583 the Archbishop of St. Andrews, Patrick Adamson, approached the local kirk session anent Alison Pearson, then in prison under suspicion of being a witch, and the session in its turn requested "Mr. James Wilky, Rectour, [and] George Blak to pas the morn to the Prisbittrie, and desyre thair gude consall and advis thairin, that God may be glorifiit and vice punischit according to the Word of God".[44] Now, this action by the Archbishop is rather odd since, as article 6 of her dittay informs us, Alison had actually been treating the Archbishop for several illnesses from which he had just been suffering.[45] Adamson, however, was not a person to be trusted. "Despised by nearly everyone, admired for little else than his poetical skills" is one modern summary of his character.[46] Ambitious for personal advancement in the Kirk, anti-Catholic but at the same time careless of presbyterianism,[47] he

43 On Seton, see Lee: 'King James's Popish Chancellor', in Cowan & Shaw: *The Renaissance and Reformation in Scotland*, 170–82. On Maitland, see MacDonald: *The Jacobean Kirk*, 30–1, 47–9.
44 *Register of St. Andrews Kirk Session* 2.508. George Black, a reader, was to all intents and purposes filling in as minister during a vacancy in the living until a suitable clergyman could be appointed.
45 Pitcairn: *Criminal Trials* 1.2.164.
46 Mullan: *Episcopacy in Scotland*, 73. Cf. M'Crie: 'Next to Arran, no individual in the nation was so universally disliked as Archbishop Adamson', *Life of Andrew Melville* 1.270. My account of Adamson in the rest of this paragraph is based upon Mullan's chapter.
47 His anti-Catholicism can be seen in his early poem, *De Papistarum superstitiosis ineptiis* (The Silly Superstitions of the Papists), addressed to the Catholics of Aberdeen and produced in St. Andrews in early September, 1564. In this, it is interesting to note, he refers to the priest directly as a magician who utters 'incantations through the arts of magic' (*magicas incantamenta per artes*). This helps to illustrate the point I have been making on several occasions, that Scottish Protestants were quite capable of viewing aspects of Catholic practice as little more than magical operations, and thus allowing themselves to regard Catholicism and magic as sisters under the skin; and the fact that this made good propaganda does not necessarily mean its proponents did not also believe what they were saying.

ran foul of Kirk discipline during the early 1570s because of his lax behaviour, and when he became Archbishop of St. Andrews in 1576, he refused point blank to answer for his faults before the General Assembly. But he managed to weather this storm and eagerly courted royal favour by announcing his conviction that the King should rule the Church along with bishops, as Constantine ruled the Church in ancient times. During the winter of 1583–4 he was in England, ostensibly for the betterment of his health, but possibly to act as an ambassador between King James and Elizabeth Tudor, thereby engendering further suspicions about his motives and conduct; and the result was that by 1586 he had made himself so unpopular at home that in April that year he was actually manhandled by several lairds and excommunicated by the Kirk.

Now, Melville tells us that between April 1582 and August 1583, "Bischope Adamsone keipit his castle (lyk a tod in his holl), seik of a disease of grait fetiditie, and oftymes under the cure of women suspected of witchcraft".[48] According to a scurrilous pasquinade by Robert Sempill, *The Legend of the Bischop of St. Androis*, produced in 1584,[49] Adamson had gulled land out of an unfortunate man and then frightened him to such an extent that the man ran away and died. His widow soon followed, leaving a curse on the Archbishop, whereupon Adamson fell very ill and sent for a witch to cure him,

> With sorcerie and incantationes,
> Reising the devill with invocationes,
> With herbis, stanis, buikis, and bellis,
> Menis members, and south running wellis;
> Palme croces, and knottis of strease [straws],
> The paring of a preistis auld tees;
> And, *in principio*, sought out syne [signs, tokens],
> That under ane alter of stane had lyne,
> Sanct Jhones nutt, and the fore-levit claver [four-leafed clover],
> With taill and mayn of a baxter aver [baker's horse],[50]
> Had careit hame heather to the oyne [oven],
> Cutted off in the cruik of the moone;
> Halie water, and the lamber beidis,[51]
> Hynteworth [hogwart], and fourtie uther weidis:
> Whairthrow the charming tuik sic force,
> They laid it on his fatt whyte horse.

48 *Diary*, p. 97.
49 For details of Sempill, see *DNB* 51.238–9.
50 Adamson's father had been a baker: hence the jibe.
51 Amber beads, worn round the neck or carried on the person as an amulet for sore eyes.

As all men saw, he sone deceissit:
Thair Saga[52] slew ane seikles beast.

Granted this is meant to be a lampoon, its tenor and some of its details are remarkably interesting. Sempill was a presbyterian and wrote on behalf of that religion. Moreover, he was satirising a bishop, the holder of an office still closely identified with the Roman Church. So the anti-Catholicism of his poem is not surprising. But the interweaving of Catholic custom and magical practice which we see here is at one with the deep suspicion of the Kirk as a whole that Catholicism and magic were, in many ways, not too dissimilar. Thus, raising the Devil, using herbs of various kinds, stones, penises, straw knots, toenail clippings, a horse's mane and tail, and an amulet consisting of amber beads are mingled with the book and bell of ecclesiastical exorcism, palm crosses, a reference to the beginning of St. John's Gospel in the Vulgate version, a stone altar, and holy water, not to mention the priest from whom the toenail clippings were taken. Exaggerated for comic effect, the passage still conveys its serious triple message: (a) Patrick Adamson (not actually a Catholic archbishop, we have to keep reminding ourselves) is a superstitious fool; (b) witchcraft is both disgusting and grotesque; (c) magic (especially in its manifestation as witchcraft), and Catholicism are as ridiculous and un-Christian as each other, since they co-exist and intermingle on equal terms.

When this witch failed to satisfy him, however, Adamson turned to a second who lived in nearby Anstruther. Sempill does not explain the exact reason for the Archbishop's dissatisfaction, but perhaps

Medusa's craftis scho had plane,
That could mak auld men young agane

is meant to hint at Adamson's motive for consulting her.[53] The rumour that he was keeping witches' company reached the ears of the kirk session, so its members summoned him before them and reproved him for believing in witchcraft to the peril of his soul.[54] But, although both he and the witch

---

52 *Saga* is one of the Latin words for 'witch'.
53 He was 45 at the time of his consulting Alison Pearson. We have no means of telling exactly how old he was when he sought out the witch from Anstruther, or even if he really did such a thing.
54 One should not, however, necessarily take this as an indication that the ministers and elders were sceptical of the reality of magic in the way we should understand. People at the time had no doubt about the existence of Satan and his demons, or about their greater than human powers to wreak havoc in nature and put human souls in danger. It was the proposition that humans could control these spirits, which often caused doubts to be expressed (and not only by Protestants), as well as the means used by magicians and witches, which were often regarded as insufficient instruments in themselves to bear the burden of preternatural performance and thus incapable of working the marvels demanded of them.

confessed they had seen each other, she strengthened what appears to have been his weak resolve, and compounded a drink which put fire in his belly and made him answer the elders with insolent defiance. The kirk session thereupon demanded that he burn both witches the very next day, but in fear of what more they would reveal about his dealings with them, Adamson arranged for them to make their escape from prison, and explained their absence by claiming that they must have been rescued by the Devil himself. No one believed him, although no one could prove his part in the witches' escape, and so people had to content themselves with urging Adamson to amend his life and stop putting his faith in witchcraft.

No sooner had the minister and elders finished having their say than Adamson went back to the castle and hired the services of a third witch, Alison Pearson whom Sempill describes as

> Ane carling of the Quene of Phareis,
> That ewill win geir to elphyne careis.

This reference to *sithean* is interesting because it invites comparison with the earlier trial of Elizabeth Dunlop, and indeed there are several points of similarity between them. Alison, like Elizabeth, was accused not only of using sorcery and witchcraft, but also of "the Invocatioun of the spreitis of the Dewill; speciallie in the visioun and forme of ane Mr. William Sympsoune, hir cousing and moder-brotheris-sone".[55] The inference of the wording of this part of the dittay is that William Simpson was not a physical (and therefore a living) presence although, since it is nowhere overtly stated that he is dead, it might be argued that the meaning of the dittay is that an evil spirit used to come to Alison in the form, that is, in the guise of her kinsman; and attendant circumstances when Simpson appears in the evidence suggest that he could have been a spirit-guide along similar lines to Thomas Reid.

According to Alison's testimony, William Simpson was a medical doctor, or at least learned in medical matters, who had treated her for an illness when she was twelve. He lived in Edinburgh at the time, and for the next seven years Alison travelled back and forth between her home (perhaps in Fife, although we do not know how long she was actually resident there) and the capital until eventually Simpson's ministrations began to effect an improvement in her condition. The problem is described as a lack of strength in her hand and foot.

---

55 There seems to have been some confusion about the exact family relationship between Simpson and Pearson, since he is described in article 3 of her dittay as her paternal uncle. But the dittay gives ample evidence of having been composed from separate pieces of information probably gathered on more than one occasion, so the discrepancy may be little more than scribal error, 'paternal' for 'maternal', although this would not entirely account for the apparent mistake.

Simpson was born in Stirling. His father was the King's smith, and it is worth noting that he was executed for reading or looking at a Missal. Whether this means he was a Catholic, or a Protestant too curious for his own good and safety, is not quite clear, but the former seems much more likely. Simpson himself had been stolen by a big gipsy while he was still a child, and remained in gipsy encampments for the next twelve years. It was soon after he left them, or escaped from them, that he began to treat Alison's physical infirmities; so he would have been quite a young man at the time, and indeed he is later described so: "nocht sax yeiris eldar nor hirselff", as Alison ventures in her deposition.[56] Alison acknowledges that it was Simpson who taught her how to diagnose illnesses and how to cure them, and that it was he who informed her what was wrong with Archbishop Adamson and told her what remedies were best to apply in his case.[57] In what may be a significant phrase, she says that Simpson "gewis hir his directioune att all tymes", and one is reminded of Elizabeth Dunlop's complete dependence on Thomas Reid for knowledge of what to do in any of her magical operations.

The evidence which suggests most strongly that Simpson may have been more of a spirit-guide than a living adviser, however, is his close association with the *sithean*. Alison says that they told her Simpson was with them (that is, one of their number), which certainly implies that at the very least he was able, like her, to cross the boundary between this plane of physical existence and that other called 'the Court of Elphame' or 'Middle Earth'. We know she had this gift, for she says she frequented "the good neighbours" and kept company with the Queen of Elphame for several years,[58] and that while she was at the Court of Elphame she saw Simpson there. He explained to her how he was carried thither, and knew when the *sithean* were going to come to her by the sign of a whirlwind passing over the sea.

Such, then, is the evidence relating to William Simpson. It is ambiguous in as much as it is never explicitly stated that he is dead, and yet he seems to act

56 Since his father would not have been executed for reading or using a Missal in any reign earlier than that of James VI, he must have been smith to him at the time of his execution. James was born in 1566 and Alison's trial was taking place in 1588, and as we are told that William Simpson had been with the gipsies when his father was put to death, there is every likelihood that Simpson could have been in his twenties or early thirties while he was treating Alison in Edinburgh. Such an age would make Alison herself a relatively young woman at the time of her trial.

57 According to the dittay, the illnesses consisted of fever and ague, palpitations, weakness in his back and loins, and some kind of severe discharge, possibly diarrhoea. For these Alison gave the Archbishop ewe's milk, copious draughts of wine and herbs, and boiled chicken.

58 In another part of her deposition she says seven years.

in relation to Alison in ways very similar to those of Thomas Reid, being her sole teacher, mentor, and protector against hostile occult forces, and we must therefore entertain two possibilities: (1) that when the court designated him a spirit of the Devil, it was relying on a description of him which led it to believe he was not (or was no longer) human; or (2) that he was a living human being who seemed frequently to exercise his power of entering into a trance during which certain visions occurred, and that he transmitted this same gift to Alison herself, or opened in her her own innate visionary potential. But whichever possibility we accept, William Simpson still seems to have been Alison's guide to or in the spirit-world.

He was not, however, her only one. Once, when she was in Grangemuir with other people, she felt ill and lay down by herself while the others went on about their business. A man in green clothes approached her and offered her help in return for her service to him ("gif scho wald be faithfull, he wald do hir guid"). She was frightened and cried out for help, but no one heard her, so she spoke directly to the man and said that if he came in God's name for the good of her soul, he should say so; at which he went away. The green clothes suggest he was a *sith*, but his departure when he was challenged in the name of God is obviously meant to suggest that he was actually of diabolic origin. On another occasion she was visited by a second man who was accompanied by many men and women. Alison made the sign of the cross and said a prayer, but then went with them "fordir nor scho could tell" to somewhere in Lothian and saw the *sithean* making merry with music and feasting, but her presence made them angry and one of them hit her hard, depriving her of strength in her side. The blow, she said, left her badly bruised, and yet it was not the bruise which hurt her so much as her side.

Such seems to have been characteristic of her experience of the spirit-world. Once, she says, she watched while the *sithean* made their salves from herbs they had gathered at dawn, but when she spoke of it they came and hit her and she lost strength in her side again and lay ill for twenty weeks. No wonder, then, that she says she cried when the *sithean* came to her. They made her fearful as, apparently, did Simpson, too, when she saw him. Clearly she associated him very closely with the unpleasant experiences she had with the *sithean*.

Sometimes, she says, they came to her once a week. They did not always threaten her, but often promised to do her good, and she actually attributes at last one of her periods of better health – she calls it a 'cure' – to their intervention "under God". The state of her health, however (or perhaps she means those periods when she was subject to trances and those when she was not), does not seem to have been consistent: "bot scho wes quhyles weill and quhyles ewill, and ane quhyle with thame and ane uthir quhyle away; and . . .

scho wald be in hir bed haill and feir [healthy], and wald nocht wit quhair scho wald be or the morne"; and this waking up in a confused state after making a journey in trance can be paralleled by similar experiences undergone by witches elsewhere in Europe, sometimes interpreted by contemporary records as transvection to and attendance at a Sabbat.[59]

Herein lies one of the principal problems of interpreting evidence about the Sabbat, both for modern commentators and for early modern demonologists. The latter had to decide whether the accounts they were given of such journeys and meetings had objective reality, or were the product of fantasy, or illusions created by the Devil by which the confessing participant was deceived and meant to be deceived as much as his or her audience. But modern commentators, too, as Eva Pócs points out, are presented with a dilemma. Was the witches' Sabbat "an experience or narrative, communication with the dead or literary topos?"[60] The assize which was listening to the account of Alison's experience with the *sithean*, like that which heard Elizabeth Dunlop's experiences, cannot have been unaware of the traditional beliefs prevalent both in their own and in neighbouring communities regarding such contact with preternatural beings, so the question for the assizers (should they decide that Alison was recounting a version of the truth, and not merely constructing a fiction for the court out of simple-mindedness or fear of ill-treatment) was whether to accept that she had genuinely made contact, or whether she had been deluded by Satan and co-operated with him, knowing herself to be deluded.

But the prevailing religious ambience, it may be argued, is likely to have brought pressure upon the assizers to interpret, or re-interpret, encounters with *sithean* as meetings with evil spirits,[61] nor can Alison's association with the Archbishop have done her any good in the eyes of those present in court, for at the time of her trial Patrick Adamson himself was in bad odour with the Kirk.[62] Nevertheless, she was not unknown as a healer to the residents of St. Andrews, for she had been coming and going thither for the past sixteen years without, it seems, anyone's objecting to the extent of fetching her into a criminal court before now.[63] But the ability to heal magically was always two-

<hr/>

59 See Pócs: *Between the Living and the Dead*, 73–5, 88–91, 111.
60 *Op.cit. supra*, 96.
61 Her odd statement that Simpson told her that a tenth of the *sithean* go to Hell each year may reflect either her own fears about their possible diabolic origin, or an effort on the part of her interrogators to put this thought into her head.
62 *BUK*, 736.
63 The wording of her dittay is expressed in conformity with the 1563 Act, accusing her of 'dealing with charmes, and abusing of the commoun people thairwith, be the said art of Wichcraft, thir divers yeiris by past'. The assize consisted of 13 men: 6 came from St. Andrews itself, 4 from Pittenweem, 1 from Anstruther, and 2 from Cairnpykes.

edged and might easily be regarded merely as the acceptable face of witchcraft, masking the same individual's negative ability to work malefice if she or he chose to do so.[64] The assize found Alison guilty and she was duly executed. Since the details of the medical treatment she gave the Archbishop reveal nothing magical at all – and had they done so, one would have expected to find this recorded in her dittay – the offences of which she stood condemned appear to have related to her experiences with the *sìthean*. It is possible that evidence of these came as a surprise to the court. Alison could have healed and been known as a healer without her trances and other-world journeys playing any overt part in her curative activity. But a revelation that she had had dealings with *sìthean* would scarcely have been enough by itself to tell against her to such fatal effect unless the assize had been willing to see the *sìthean* as evil spirits, although without evidence from the assize-room one cannot usefully speculate further on this point.

There is also, however, the possibility that Alison was a Catholic, and this needs to be taken into account. She blessed herself (that is, made the sign of the cross) before going away with the *sìthean* on one occasion, and whenever William Simpson came to warn her that the *sìthean* were about to visit her, he would tell her to make the sign of the cross so that she would not be taken away with them again.[65] So we have a possible situation in which the following points combined: (a) the Kirk as a whole was fighting ever more forcefully against what it saw as a resurgence of Catholicism at home and a constant support of Catholics at Court shown by the King; (b) a recalcitrant Archbishop who stood upon the rights of his office against the superior jurisdiction claimed by the Kirk and retained (at least for the moment) the favour of the King; (c) a possible Catholic demonstrating by her magical behaviour and experiences those links between idolatry and superstition, Catholicism and magic, which had been agitating and continued to agitate the Kirk. It is a situation tailor-made to be interpreted in the worst possible light. Alison's condemnation and execution, therefore, could be viewed as a reaction of her local community to the religious and political conditions obtaining at just the time she found herself in court; and so perhaps it is no accident that her trial and its outcome could have been seen as conveying a message to Adamson and, through him, to higher authorities that the Kirk

64 Pócs: *Between the Living and the Dead*, 107–9.
65 It is possible, of course, that she was a Protestant who simply used Catholic signs in moments of extreme emotional agitation. But if, as I have suggested, she was a relatively young woman, she is unlikely to have been a Catholic remembering and reverting to the practices of her childhood; and if, as seems likely, she had been brought up in Fife where the Reformation had shown itself strong from the start, her Protestantism would surely have been made of sterner stuff. So the likelihood of her making Catholic signs because she actually was a Catholic is a little more convincing than the alternatives.

was determined to exercise what she considered to be her proper authority, especially in matters ecclesiastical, no matter who might be involved, and regardless of his or her powerful patronage.[66]

66 The witch from Anstruther, whom Adamson had also consulted, had been in prison since February. Her name was Agnes Melville and she was the daughter of Andrew Melville, lately reader in the kirk of Anstruther. She was 34 or 35 years old, and had been married twice, the first time to a mariner from Anstruther, the second time to a David Bains of St. Andrews, by whom she had had a son. This second marriage does not seem to have lasted, for we are told that for some time she lived in various places with various people before finally settling down in St. Andrews where she had been arrested. At the kirk session of 17 July, those present were informed of her skill in the use of herbs, which she had learned from an old man called 'John' in North Berwick. There is no indication in the kirk session record that 'John' was other than a human being. Agnes, then, was a healer and the session heard details of people who had used her services. On 13 November, she was warned that she would be tried within the next week, and later evidence tells us she was found guilty, for she is referred to as 'condemned witch' and 'umquhile'. See *BUK*, 725. Calderwood: *History of the Kirk of Scotland* 4.669. *Register of St. Andrews Kirk Session* 2.620–3, 628, 799–800.

5

Sithean in the South and Malice in the North

The years 1589 And 1590 were momentous ones for James VI. In the first, he married Anne, Princess of Denmark, and in the second he brought her back to Scotland where, by the end of the year, he was to undergo the deep of shock of discovering that there had been attempts during his absence to kill both him and his bride by means of magic.[1] The marriage came as a relief to a good many people. Negotiations with Denmark had been going on throughout the 1580s, but in 1585 the Danes decided to take the initiative and by 1588 the matter had more or less been settled. Even so, delay followed delay until 28 August, 1589 when James was surprised, though delighted, to learn he had actually been married by proxy to the Danish Princess Anne a week before. The new Queen immediately prepared to set out for Scotland and left Copenhagen on 5 September, rumours that she had sailed on the 1st precipitating a premature excitement and anticipation in Edinburgh. Storms, however, blew her ships back and forth and her flotilla was soon obliged to put in for a while at Mardø on the southern coast of Norway.[2] A long delay in finding out what had happened first caused and then increased the King's agitation until finally he decided to set out for Denmark and bring back his bride himself. So on 22 October, after a yet further delay because of a storm over Leith, he set sail for Scandinavia, leaving behind his closest kinsman, the Duke of Lennox, and Francis Stewart, Earl of Bothwell, his cousin, as the principal figures in a Council of Regency.

This concatenation of storms was greeted rather differently in Scotland and in Denmark. James seems to have regarded them as stemming from natural causes. "Contrarious winds stayed [the Queen]", he announced in October, 1589 and "she was stayed from coming through the contrarious tempests of winds and . . . her ships were not able to perfect their voyage through the great hurt they had received".[3] In Denmark, on the other hand, there was embarrassment that the Queen's ships had been unable to withstand the force of the winter gales, and the admiral in charge, Peder Munk, deflected blame from himself on to the Governor of Copenhagen, Christofer Valkendorf, on whom fell responsibility for keeping the Danish navy in good repair. Valk-

---

1 The subsequent section follows the accounts given in Stevenson: *Scotland's Last Royal Wedding*, and Maxwell-Stuart: 'The fear of the King is death', 209–25.
2 Norway should have been little more than three days' sailing from Scotland in favourable weather. See Calderwood: *History of the Kirk of Scotland* 5.84.
3 Akrigg (ed.): *Letters of James VI*, 84.

endorf, in his turn, blamed local witches for raising contrary winds, and a series of trials began in April, 1590. Meanwhile James, pleased perhaps to be on holiday for a while from the dangerous adventure which constituted Scottish regal and political life at the time, lingered in Norway and Denmark until 21 April when he and Anne set out from Copenhagen and made a stormy passage back to Scotland, landing at last in Leith on 1 May; and from then until late autumn, the King's mind was directed to matters quite unconnected with magic or witchcraft.

During the King's absence, Scotland had been fairly tranquil, apart from a flurry in January, 1590 as Edinburgh decided to worry about the sudden presence of strangers in the country: "Upon Moonday, the fyft of Januar, there was a great feare of surprising Edinburgh in the night by the Papists, who were thought to be in the toun with their freinds, very frequent. The repaire of Crawfurd, Claud Hammiloun, the Setouns, and others evill affected to religioun, and the sight of manie uncouth [unknown] faces, bred this suspicioun. The suspicioun was augment by a brute [rumour] of some Spaniards to be sent from the Duke of Parma to Leith . . . And in the meane tyme, a Spanish shippe arrived at Wigtoun with gold, as was suspected, to the Scotish erles . . . There were sindrie presumptiouns, that [the Spaniards] were come to plumme our waters, and to try where the Spanish fleete might land".[4]

But the incident passed, although it must have served to confirm the Kirk's conviction that Scottish Catholics in general, and those in high places in particular, were not to be trusted and were determined to destroy the Reformation in Scotland if they could. Indeed, the Kirk was fulminating ever more frequently about the danger posed by Jesuits, seminary priests, and Catholics as a whole. A General Assembly held in January, 1589 asked the King to issue commissions to members of the Privy Council "to search, seek, and apprehend and present to justice, all Jesuits and uthers privat or publick seducers of his Hienes lieges", and listed for him three grades of enemy: (1) "cheiff mantainers of Papists and Papistrey", (2) those who supported Jesuits and seminary priests, and (3) "allowers, receivers, and intertainers of these in their houses, and partakers of their purposes and idolatrie".[5] In view of the perils posed by all these hostile groups, the Kirk thought it appropriate and necessary to have its commissioners and ministers warn "all Gentlemen well affected to religion" to beware Catholic conspiracies and make sure they themselves frequently attended meetings of Protestants.[6] The same theme

---

4 Calderwood: *History of the Kirk of Scotland* 5.70–1.
5 On 7 and 8 May, John Lowrie living at the West Port of Edinburgh was put on trial for 'mantening, intercomoning and furnesing of meitt, drink and herberie to Mr Robert Bruce, confessit and avowed Papist and Seminarie Priest', Pitcairn: *Criminal Trials* 1.2.167–8.
6 *BUK*, 741–3.

dominated an Assembly the following month, reports from the various provinces and presbyteries illustrating "how the land was defiled all throughout, specially the North and South, with popery, superstition, bloodshed, and all kind of villany".[7]

After the 'strangers and Spaniards' incident of January, 1590 one is therefore not surprised to find that at the General Assembly held on 3 March, the first act passed there was "an Act concerning discipline to be used against accepters of Jesuits, Seminary Priests, and excommunicats", along with a Protestant bond by which the subscribers promised to take order against all Catholics "conform to the acts of the Kirk"; and so ministers and gentlemen in authority throughout the realm were instructed to see the laws against Catholics enforced, and to assist the Kirk's commissioners in the execution of this special duty.[8] In August the commissioners were quizzed on what they had done in response to this instruction, and when the King attended the eighth session of the Assembly, the brethren took the opportunity, through the voice of the Moderator, to ask that he purge the realm of Jesuits, priests, and Catholics in general.[9] The King replied that he was very keen to rid Scotland of its Catholics, but he did nothing substantial, for the Assembly petitioned him to the same effect yet again on 12 July, 1591.[10]

It must be said, however, that certain presbyteries at least were less than diligent when it came to co-operating with the Kirk's higher authorities. The Synod of Lothian and Tweeddale, for example, certainly tried to press for action against Catholics – it directed specific questions thereanent at the presbyteries of Dunbar and Lothian in April, 1589[11] – but in 1590 it discovered that nothing was being done in particular instances. On 7 May, the presbytery of Haddington had to explain that it had not proceeded against George Ker, a Catholic, on the grounds that he was not resident within the bounds of the presbytery; and so Edinburgh was instructed to deal with the matter. Quite clearly Edinburgh, too, refused to accept responsibility because in April, 1591 Haddington had to be told once more to summon Ker to appear before the presbytery, a summons which seems to have had little effect, for in October, 1592 Haddington was having to explain to the synod

---

7 *Op.cit. supra*, 744.
8 *BUK*, 748. Cf. 749 referring to the excommunication of anyone receiving Jesuits and seminary priests. Details of the act and bond appear in the record of 6 March, 750–61.
9 *BUK*, 768, 771–2. The General Assembly's instructions filtered down to parish level in at least some instances. On 1 April, 1590 St. Andrews noted that every gentleman be asked to inquire diligently into the local presence of Catholics and Jesuits between that date and the 22nd, *St. Andrews Kirk Session Records*, 662.
10 *Op.cit. supra*, 784.
11 *Records of the Synod of Lothian and Tweeddale*, 3,7.

that it had indeed summoned George Ker and Lord Seton to come before the brethren, but that neither man had done so.[12]

It was a similar story from Dunbar. In April, 1591 the presbytery had to answer a complaint that it had done nothing about Thomas Tyrie, a Catholic, and a servant of Lord Hume; and although the brethren said they had put in motion a process against him, they can scarcely have been diligent in following it through because in October they were telling the synod that in fact they had not actually done anything positive, because Tyrie was no longer resident within their bounds and had come to live in Edinburgh. Nor, for more or less the same reasons, had Lord Hume been summoned, and Dunbar had still failed to deal with either man by the time the synod met again a year later.[13]

This, then, was the situation with regard to Catholics between 1589 and 1593. Official attitudes were as rigorously hostile as they had ever been, indeed perhaps rather more so as the Kirk's preoccupation with the apparent threat to its own régime from Jesuits and seminary priests seems to indicate. Yet the King, despite his protestations to the contrary, did little or nothing to see that the relevant Acts of Parliament were properly enforced against them and Catholic landowners cocked a snook at presbyteries which tried to discipline them, while protecting their Catholic servants and dependants in similar fashion, taking their cue, perhaps, from the King's apparent double standards.

So it is interesting to note that the Kirk was having just as little success when it came to dealing with certain people accused of witchcraft. Indeed, the presbytery of Haddington features once again; for on 1 April, 1589, the Synod of Lothian and Tweeddale, sitting at Linlithgow, received a complaint that the presbytery had not summoned Agnes Sampson, described as "ane indweller in Keyth Merschell within the boundis of thair presbyterie", to answer for being suspect of witchcraft. Responding to the Synod's complaint, the presbytery explained that it could find no grounds on which to pursue a charge against her; but the Synod was not satisfied and instructed the presbytery to summon her again, "and efter tryell if ony may be had, that they tak ordour with hir, and for furdering heirof it is ordanit that all brethren that can get ony thing tryit aganis the said Anny,[14] suspect as said is, gif in the samin within xv dayis nixt efter the dait heirof".[15] In other words, the Synod was having no nonsense about lack of evidence. If evidence was not forth-

---

12 *Op.cit.* supra, 22, 28, 46.

13 *Ibid.*, 28, 30, 45. Lord Hume was summoned again in April, 1593 but did not appear, *Ibid.*, 54.

14 Agnes appears as 'Anny' in more than one record, but it is clear that only one person is involved.

15 *Synod Records of Lothian and Tweeddale*, 5.

coming, it should be found.[16] Members of the presbytery, however, were either made of stern stuff or people were unwilling to testify, for on 16 September the Synod, now meeting in Edinburgh, noted that Agnes had not yet been summoned before the Haddington elders, and therefore instructed the presbytery that this must be done; and to make sure it was done, Adam Johnston and George Ramsay were deputed to go to Haddington and assist the ministers and elders in setting up the investigation.[17]

Johnston and Ramsay, both members of the presbytery of Dalkeith, were figures of some importance. Johnston had been one of the Kirk's commissioners in Lothian in 1579 and in 1584 had been imprisoned for refusing to accept episcopacy. Soon released, however, he was employed in helping to prepare cases of slander to be heard during the General Assembly of May, 1586, and in 1588 he was a member of a commission to seek better provision for ministers of the Kirk.[18] Ramsay, Dean of Restalrig, was not a person to be afraid of authority. He accused the Lords of Session of selling justice but, when brought before them in 1593, managed to leave their presence unscathed, the case against him having come to nothing.[19] Nor was the minister of Haddington itself any less a figure. James Carmichael assisted the Kirk with revisions to the *Second Book of Discipline*, and was one of a committee of four who prepared the Acts of the Kirk for general use. In 1584, however, secular politics had obliged him to go and live in England for a while, and he returned only in 1587 when he resumed his editorial work for the Kirk's Assembly.[20] But the parish of Keith Marischal where Agnes lived was in a poor state. John Nimmill (or Nimmo), the minister at the time, actually lived in Edinburgh and walked to Keith Marischal each Sunday to conduct the services, a labour for which he received no stipend.[21] Clearly he was in no position to exercise much, if any, discipline over the members of that parish, and this may help to account for the inability of the presbytery to find witnesses to accuse Agnes Sampson. If her local kirk was not exercised by her behaviour, and her neighbours remained unmoved by appeals for damaging testimony, there was little the district clergy could do about it.

But on 28 April, 1590 the trial of Meg Dow from Gilmerton on charges of sorcery, witchcraft, and infanticide[22] may have combined with the presumed

---

16 Which is not the same as saying it should be manufactured. There are no
   indications of corrupt practice in the Synod records anent these complaints.
17 *Synod Records*, 12.
18 *Fasti*, 1.311–12. The Assembly that year dealt with a slander against the Bishop
   of Aberdeen, accusing him of adultery with Elspeth Sutherland, *BUK*, 650.
   Johnston was certainly present at the Assembly: see *Ibid.*, 655.
19 *Fasti*, 1.328.
20 *Fasti*, 1.369.
21 *Fasti*, 1.378.
22 Pitcairn: *Criminal Trials* 1.2.186. See also *infra*, pp. 122–4.

visit of Johnston and Ramsay to Haddington to stimulate the presbytery and get it to take some preliminary steps. For on 5 May, the Synod in Edinburgh, "finding sum diligence ussit be thame hes ordanit thame to use farder diligence . . . and also to sute of the kingis majestie a commissioun for apprehending of hir";[23] and two days later, the Synod increased its pressure. "In the tryell of the brether of the presbyterie of Hadingtoun, they being inquyrit how farr they had procedit with Anny Sampsone and Jonet Ga, suspect of the art of witchecraft, answerit as for Jonet Ga they had done nothing, bot with Anny Sampsone they wer begun and enterit. The assemble hes ordanit that they insist prosequuting the sam".[24] Since Agnes was still at liberty and able, according to later testimony, to attend a Sabbat on 31 October that same year, however, it seems the presbytery failed in its efforts to press her case much further.[25]

Clearly one should raise the question whether the presbytery of Haddington's failure to press the existing laws against Catholics was linked in any way with its apparent reluctance to pursue diligent inquiries into certain people accused of witchcraft. Agnes Sampson, as we have noted earlier,[26] was accustomed to use prayers or charms employing Christian phraseology as part of her method of magical curing, and although there is nothing specifically Catholic about these, one wonders if she had powerful local contacts, such as the Kerse famly, who might bring some kind of pressure to bear on her behalf. Certainly Agnes had at least one good connection with a Kers at Court, for she was able to ask John Kers, one of the gentlemen of the King's bedchamber, to let her have an item of the King's dirty linen which she intended to use for magical purposes.[27] How had she become acquainted with him? Item 31 of her dittay tells us she cured a Robert Kerse in Dalkeith by taking upon herself the disease with which he had been afflicted by a male witch in Dumfries.[28] If Kers and Kerse were related (and the variant in spelling is not significant), then it may indicate that John Kers felt obliged to her for working such a potentially dangerous cure on behalf of his kinsman. These interconnections are, of course, highly speculative and may actually

23 *Synod Records*, 17.
24 *Synod Records*, 22. Janet Ga makes no further appearance in the records.
25 Visitations by the presbytery turned up two possible cases of witchcraft. On 12 June, 1588, the parishioners of Garwald delated a John MacGill on suspicion of witchcraft, *CH2*/185/1. fol. 11r; and on 27 August, 1589 the parish of Gullane reported that Bessie Gray, a witch, had fled from another parish and come into theirs, *Ibid*. fol. 42r. In neither case, however, is there a further report in the presbytery records. Perhaps the local kirk sessions dealt with the problem; perhaps, in tune with the general dilatoriness of the area, nothing further was done.
26 *Supra*, pp. 20–1.
27 *Newes From Scotland*, in Pitcairn: *Criminal Trials* 1.2.218. Kers was also charged with looking after James's dogs, *Exchequer Rolls* 22.160.
28 Pitcairn: *Criminal Trials* 1.2.234.

amount to nothing. But it may be thought that some explanation for Haddington's dilatoriness over Catholics and suspect witches other than laziness or incompetence is required, considering the pressure coming down from the General Assembly and local synod, and a counter-pressure of gentlemanly obligation may provide at least the start of a possible answer.[29]

The Spring and Summer of 1590

But if 1589 produced very few witchcraft cases in the records – the trial of John Millar in Middle Cairnie and of Marjory Blaikie in Cairnie "dilatit of airt and pairt of the slaughter of umquhile Williame Robertsoun in Cairnie in bewitching of him" was postponed from 26 July in Perth until the next justice-air; and the wife of Richard Watson in Perth was cleared on 2 November of the accusation of being a witch [30] – the following year saw a comparative explosion of references, trials and investigations even before the multiple arrests on charges of treason mixed with magic which constitute what is sometimes called 'The North Berwick Affair'. On 26 March, 1590, for example, St. Andrews "ordanis Maisters Androw Melvill, James Melvill, and Thomas Buchanan to visit the kirk of Ebdie[31] on Twysday nixttocum and to examine Nans Murit within the said parochin, suspect of witchcraft". On 6 May, the minister of Lathrisk had occasion to ask "gif anie woman may bee witnes in the sklander of witchcraft", and was told that she could indeed; on 28 May, the presbytery issued instructions that "forsamekill as [in as much as] Euphame Lochoir in Craill is suspect of witschcraft, the presbitrie ordanis everie minister to try the same sa far as thai can, and speaciallie the sessioun of Craill to be diligent in trying of the said matter"; and on 3 June, Janet Husband was made to apologise to Elspeth Lyall for calling her a "wiche carling", a slander, we have seen before, which was capable in some instances of further development to the peril of the person slandered.[32]

---

29 In 1588 it had been thought necessary to call for an assize within the sheriffdom of Haddington 'to delait the names of the persones suspectit to be the principall ressettaris and supplearis of . . . all jesuittis, seminiarie priestis and excommunicat papistis, the notorious committaris of the said filthie vices of incest and adulterie, all comoun sorceris, ydill and sturdie vagabondis, and the saidis theves and abusaris calling thame selffis egiptanis, hauoldand and remanand within our said schirefdome', *JC26/2*. The presence of the Setons, a prominent Catholic family in the area, will probably explain, at least in part, the reason for such a summons.

30 Pitcairn: *Criminal Trials* 1.2.167. (Pitcairn dates their trial to 1588). *Spottiswoode Miscellany* 2.266–7. Lawson: *The Book of Perth* 188–9. The Cairnie referred to here is a parish in Fife.

31 'Ebdie' = Abdie, a parish in the NE of Fife, on the Firth of Tay.

32 *Records of St. Andrews Presbytery*, 31r, 39v. On 15 March, 1593 the minister at Pittenweem was instructed 'to try and inquire diligentlie within his parochine of the secreit and quyet dealing of Janot Loquhour, suspect of witchcraft, and to report the samyn again to the presbitrie', *Ibid.*, 49r. It would be interesting to know if the two women were related. *St. Andrews Kirk Session Records*, 39v.

It is in Stirling, however, that we find a clutch of cases, one of which is particularly interesting. On 21 April the presbytery heard a detailed confession from Isobel Watson who admitted to a series of experiences with the *sìthean*.[33] She was 60 years of age at the time of her confessing and had lived for sixteen years in Perth (where she married a fisherman), before fleeing the plague and having to get a living by begging from place to place: Tullibardine, Muthill, and Glendevon, all places in Perthshire, are mentioned in particular. She had some kind of scar on her head, because the brethren asked her how she came by it and were told that when she was 18, she was doing the work of a shepherd near Tullibardine, fell asleep, and "was takin away be the fair folk and hauldin with thame 24 houris", during which time she passed through a rock beneath the earth and so came into a fine house where there were many people both tall and short. A woman offered her a piece of bread but Isobel, in response to a warning from her aunt, refused it,[34] and for the three days and nights she stayed in that house, she ate and drank nothing. But while she was there she was marked on the head with a knife, the wound being deep enough to last and require attention, for the record says that "James Watson, hir brother, haillit [it] within the speace of thre ouilkis [weeks]".

Further examination by her interrogators revealed that she gave the *sìthean* her own child, aged two, in exchange for their curing her husband of a long illness brought on because he had fallen asleep on a fairy hill. By way of compensation, the *sìthean* laid a changeling in her cradle, but although it looked like her own child she refused to feed it and her husband actually threw it into the fire, a violence which precipitated a scattering of burning fuels and almost burned down the house. Finally, Isobel agreed that she would serve the *sìthean* if she could have her own child restored to her. She then received the mark on her head, which was given to her by one Thomas McRory, a man with whom she had once had sexual intercourse, and whom she described as 'being with them'. 'Being with' the *sìthean* is a phrase not easy to interpret. It may mean that Thomas was dead (like the Thomas Reid of Elizabeth Dunlop), or that he was alive but, like a witch at a Sabbat, joined their company every so often, and it is worth noting that the brethren of the presbytery, after hearing Isobel's confessions, decided to accuse her not only of consulting the Devil but also of consulting the dead; so it is possible that not only Thomas McRory but also some of the others whose names she gave were not necessarily those of living people.

Names turn up frequently. Isobel told the presbytery that she joined the

33 *CH2/722/2.*
34 It is not clear from the text whether her aunt was present with her in the *sìthean* house, or whether Isobel was remembering advice which her aunt had given her at some previous time. Eating food provided by *sìthean* put one in their power. See Briggs: *A Dictionary of Fairies*, 143–4.

sithean at each change of the moon, and that several people there would offer her food and drink. She named them – James Hog, Isobel Leith, James Brown, Margaret Bill, and James Tod who played the fiddle while they danced. NicNevin, she added, was appointed midwife to the 'elf queen', and she herself was also appointed to that post. ('NicNevin' is a generic rather than a personal name and seems to have been used as a kind of title for any witch.[35]) James Kynard sent his wife to her and asked her in God's name to cure his toothache, Isobel gave him some wheat, a piece of woollen cloth which she said came from the elf queen, and a bone or finger-joint she said she had got from John Row, the minister of Perth. It is not quite clear which minister she had in mind, for there are two possible candidates. The first was born in about 1526 and died in 1560. He began life as a Catholic but later became a Protestant, rising high in the ranks and estimation of the Kirk. The second John Row had been a minister at Forgandenny between 1572 and 1574, and again between 1580 and 1585. He died in 1588.[36] Isobel could have received the bone from either during the lifetime of each or after they were dead. But there are two slight indications which make one incline to the earlier John Row's being the minister in question. First, the record refers to him as 'Sir' John Row. This title is customarily used of Catholic priests. The record also calls him 'minister of Perth', and this fits better with the earlier man since he was actually attached to the East Church in Perth. One would have expected the later man to be called 'minister of Forgandenny'.

The bone is clearly significant. It may have been a saint's relic (in which case Isobel would certainly have received it from a Catholic John Row), or it may have been an instrument of magic. Later that year, for example, the witches meeting in North Berwick were going to be accused of opening graves within and outwith the church in order to remove bones from the bodies deposited there, which they were told to keep "quhill [until] thay wer dry, and thane to mak ane powder of thame".[37] But whether the bone was a relic or a piece of magic, the presbytery regarded it with much disfavour, and indeed the brethren were shocked by the claim that a clergyman could have been involved, even marginally, in Isobel's dubious operation, for we find that she changed her account and said first she had got both the bone and the other things from her own aunt while they were both at the *sitheans*' Court – the intention of the gift being, apparently, "to keip hir fra all straikis [blows] of

35 See, for example, Dalyell: *Darker Superstitions*, 233. The name is derived from
    Gaelic *nic* = daughter of, and *naomhin* = little saint, and bears the hall-marks of a
    false honorific, intended to placate a power feared for its potential malevolence.
    Cf. 'Eumenides' in Greek.
36 *Fasti* 4.229, 209, 213.
37 Pitcairn: *Criminal Trials* 1.2.239 (item 50). Cf. *Ibid.*, 233 (item 26) and 237
    (item 42).

the fair folk (quha usit to straik hir sair) in the chainge of the mone"[38] – and secondly that she received them from the fairy queen's daughter. The fairy queen, it seems, had also bidden her deny God and stay with the *sithean*, since she would have a better life with them.

Isobel then gave further details and yet more names. She had seen William Finton and his wife helping *sithean* to lift large stones and had more stones been lifted, James Hog's wife would have travelled with them. She herself sometimes danced with the *sithean* and had seen several of them in the mercat place, "quhome na uthir folk will ken bot sic [such] as hes bein in the court".[39] James Watson, a bowman, had been taken away by the *sithean* three years previously; only God kept Peter Lambert on his feet, and Peter's brother-in-law had been a disruption in his house for the past twenty years.[40] She showed the presbytery a mark on the middle finger of her left hand where one of the *sithean* had bitten her, and another mark on her arm, also caused by a *sith*. Anyone who stays with the *sithean* for seven years, she told the brethren, is given to the Devil as a tithe[41] – and thus her preliminary (though not necessarily first) encounter with the presbytery came to an end.

The account seems to degenerate fairly quickly into a near-incoherent ramble through entirely disparate pieces of information, but this impression may be misleading, at least in part. It is clear that the record has been put together from the results of more than one occasion, for every so often it says, "in the tolbuith scho confessit that scho was midwyf to the elff quein . . . in the tolbuith scho confessis scho gat the premeiss fra the quein of fareis dochtir . . . in the tolbuith scho confessit that scho was thair" (at the lifting of the stones), and indeed the account of her appearance before the presbytery begins, "eftir *farder* examinatoun" (my italics). So the apparent incoherence may mirror Isobel's growing confusion during these several sessions of interrogation; or it may reflect the disconnected nature of the questions she was asked; or it may point to a failing of the clerk himself. Isobel was

---

38 This reminds one of the violence Elizabeth Dunlop claimed she received at the hands of the *sithean*. The picture was the same elsewhere in Europe. Cf., for example, 'In the 1570s, a girl from a Neumark village claimed to have been fed by the Little People for almost four years. She did not consume any ordinary food during this period. The Little People, however, were not only her benefactors but hurt her as well', Beyer: "A Lübeck prophet", 173.

39 Again one is reminded of Elizabeth Dunlop who said she saw Thomas Reid in the kirkyard of Dalry and in an Edinburgh street walking unseen, apparently, in the midst of the crowd.

40 On being asked what could be done about that, Isobel gave the non-magical answer that they should change the doors (i.e. locks).

41 One is reminded of a phrase of Alison Pearson's, that a tithe of the *sithean* themselves goes to Hell every year, Pitcairn: *Criminal Trials* 1.2.164. Could this be a mistake on the part of the clerk? Did Alison mean to say, or did she actually say, that a tithe of those who stay with the *sithean* go to Hell each year?

providing a great deal of information, and it is quite possible that the clerk was not skilled in the art of précis and so failed to produce a decent, well-structured account for the presbytery records.

But Isobel's ordeal was not yet over. On 3 May she was examined again in the tolbooth and confessed that on two occasions the fairy king gave her some oil which looked like the yolk of an egg. First he anointed her head and then her arm, throat, and breast, saying "sa lang as ony of that oyll was on hir, na mane suld haif powar to do hir skayth [harm]".[42] (The oil, she assured her interrogators, had now completely gone from her.) It was on the occasion of her anointing, apparently, that the royal daughter gave her the wheat, cloth, and bone she had mentioned before; and we learn further that as well as rubbing her head, throat, breast, and arm with oil, the king also removed her hair – whether all of it or only some is not made clear, although certainly if we conjecture that Isobel was having visions during the course of a long period of stress, there is no reason to suppose that a temporary loss of hair might not have happened.

Isobel also confessed that the previous Thursday, before she went to bed, the Devil came to her in the guise of an angel and said that if she would serve him he would rescue her from her present danger. Isobel replied that the period of time during which she had promised to serve him had now run out and that she had given herself to God; whereupon, she told the presbytery, she suffered great physical pain "and gif scho hade bein out of the houss scho wald have gane wod [mad]". This reference to the house strikes one unexpectedly, for it implies that Isobel was not under arrest but was being fetched into the tolbooth whenever members of the presbytery wanted to question her further. But again the record gives evidence of incoherence. There was a woman in Stirling, said Isobel, with whom she saw the fairy king have sexual intercourse; and asked how she knew who had stolen some property belonging to Thomas Boyd, she answered that Jesus Christ came to her in the likeness of an angel and told her. The presbytery must have been taken aback by this presumption and clearly sought to change Isobel's mind about certain details, for the record goes on to say that "eftir farder examinatione [scho] confessit that it was the devil quha schew hir the samen".

The session ends with further names of people Isobel had seen in company with the *sithean*, and when the record resumes on 12 May this is still the presbytery's concern, for still more names appear. One may turn out to be particularly significant: "Confessis scho saw with the fair folk Richie grahame four severall tymes". Richard Graham was the name of a magician prominent in the North Berwick affair of treason and witchcraft, and although the two

---

42 A marginal note adds that the elf queen held Isobel's head down while something like oil was put on it.

men may not have been the same person, it is intriguing to find the name closely connected with meetings of *sìthean*. By 10 June the presbytery had made up its mind about Isobel and judged her to be "ane abusar of the pepill, consultar with the devill and the dead, and thairfor worthie to die according to godis law, and requyris the civill magistrat to put hir to the knawledge of ane assyss".[43]

It is difficult to know what one should make of Isobel. Because the account of her several interrogations has been rushed on to paper pell-mell, it would be easy to dismiss it as the ramblings of a confused, frightened woman who was perhaps not quite right in the head, and certainly there may be an element of truth in this. Nevertheless, the details of her meeting *sìthean* and their behaviour towards her agree with other accounts, as we have seen, and can be paralleled from folklore over a long period of time. In other words, the narrative is actually coherent in itself, despite its being broken up by the manner of its recording. Moreover, one can detect the pressure her interrogators were bringing to bear on her account as they sought to reinterpret the *sìthean* as evil spirits or spirits of the dead, and her visions of angels as devilish impostures. Now, as I have remarked before, neither the officers of the Kirk who were usually the first to undertake investigations into charges of witchcraft, nor the members of the assize who composed the audience for the final, official version of those charges and passed judgement upon the truth or falsity of it, were immune from the general beliefs and practices of their communities and of society at large. All would have been aware that many, if not most, of their neighbours accepted the reality of *sìthean* and of magical operations, even if they themselves did not, or had surrendered their former beliefs to the requirements of a Christian creed which condemned all forms of what it called 'superstition'. Even so, it is asking too much to accept that every minister, every kirk elder, and every member of every assize had left such beliefs behind. Indeed, had they all been sceptical or disbelieving, their condemnation of so many women and men on charges of witchcraft would have been unthinkable cruelty. The simple fact that they brought in verdicts of 'guilty' is an indication that they accepted the reality of what they were being told, just as their verdicts of 'innocent' demonstrate that they were prepared to exercise their judgement in the hearing of such cases and were not ready to condemn one of their own community − a person whom some of them at least had known for years, and of whose magical activities they had also been well aware − merely because she or he had been accused of a series of particularly heinous offences.

---

43 This, it seems, happened and the result was a verdict of guilty, because an entry in the record for 23 June notes that Isobel 'is convict and hes sufferit for witchcraft'.

So the men who were examining Isobel were clearly not questioning the reality of her experiences (not all of them, anyway). Rather, because of their personal religious commitment, they saw them in a different light and were anxious that Isobel make no mistake about the nature of those experiences, but see them in their light, too. She could not, therefore, have seen Jesus Christ in connection with so trivial a matter as Thomas Boyd's lost property. What she took for an angel must have been Satan, a re-interpretation she seems to have been willing to accept especially since, having given herself to God, as the record says, she was able, without external assistance, to recognise another angelic visitation as an appearance of the Devil. Such re-interpretations by the Kirk seem to have been quite common and indeed are to be expected because, as Diane Purkiss explains, they enabled officialdom to do one of two things: "to understand the practices of others or to legitimate their own".[44] Conversation and dealings with the *sithean* might be undesirable, but were they necessarily wicked, and did they transgress either Church or civil law? Conversation and dealings with Satan, on the other hand, were clearly iniquitous and did indeed break both God's law and an Act of Parliament. Hence the need, as well as the personal inclination, to see *sithean* as evil spirits and angels as devils.

Isobel's various examinations had repercussions. On 2 June, a week before the presbytery decided to send her for criminal trial, William Wilson and Elspeth Stalker, both from the parish of Dollar, were ordered to present themselves before the brethren because each had accused the other of practising witchcraft and consulting with witches.[45] When they appeared on the 23rd, William confessed he had indeed consulted Isobel because his cow had ceased to give milk. Isobel for some reason did not undertake his case herself, but recommended that he go to Elspeth, which he duly did, "and mait with hir on the hie fieldis quhair upone his kneis askit fra hir the proffeit of his cowis milk quhilk [which] was tane fra him". His appeal was evidently successful, for within two days his cow started providing milk again. Elspeth must have had a reputation for skill in dealing with this kind of problem,[46] because William's brother John told him that Donald Brown from the parish of Crombie[47] had also consulted her for much the same reason.

Elspeth, however, refused to accept these accusations. She admitted that William had paid her a visit, but said she did not hear what he said, that she had no power to restore a cow's milk, and that she had no knowledge of

---

44 *The Witch in History*, 160. Purkiss is writing here about the situation in England, but her remarks equally apply to Scotland.
45 *CH2/722/2*. Dollar is a parish in Clackmannanshire.
46 Favret-Saada points out that some magicians may possess only one secret and are therefore consulted only when their special skill is required, *Deadly Words*, 45.
47 Probably the one in Fife.

witchcraft. She also agreed that David Brown had come to her and asked her to cure (or probably unwitch) his cow, but again protested her innocence on this point. The presbytery decided she should be subject to further investigation "and ordanis hir minister to seik diligentlie in his parochin gif scho hes ony wiche craft and give [if] scho wsis the samen". Meanwhile, William was to perform public penance until the next meeting of the presbytery for consulting both Isobel Watson and Elspeth Stalker.

July brought yet another accusation of witchcraft before the brethren.[48] On the 21st, Janet Mitchell, the wife of William Mayne, offered charges against Marion MacNab. There were three: (i) Marion had bewitched William Mayne's barley, but had accepted a peck of it in return for lifting her bewitchment. This Marion denied. (ii) She also denied curing William Mayne of sickness. (iii) She confessed to setting out with Janet to visit a woman who specialised in unwitching barley, but said she changed her mind and turned back homeward before they reached the woman's house. Janet, however, maintained she could prove her accusations in spite of Marion's denials, and the presbytery decided she should be given the chance to do so. Marion was therefore handed over to the baillies of Stirling to be kept in confinement until the 28th.[49]

Further sessions of the presbytery on 28 July, 18 and 25 August, and 8 September saw the matter proceed no further than the production of a large number of witnesses to testify for Janet Mitchell. Marion, meanwhile, was warded in prison, and it may have been this experience which induced her to confess to the brethren meeting on 17 September that she was able to persuade a cow which had lost her calf to accept another calf, by laying the skin of the dead calf in front of her with a lick of salt sprinkled on it, and saying thrice, "In the name of the Father, the Son, and the Holy Ghost"; or by spreading the dead calf's skin over a living calf and repeating the same formula. It was magic, but scarcely trafficking with Satan. The presbytery therefore decided to have the matter investigated further, but allowed Marion to come out of prison on bail: at which point the record stops.

Once again there is evidence enough to provide some indication of the way these ministers' minds tended to work when faced by the possibility that they were dealing with instances of witchcraft. Witchcraft was defined for them by texts in the Bible, by an Act of Parliament reinforced by others which dealt with examples of magical operations by gipsies and vagabonds, and by the writings of foreign demonologists, should they wish to consult learned

---

48 *CH2/722/2.*
49 It is perhaps curious that the presbytery did not, apparently, pursue Janet Mitchell and her husband for consulting a witch, but it may be that the brethren were waiting to see if the charges against Marion MacNab could be proved or not.

opinion. Marion MacNab was clearly a quite different case from Isobel Watson. Here were no *sithean* or disturbing visions, merely an alleged bewitchment of barley and an accusation of curing illness – the kind of everyday magic the brethren would recognise and with which in a sense they could feel at home. The allegations might turn out to be no more than slander, since it was obvious the two women had fallen out; on the other hand, magic was undesirable, and so Marion was put in prison to await the outcome of events. The emergence of a long list of people willing to testify against her must have kept her there but when, after nearly two months presumably in the tolbooth, she confessed to no more than a practice which may have smacked a little of Catholicism but was scarcely, if at all, magical, the ministers were prepared to release her from custody, although they set a rather high bail (£500)[50] and certainly intended to take their investigations further.

We now come to the case of Meg Dow from Gilmerton, a village just south-east of Edinburgh, who was accused, along with Janet Pook,[51] of murdering two infants. Sixty years old, like Isobel Watson, at the time of her trial, Meg originally came from Kippen in Stirlingshire but had recently been living in Pleasance, a village in Fife, not far from Auchtermuchty. Janet Pook came to see her there, explaining that she had had a child out of wedlock, that the father was refusing to recognise it, and that she did not know what to do. The two women stayed in the house all night and then, at 9 o'clock next day, made their way into the countryside with the child wrapped up in a shawl, and once there threw the baby into a hole in the ground, being careful to keep the shawl. Since this had been Meg's solution to Janet's problem (although clearly Janet had been a willing party to it), Meg was the more culpable of the two, and one can therefore understand why she was found guilty and sentenced to death. Janet, by contrast, was put in prison. Whether she stayed there, or was later released, or executed, is not recorded.

Meg's sentence – that she be strangled, her body burned to ashes, and her movable goods escheat to the Crown – was the one usually applied to condemned witches, so it was not only her action in killing Janet's child (not to mention another belonging to Bessie Rae from Gilmerton) which brought her to the stake, but her admission that she had also been a servant of the Devil. For on 1 April, after giving an account of how she and Janet Pook had committed infanticide, Meg went on to say that "ane mekill [big] blak man come to hir thair about xii houris at evin and said to hir, 'Will ye go with

---

50 The contemporary value of this sum may be gauged by a comparison with ministers' stipends. About 500 merks would have given a satisfactory annual minimum. A merk = two thirds of a pound Scots, so 500 merks = £333. 6s. 8d. See Foster: *The Church Before the Covenants*, 157–8.

51 Not 'Pollok' as it appears in Pitcairn. Details of her confessions come from *JC26/ 2/27*.

me, and ye sall get yow geir aneuche [enough]?'" Meg answered that she would indeed serve him because he would give her a life better than the one she was living; whereupon he lifted her up and carried her until dawn. Nor was this his only visit. He came to her again on six nights in a workman's hut near Edmonstone, a village south-east of Edinburgh, "and gave hir quhatt to put doun bairnes". This information that Satan − Meg calls her visitor "the Innemy" − assisted her in doing away with unwanted children by giving her something, presumably drugs or herbs to be made into a salve or a drink, seems to indicate that Meg could have been an abortionist, which may be as much as to say she was also a midwife, although the record does not say so.[52]

So it is noteworthy that it was Satan himself who appeared to her, for hitherto in the literature the man has not been so easily identifiable: and indeed in one or two cases had been a ghost or or *sith*-like guide rather than 'the enemy of mankind'. Meg's reference to her transvection is also unusual, especially since the journey appears to have lasted a long time and yet no details are given of where she was taken or what she saw on the way. Either her interrogators did not pursue these questions further, or they did not ask them in the first place. Yet one would have expected them to do both, in the circumstances, because Meg's experience is the closest we have encountered so far in the Scottish records of the sixteenth century to the type of transvection attributed to Continental witches in works such as the *Malleus Maleficarum* or the illustrations which accompany Ulrich Molitor's treatise on witches.

Meg dated these events to "the tyme of the gret pest", a reference either to the plague which ravaged part of the east coast of Scotland in 1585, or to that which broke out in 1587. Melvill attributed the former to the direct intervention of God: "First in the simmer he send a Pest, quhilk past throw the principall Townes, and raget till almaist utter vastation in the Townes of Edinbruche, St Andros, St Jhonstoun, and Dondie . . . and at the hervest, togidder with the raging pestilence incressing mair and mair, namlie in Edinbruche, the Lord send . . . a tempest of wather and rean". The second started in Leith at harvest-time, "and continowit all that wintar, quhilk strak a grait terrour in Edinbruche and all the cost syds".[53]

Nearly a week after this confession, Meg deponed on the 20th that Satan had told her to prevent a cow from giving milk and to "put ane evill betuix a man and his wyfe", that is, either make them quarrel or stop them from having sexual intercourse. She was also to take a fedder − part of a plough-share − and place it next to the cow, for what exact purpose is not explained. At some

---

52 Rue, juniper, dittany, and birthwort, for example, are all herbs which can produce abortions and were known to do so from ancient times. See Riddle: *Eve's Herbs*, 48–50, 54, 56–7, 58–9. The supposed connection between midwifery and witchcraft, however, needs to be treated with great caution.
53 *Diary*, 148, 173.

point, Satan gave her his mark by biting her little finger. Meg says this happened at dawn and that the teeth-marks bled rather a lot. Again her confession is somewhat unusual in that those of earlier Scottish witches have made no mention of any such mark, and one wonders whether any of her interrogators had been reading the Continental demonologists.[54] Meg's mark is, however, quite typical of those which appear more frequently in seventeenth-century Scottish confessions in that it was not concealed in her private parts. The neck and the shoulders were the most common places to find Satan's marks on Scottish witches. Once he had marked her, the Devil then told her to "tak ane womanes sark [shirt], and wasche in ane sothe runnen watter on setterday, and put it on hir husband on sunday in the morning". Again, no explanation is offered for this piece of magic, but south-running water was regularly attributed with power to cure the sick and there is therefore a strong possibility that such was Meg's intended aim.[55]

It is clear from the narrative that Meg's involvement in infanticide was not an integral part of her operation as a witch – she was not, in other words, killing the children in order to render their flesh into grease for incorporation into magical salves, a common accusation levelled against many Continental witches – and if the infanticides are set apart from the rest of her record, she seems to conform to the standard image of a witch, someone believed capable of exercising preternatural power for both maleficent and beneficent purposes according to her or his personal desires.

A series of trials based upon magical activities in Aberdeenshire, however, affords a view of witchcraft to be used as a weapon in family disputes. The first begins with a confession by Barbara Kaird *alias* Leslie who was convicted and condemned to death on 20 June.[56] She was examined on the 17th in the tolbooth of Aberdeen, where she was being held prisoner, by seven men including Peter Blackburn, the minister of St. Nicholas's parish, Walter Stewart, Principal of King's College, Thomas Cargill, master of the grammar school, and two of the town's baillies. Her story was quite straightforward. John Leslie, Laird of Boquhane, had quarrelled with William Leslie of Crethie.[57] William Leslie wanted revenge and so he and his servant, Bessie Roy, came to Barbara in the summer of 1587 "to solisit and intreat hir, being off all estemit a wiche, to tak in hand be witchcraft primarlie to distroy him". But Barbara had ties of obligation to John Leslie's family – one wonders whether her alias 'Leslie' indicates she had married into it – and so refused

---

54 But in that case, why had they apparently not picked up her narrative about being carried by Satan?

55 See further Dalyell: *Darker Superstitions*, 84–6.

56 *JC26/2/25*. This record was made after her death.

57 The reason seems to have been a dispute over land in Meikle Durno which is twenty miles or so north-west of Aberdeen.

point blank. Bessie Roy then said something to William (we do not know what), and the two of them left, William threatening to break every bone in Barbara's body if she mentioned to anyone else the purpose of his visit or, indeed, if he ran across her again.

With his problem still unresolved, William then sent Bessie to another witch called Janet Grant who lived in a village in Cromar, a small district on the north side of the middle reach of the Dee. Janet happily agreed to do as she was asked and made her way to Crethie where she fashioned a wax image of John Leslie and roasted it over a fire. Somehow Barbara got to know about this magical operation and came at once to John to offer him advice and warning. Wrack and destruction, she said, awaited him and therefore he should not go riding along a certain route he was intending to take, "els the ewill suld strik him to the hart giff he raid that way". But he, "being vilfull and contemning all sic ewill, raid that way upon the morne and metting thair Alexander Mitchell with ane uthir man . . . Allixander Mitchell knew na thing off the ewill, bot the man that wes with him brocht the ewill upon the said Johnne". Not long after this meeting, the evil struck John to the heart and thus he "languished and wis consumied, pece and pece to death".

Such, then, was the version of events given by Barbara on more than one occasion during her imprisonment, and again when she was bound to the stake. John Leslie's death seems to have been resented by the crowd present at her execution, for there were cries that he should be revenged and that those who had encompassed his death were being rightly punished. At first it may seem odd that people should be calling for Barbara's death when she was the person who had alerted John Leslie to his danger and had refused to undertake the murderous commission when it was offered to her. But if Barbara was indeed widely known to be a witch, as the record puts it, and since William Leslie felt confident enough to approach her in the first place, and since the ground for her refusing his request was her obligation to John Leslie rather than revulsion at the suggestion she murder him by magic, it may well be that the crowd had a more exact estimation of her character and past performances than is available to us, and that justice was actually being served, after its fashion, in spite of the apparent anomaly we see in the surviving records.

But Barbara did not suffer alone. On 23 July, a summons was issued for the arrest and trial of the others involved in this affair: Bessie Roy, Janet Clerk *alias* Spaldarg, and Janet Grant.[58] These three "common and notorious witches, at the earnest sute, pirsuasioun, and onlie instigatioun of the said William Leslie in Crethie, and Wiolatt Achinlek his spous, in the monethis of June, July, and August the yeir of god 1587 yeiris . . . consultit, dewysit, and

58 *JC*26/2/26.

intirprysit the cruell murthor, slauchter, and distructioun of the said umquhile [late] Johnne Leslie within the toun and boundis of Crethie or thairabout, and in Cromar". It was not until September that their plans were put into execution, but thereafter John Leslie "contraktit deidlie seiknes and lay continwallie seik and bedfast, dwynand [wasting away], consumit be sweyt and thair develische craft foirsaid be rosting of his picture in wax at the fyre in Robirt Swapis hous". John Leslie lingered until November when at last he died, the alleged victim of these people's premeditated murder.

Witnesses and assizes were summoned in the last days of July and during the first week of August, William Leslie and Violet Auchinleck also being arrested. The dittays of the three accused witches reveal the extent both of their reputations and of their activities, and since Janet Grant was named in Barbara Kaird's confession as the person actually responsible magically for John Leslie's death, let us begin with her.

There are fourteen articles in one version of her dittay and she was acquitted of six of them.[59] Her magical activities were wide-ranging, but may be grouped under three broad headings: (a) treating the sick, (b) murder or attempted murder, and (c) malicious magic in return for payment. Anent the first we are told that she claimed she could tell at a glance whether a sick person was going to live or die, and it was said by others that when she helped anyone who was ill, she did so by exchanging one life for another. Apparently she used to travel about the countryside as a kind of itinerant healer, and on at least one occasion in Alford employed medicines which were accounted quite extraordinary. Six or seven people who consulted her, however, found themselves denounced to the local kirk session and were made to sit on the stool of repentance by way of punishment.

The nature of her healing activities may be gauged from two separate incidents. The late John Panton's wife was sick and Janet said she would cure her. So at night she took her patient to John Nairn's house and there gouged out a big hole in his yard-dyke, the low drystone wall running round a small piece of land next to the house. Then she hauled the sick woman thrice through the hole, after which they went back to John Panton's house where Janet washed the invalid with a mixture of herbs and water, telling John to wash himself likewise. John Nairn, however, found out why there was a large hole in his dyke and came looking for Janet, along with two other men, all three of them carrying weapons. They seized hold of Janet, pinioned her, and then forced her to throw water back into John Panton's house (thus returning the illness which had been magically washed away), and in consequence John

---

59 *JC*26/2/30. A marginal note on *JC*26/2/26 seems to suggest that Janet Grant was acquitted on every point, but this is contradicted by the marginalia of her dittay. Four more items appear in another pre-trial paper, *JC*26/2/29.

Panton's wife died.[60] But if Janet's methods in this case were recognisably those of conventional magic, her treatment of Duncan Richie were somewhat more extraordinary. He was ill and it was assumed he had been bewitched. Janet was therefore summoned to explain how this had happened and (presumably) to lift the enchantment.[61] Janet answered the call and, again at night, went to the Bog of Cults with Merslie Richie who may or may not have been Duncan's relative. The record is careful to describe her as respectable. When the two women arrived at the marsh, Janet told Merslie to sit down and then seems to have embarked on some kind of evocatory ritual, because we are told that "the clamur and rumling and crying of the divillis and thi self [i.e. Janet] was so odious and execrable that it constranit and compellit the said Mersly Richie to run awa for feir and durst not abyd thi coming to hir". In fact, Merslie ran back to Duncan Richie's house where the sick man was being visited by some of his friends. Janet herself arrived not long afterwards, but brought no good news. There was no hope for him, she said: Duncan was going to die.[62]

Janet, then, was known both as a healer and an 'unwitcher', and was often consulted in both capacities. Some of her methods of healing the sick were conventional, in the sense that they belonged to magical traditions her clients and their families and friends could easily have recognised, and with which they may have been familiar. Her evocation of evil spirits at night in a deserted, marshy countryside, however, appears to have been much more unusual, so that it comes as little surprise to find that one of the items of her dittay says "that thow art oft and diverss tymes sene be sundry personis quhair thow resortis that thow converssis and lyis with the divill in sindry monsterous liknes terrable for to declair".[63]

---

60 Water absorbs disease which can therefore be thrown away with the water. But if anyone passes over the spot where the water has been thrown, he or she can be infected by it. See Dalyell: *Darker Superstitions*, 104. This clearly explains John Nairn's fear and the reason for his wanting the 'infected' water magically returned whence it came. On the custom of passing sick people through circles, see Dalyell, 121–2.

61 Cf. Favret-Saada on an 'unwitcher', *Deadly Words*, 49–51.

62 One is reminded in some measure of Horace's female magician, Canidia, uttering long, drawn-out cries at the top of her voice (*ululantem*: the Greek verb from which it is derived implies that coherent words were spoken), in order to summon spirits from the world of the dead to answer her questions (*animas responsa daturas*), *Satires* 1.8.23–9.

63 Even so, she was acquitted on this point. It is difficult to know why. Perhaps the suggestion that she had had sexual intercourse with the evil spirits had been suggested by her interrogators, eager to associate her actions with the conventionalities of Continental witchcraft. Nevertheless, it does not explain why the assize chose not to accept the veracity of this item. We are also told that Janet and nine other witches, of whom she was the principal, were called in to cure James Ogilvy of Woodfield, but it is interesting to note that she was acquitted of this article, too.

But, as her dittay makes clear, there was an even more sinister side to Janet, for she was asked on more than one occasion to commit magical murder. One involved William Leslie and Violet Auchinleck, the case in which she was named by Barbara Kaird. Apparently Janet asked William and Violet about John Leslie's present condition and was told that he sweated during the week but had a respite on Sunday. To this she observed that if William and Violet were the cause of this, John Leslie would soon be dead, and the dittay adds, "because thow wald not adverteiss the said young laird of Wardiess, thow art airt and pairt, and ane of the principall distroyaris of him be inchantment and witchcraft". Interestingly enough, however, the assize did not accept this argument and acquitted Janet of both the articles which sought to inculpate her. So we are faced with a problem. Was Barbara Kaird lying when she named Janet Grant as the witch who accepted William Leslie's commission, or did Janet Grant's assize make a mistake when it found her not guilty of this crime?

Still, Janet was found guilty of magically causing the deaths of John Reid and his son James at the instigation of certain of their neighbours who wished them harm; she was also found guilty of offering to kill Patrick Mortimer's brother and nephew so that the way might be cleared for Patrick to become Laird of Craigiewar, although Patrick refused her offer and submitted written testimony against her; and she was found guilty of killing Duncan Ingram's wife and children by magical means. This episode dated back a long way, to 1565. Janet and Duncan had committed adultery in Easter Foulis. The text seems to imply that Duncan had left his family for this purpose, because it goes on to say that Janet told him to go home where his wife and children lived, and then came within half a mile of the place herself. He was to look in at a window or a door, "and he suld sie ane sicht of his wyff that suld content him". Duncan did as he was instructed, but as soon as he had come back thence, "the haill hous, wyif, and barnis war altogiddir brint by the witchcraft and divilische dewys" – a crime, the dittay adds, which was notorious throughout the whole district.

At first glance, we seem to have here an example of malefice by means of the evil eye, but there is a difficulty in this interpretation. The evil eye is commonly associated with envy, but whereas Janet might well be credited with envy of Duncan's wife and children, Duncan himself can not, so the glance or stare by which the damage was done should have come from her and not from him. For there does not seem to be any evidence that the evil eye can be transferred, so to speak, except between members of the same family, and so it is highly unlikely that Duncan could have been invested with this particular magical force. Moreover, even if such a transference had been possible, Duncan does not seem to have been aware of it. Janet's instruction to him, one notices, was accompanied by a completely misleading and deceitful phrase – "he suld sie ane sicht of his wyff that suld content him"; and yet she herself does not appear to have come near enough the house to be able to exercise the power of the evil eye. Some other method of magical operation must, therefore, be posited: exactly what, however, the evidence will not permit us to say.[64]

Two other instances of her activities illustrate her willingness to work malefices in return for payment. In 1565 someone paid her a small fee and a number of women found that milk was coming out of their straw. They threw the milk away, but it continued to appear, in large quantities, in their pestles. Then, together with Janet Clerk, she was accused of killing seventeen cattle belonging to William Ross, being paid half a scraped hide and twenty silver shillings by one John Adie, although on this latter charge the assize brought a not guilty verdict.[65]

This was not the only occasion she worked with Janet Clerk. Together they came to Margaret Ross, a relative of William Ross, who had contracted some form of disease, and promised to cure her by enchantments and sorcery, as the dittay puts it. She obviously agreed to their terms, because they were engaged in their magical work when Elspeth Reith "came in to the houss be accident, and ye keist the haill seiknes on hir". Such a transference of sickness was standard magical practice and Elspeth became seriously ill. Janet Clerk then had the nerve to offer to cure her, provided she and Janet Grant were paid, and again a bargain was struck. Once the fee had been handed over, however, it was explained to Elspeth that her daughter would have to die in her place, "and then scho ansrit to yow that scho had rather abyid godis will nor that hir barne suld die for hir caus": as a result of which refusal, Elspeth slowly wasted away and died.

Now, Janet Clerk clearly had much in common with Janet Grant. Both were undoubtedly professional operators of magic, and both seem to have been rather unpleasant characters. Janet Clerk had three aliases, Spaldarg, Bane, and Keith, and there are ten items on her separate dittay, as well as the

---

64 On the evil eye, see Roberts: 'Belief in the evil eye in world perspective', in Maloney (ed.): *The Evil Eye*, 223–6. MacLagen points out that the evil eye can be transmitted within the immediate family, *Evil Eye in the Western Highlands*, 102–3. Duncan was, it appears, only one of Janet's many adulteries. An additional item on her dittay says, 'ye have beine saxtene tymes mareit and hes four sundrie men yit levand [still living], stryvand for yow . . . quhairthrow ye have committit mony adultereis desyrving thairthrow the deid [death] be the lawis of the countrey and actis of parliament', *JC* 26/2/29.

65 Something also seems to have happened to a charge that they were occupied in a magical cure of John Adie in his house when a woman (William Stewart's wife) interrupted, realised what was going on, and threatened to see both Janets burned if anything happened to her. The item has been crossed out, presumably either because it could not be substantiated, or because it was withdrawn at some point for reasons we do not know.

joint operations with Janet Grant recorded on another paper.[66] Like Janet Grant, Spaldarg (as I shall call her for easy identification) was employed as a healer and used to scrutinise a patient's shirt as part of her *modus operandi*. In the case of James Callider, however, she did rather more than this. First she removed the shirt from the house and took it somewhere else, presumably hoping to do her diagnosis in private. But if this was her hope, it was disappointed because several people observed her throw the shirt thrice into the hair above her head. On the third occasion, we are told, it spread out in the air and seemed to catch fire. Whereupon Spaldarg returned to James Callider's house with the melancholy news that he was destined to die: which indeed he did fairly soon afterwards. John Root also sent for her in the hope she would be able to cure him of his illness, and paid her twenty merks on her promise she would do so. But she left his shirt behind and very shortly he died. It is scarcely surprising, therefore, to find that the tenth article of her dittay says, "Thow art commonlie haldin throw the haill contrie quhair thow duallis for ane commoun notorious wiche in respect of ye deilling in sic caussis".

Of one charge of magical healing, however, she was acquitted. It was alleged that when she lived in Auchinhouse, she laid a piece of maleficent magic (probably in the form of some enchanted object or objects) under the threshold of a house, intending thereby to bewitch the lady of the house. Unfortunately, "the nourishe [nurse] quha wes fosterand the barne came first out at the dure, quha immediatlie grew licht and furious". Spaldarg and her sister then claimed they could restore the nurse to her former health, or be burned as witches, and within three days made good their boast, to which the dittay adds the grim remark, "thy sister yit lyve als grit ane witche as thy self".[67]

Spaldarg also appears to have specialised in making men impotent, as she travelled about the area: John Crathy in Cromar and John Watt are named as particular victims. The last case involved magical revenge. John Watt "lay in fornicatioun with thy frendis" and when, later on, he married he found he was impotent with his wife. She thereupon complained to the kirk and Spaldarg "wes then compellit to restore him to his awin hability".[68] It is an interesting

---

66 *JC26/2/28*. The alias is 'Spaldarg' and not 'Spalding' as Pitcairn has it, *Criminal Trials* 1.2.206. Janet Grant, too, had an alias, 'Gradoch'.

67 On thresholds as foci for magic, see Merrifield: *The Archaeology of Ritual and Magic*, 119–20. Cf. Martín Del Rio, quoting Paolo Grillando on ligatures intended to cause impotence, which may be put in the intended victim's clothing, concealed under a pillow, or hidden beneath a threshold, *Disquisitiones Magicae* Book 3, part 1, question 3, section 1.

68 Item 4 of her dittay says, "thow had in thy awin hous ane kist [box] full of mennis secreit memberis and maid merchandice thairof". Dried and then reduced to powder, these, presumably garnered from graves, would have constituted an obvious form of love-magic.

comment on the way the local kirk session appears to have been willing to co-operate in practical magic by approaching the person accused of causing the bewitchment and insisting that she remove it, and not, as far as one can tell, take the matter further. But it also indicates that certain kirk sessions, even if they were active and effective enough to provide people with an immediate source of authority to which they felt they could turn for exercise of local discipline, accepted the reality of a magician's preternatural power to bewitch and to unwitch — a small indication of the problem faced by the higher authorities in the Kirk who were trying to stamp this out.

Another accusation made against Spaldarg, which looks as though it too involved some form of love-magic, is contained in the first article of her dittay which says that she agreed to give Isobel Carnegie 'enchantments' (probably in the form of powder)[69] to put into her master's food. Isobel's husband and another man, John Turner, found out, however, and would not let her proceed with the magic. Although Spaldarg confessed this point to Robert Young, minister at Kinbattock in south Aberdeenshire, the assize decided to acquit her of it, perhaps because the operation was not actually carried out.

Finally, there is her alleged involvement in the magical murder of John Leslie. The article is vague about certain points — "thow art indytit for the comming to the place of Wardes be the desyre of sum ungodlie person" — and suggests that John Leslie died 28 hours later, whereas we have been told by Janet Grant's dittay that it took the young laird several weeks to die. But the item goes into magical details which do not appear in either Barbara's or Janet's account. Spaldarg spoke to John Leslie's wife and told her what to do if she wanted her husband to live. She should cut his fingernails and toe-nails,[70] take nine slivers of wood from different kinds of tree, and water from a stream running nearby, steep the nails and wood together, and then wash her husband with the water; after which he was to be dried, not with a cloth, but with the fluttering of a cock's wings.[71] We have noted already that Janet Grant and Spaldarg occasionally worked together, and that although Janet Grant was supposed to have been the one hired by William Leslie to kill young John, the assize found her not guilty of the attempt. It is possible that the clerk made a mistake and confused Janet Grant and Janet Clerk (Spaldarg) when he recorded Barbara Kaird's confession, as it is also possible that Barbara (who was not present during the operation but seems to have relied on hearsay for her evidence) mistook one Janet for the other. Some such confusion would

69 Cf. the passage from Del Rio, cited in note 66. See also Sprenger & Institoris: *Malleus Maleficarum*, part 1, question 8 and part 2, questions 6 and 7.

70 Cf. the priest's toenail clippings to which Sempill refers in his satire on Patrick Adamson, *supra* p. 100. It is interesting to see how accurate Sempill is in his detail, even if his intention is to mock.

71 I.e. the live bird was to be held near him while it struggled.

also help to explain a marginal note on one of the pre-trial papers to the effect that Janet Clerk was found guilty on every point of her dittay, a note which is not altogether accurate but does distinguish between the two anent their guilt on this particular item.[72]

Bessie Roy, the third of the nefarious trio, came to trial the day after the two Janets, on 18 August.[73] She was nurse to the children of John Leslie, Laird of Boquhane – not the same John Leslie whom she and others were accused of attempting to kill[74] – and before that had been a servant in the household of William King for twelve years. One day, we are told, she went with other women to pick lint and in their presence performed a divination. To do this, she drew a large circle in the earth, dug a hole in the middle, and conjured three worms to come out of the hole. The first was big and crawled out of the circle; the second was small but did likewise; the third was also big, but could not get out of the hole and fell back into it and died. Bessie interpreted these phenomena as follows: (a) the first worm was William King whose continued life was assured; (b) the second was a child in his wife's womb, although no one knew as yet that she was pregnant. The child, said Bessie, would live. (c) The third worm was the wife, who was destined to die. These predictions turned out to be true, and King's wife did indeed give birth but died soon afterwards.[75]

Two further items refer to her opening doors and locks by magic, stealing whatever took her fancy, and then magically locking up again behind her.[76] One of the houses to suffer thus belonged to Boquhane, and something must have aroused suspicion against her because a steel box containing gold was found in her possession, and when challenged to explain how she came by it, she said that a black man had come and given it to her – "quhilk wes nothing but the illusione of the Divill", the record adds with what may be intentional sarcasm. Finally, the dittay accused her in summative terms: "Thow art indytit and estimit for ane notorious and commowne Wiche in the cuntrie, and can do all thingis, and hes done all mischeifis that devilrie of Wichecraft can

---

72 *JC26/2/26*. In addition to the crimes listed above, Janet Grant was also accused of killing Alexander Abercrombie and the son of John Gordon by magic, and Janet Clerk of bewitching Alasdair Caddell's son, Pitcairn: *Criminal Trials* 1.2.206.

73 Pitcairn: *Criminal Trials* 1.2.206–9.

74 The 'others' apparently included two women not mentioned hitherto, Marion Bruce and Bessie Paul, described as fugitives for the said crime.

75 A contradictory item in the dittay, however, says that Bessie bewitched William King's wife after leaving her service, by laying a plaid full of enchantments on her bed, and that this was the cause of her death.

76 Unlocking by magic was a feat often attributed to witches. See, for example, Johann Wier: *De praestigiis daemonum* Book 5, chapter 11, and cf. the trial of John Fian on 26 December, 1590. Fian was one of the principals in the North Berwick affair. Pitcairn: *Criminal Trials* 1.2.211–12.

devyse, in abstracking of mennis lyffis, wemennis milk,[77] bestis milk, and bewisching of bestis as weill as menne, lyk as thai diverse practisis can testifie".

It is an extraordinary fact, however, that in the face of all this evidence and of the testimony that, since she had accompanied William Leslie on his errand to Barbara Kaird, she had been at least cognisant of the plot to kill John Leslie, the assize found her not guilty on every point of her dittay. The reason, one suspects, must lie not in her actual innocence (which does not seem to be very likely), but in the superior patronage her proloquitor was able to muster on her behalf. For on the next day, the 19th, William Leslie and Violet Auchinleck came to trial on a charge of having John Leslie murdered by magic, and they had a formidable array of supporters in court, of whom Francis Stewart, Earl of Bothwell and the King's cousin, is perhaps the most notable. But there were also the Earl of Errol and Lord Home (both known to be favourably disposed to Catholics) and Bessie's employer, the Laird of Boquhane himself.[78] Had Bessie been found guilty of any part of her indictment, it would have looked bad for Boquhane – what was he doing, employing a witch as nurse to his children? – and it would have cast a dubious light on William Leslie, too, since his associating with a convicted witch must have lent colour to the accusation that he had indeed sought John Leslie's death by magic. Preferable by far (indeed necessary) to have the woman acquitted.

A hint that a great deal of local pressure was being exerted on William's behalf can be seen in the results of that particular court session. The judge was obliged to postpone the trial because the court could not find sufficient men to form an assize, large numbers being rejected on account of their relationship with or partiality for the accused.[79] Naturally, William and Violet were released on bail: their cautioners were the Earl of Bothwell and the Laird of Boquhane, and Bessie Roy appears to have sailed out of court on the coat-tails of her social superiors.

The Leslie affair became a topic of conversation in Edinburgh. On 23 July, Robert Bowes, the English ambassador, wrote to Lord Burghley, "sundrie

77 The dittay includes an account of how, in an act of spite, she deprived Bessie Steill of her breast-milk because Steill had a greater flow than she. Steill complained of this to Bessie's mistress, and Bessie was obliged to cure her. This she did by telling the woman to come to her at night and ask for her milk again for God's sake. Steill did as she was instructed and lay in the bed next to Bessie until midnight, when Bessie woke her up and told her she was cured: 'and incontinent sche walknit, and hir papis sprang out full of milk, and remanit with hir thaireftir'.

78 Pitcairn: *op.cit.* supra 1.2.209.

79 The whole sequence of these trials is dominated by Leslies. Evidently there was either some kind of pre-existing feud within the family (meaning the nexus of relationships between those in the area whose surname was 'Leslie'), or the attempted murder of John had riven the Leslies into factions.

witches were arrained yesterdaie in this towne, and are found giltie of odious crimes; chefelie that some of them made in wax the image of the yong lard of Wardhouse, and rosting the image the gentleman pined awaie by sweate as the wax melteth before the fier".[80] But William Leslie and his associates were not the only subject for gossip. The ambassador also noted that news had come from Denmark that five or six witches had been arrested in Copenhagen at the instance of the Danish admiral on charges of seeking to interfere with Queen Anne's voyage to Scotland the previous autumn, and the royal couple's return from Denmark in April just past. He also had further news of the woman from Lübeck. Apparently at the end of June or the beginning of July, a 'Dutch'[81] woman arrived in Leith with a Latin letter for the King. She had gone first to Denmark but the King had already departed, so she was now in Edinburgh, declaring that she had been sent – she would not say by whom – to tell James about a particular piece of good fortune relating to himself. Having obtained access to the Queen, she explained in German "that learned magicians of the east had met and found noble acts to be done by a prince in the north-west of Europe, having a mark in his side, whom they noted to be the King of Scots", and then asked for an interpreter so that she could say this directly to James.[82] The King appears to have thought her a witch but was inclined, nevertheless, to see her. Presumably he was curious to hear more about the noble acts he was destined to perform. He sent George Young to talk to her, but she insisted she must see the mark on the King's side and have it verified by "such wise man as she would open the matter unto" before she would say anything further.

This condition almost certainly brought the matter to an impasse, and then Bowes remarked that people were saying she had actually come to Edinburgh because she had fallen in love with one of the Queen's servants and that this revelation had destroyed her former credit. Cowan refers to her as "crazed",[83] but there seems to be no good reason for doing so. James thought she was a witch, not a lunatic, and is unlikely to have taken the trouble of sending one of his gentlemen to talk to her if it was clear she was mentally deranged. Moreover, prophecies were part of the regular currency of the day, even in royal and aristocratic circles, as the case of Nostradamus alone will bear witness. The story of her being drawn to Edinburgh by love is, however, a little peculiar. Had that been all there was, she would not have needed to concoct a story involving the King which, if discovered to be untrue, would

---

80 *CSPS* 10.365.
81 Probably Deutsch (i.e. German), since we later learn that German was her native tongue.
82 *CSPS* 10.348. The woman is described as a 'gentlewoman', which indicates that she was respectable.
83 'Darker vision of the Renaissance', 129.

have been likely to land her in grave difficulties. One notes she was able to obtain an audience of the Queen. If she knew one of the Queen's servants, this would explain her access to the royal presence, and it may also account for the origin of the tale which seems to have discredited her.

But these instances were not the only ones involving occult and magical themes, for in 1590 on 22 July, Edinburgh saw the trials of Katherine Ross, Lady Foulis, and of Hector Munro, her stepson, on charges of attempted murder by poison and magic.[84] Katherine Ross was the daughter of Alexander Ross of Balnagown and the second wife of Robert Munro, fifteenth baron of Foulis.[85] By him she had six children and from him she inherited five more from his previous marriage. Two of these last were involved in her murderous plot: Robert Munro the younger, heir to the barony and her intended victim, and Hector Munro, his brother, and her willing accomplice. The aim of the plot was simple – to kill young Robert and so clear the way for Hector to inherit the title. But this was not all. Katherine also had in mind to kill the young wife of her brother, George Ross, the laird of Balnagown, so that George could marry young Robert's widow. George Ross was therefore cognisant of her intentions but, curiously enough, never ended up in court.

None of this, however, was recent. The attempted murders and their long preparation took place mainly between Easter and December, 1577 and it was therefore extraordinary that it should have taken so long to bring the principal parties to justice. The evidence against Katherine is long and detailed, with 29 separate items on her dittay. These depend largely on the confessions of five other people involved in the plot, but as only eleven of the articles are directly concerned with magic, it is these which will merit our particular attention. The sequence of events appears to be as follows.

At midsummer, 1576 Katherine sent Agnes Roy, a witch, to consult another witch called Marjorie nighean [daughter of] MacAlasdair, *alias* Laskie Loncart anent whether or not she would meet success in her plot against young Robert Munro and Lady Balnagown. Loncart told her to go to the Hill of Nigg and there speak to the *sithean*, although whether Katherine actually did so is not recorded. But, fairy counsel or not, she clearly made up her mind to proceed, for in September she paid William MacGillivray five ells of linen, and the following Easter a further 16 shillings to obtain some kind of magical paraphernalia which were then handed over to her in a small box. William's commission also seems to have included the purchase of some rat poison from a man in Elgin, but evidently he did not buy enough because in May, 1577 Katherine had to ask him to get some more. This he refused to do unless Katherine's husband guaranteed the money

---

84 Pitcairn: *Criminal Trials* 1.2.191–204.
85 Balnagown is about one-and-a-half miles north of Nigg Bay in the Cromarty Firth, and Foulis Castle is three-quarters of a mile north-west of the the same firth.

(something he was not likely to do, since the point of the purchase was the death of his son and heir), but Katherine offered to pay William his wage in kind and to this he agreed, adding – perhaps with a view to extorting something more – that George Ross, her brother, knew all about the poison. As George was a willing accomplice in her designs, however, this information scarcely seems to have troubled her and the blackmail, if that is what the remark amounted to, fell flat.[86]

By June, she was making preparations to do away with her intended victims by magic if poisoning did not work.[87] First she needed to obtain a fairy arrowhead and sent for one from Dingwall.[88] For this she paid four shillings. Then, on 2 July, along with two female witches, Christian Malcolmson and Laskie Loncart, and a male, Thomas MacKane, she made a figure of young Robert out of butter, set it up against a wall, and shot it with the arrowhead. Unfortunately Loncart, who was acting as archer, missed her target and so the magic failed to work. There was therefore nothing for it but to try again, and so four days later another image, this time made of clay, was set up as a target. Loncart shot twelve times but missed again. Had she been successful, we are told, the image would have been buried beneath a bridge.

Midsummer came and Loncart was summoned once more. This time she and Katherine were joined by three other witches, Agnes Roy and Christian and Gradoch Malcolmson, and together they made more clay figures representing Katherine's intended victims.[89] Yet still something

86 Katherine had paid him eight shillings and four ells of linen to buy the poison which he had passed on to her via another Catherine Ross, the daughter of Sir David Ross. Katherine used William as a messenger on several occasions, and on one sent him to some gipsies to ask for their advice about how best to poison young Robert and Lady Balnagown.

87 As indeed it did not. Katherine tried bribing the laird of Balnagown's cook to put rat poison in Lady Balnagown's food. This he did, but the dose was not quite sufficient to kill her, although it made her vomit at the time and left her permanently ill thereafter. Attempts to poison young Robert were equally unsuccessful. One jar of venomous liquid which was being conveyed to his house by the nurse in Katherine's household fell and broke and the nurse, who was foolish enough to let her curiosity get the better of her, tasted the stuff and died. A second jar leaked, and the servant boy who was carrying it licked his fingers and became extremely ill.

88 These fairy arrowheads, or 'elf-bolts', were usually flint arrowheads dating back to the Bronze Age and were regarded as weapons belonging originally to the *sithean*. See Merrifield: *Archaeology of Ritual and Magic*, 16.

89 In her confession, Agnes Roy revealed that she, Loncart, Catherine Ross the witch, and Katherine Lady Foulis, had special signs they could make to one another if they found themselves in company with others who were not privy to their secrets. These signs consisted of Agnes's gripping their hands (presumably after a particular fashion) or stamping her feet. It sounds rather like a version of Freemasonry, but I think it unlikely the four women can be seen as belonging to some kind of esoteric or occult group. Nevertheless, one wonders under what circumstances these women can have met in public and why they should have required secret signs to convey their meaning.

must have gone wrong, for on 16 August Katherine was stalking Lady
Balnagown and had been joined by two others, Christian Ross and
Thomas MacKane *alias* Cassindonisch, the latter having been sent to
Katherine by her brother.[90] Katherine asked Thomas to murder Lady
Balnagown by magic in return for a good reward, but Thomas must have
had reservations, perhaps requiring confirmation that this request was
genuine or that he actually would be paid, for by the 24th both he
and Katherine had gone to see George Ross who then told Thomas to do
as Katherine bade and in return he would receive a set of travelling-
clothes. But whatever magic Thomas may have tried must have been as
ineffectual as that of Katherine's earlier attempts, because in October she
was talking again to William MacGillevray and Catherine Ross about
giving a poisoned drink for young Robert Munro. It was to be delivered to
him on All Hallows Eve, and when that time arrived, Katherine bolstered
her effort with poison by meeting Christian Ross and Laskie Loncart to
perform yet again the ceremony of shooting fairy arrowheads at a couple of
clay figurines. Katherine herself shot two at the image of Lady Balnagown
and Loncart shot three at 'Robert'. Both images broke – not the intention
of the exercise: the arrowheads were supposed only to stick in the damp
clay – and so Katherine told Loncart to make fresh images.

Meanwhile this activity had not gone unnoticed. That same month,
Katherine's husband obtained a commission from the King to inquire
after and arrest 31 individuals delated or suspect of magic, incantation,
murder, homicide, and other dreadful crimes (*aliorumque horribilium
criminum et offensionum*) within the bounds of Ross, Ardnamurchan,
and Inverness,[91] and among these names were all those we have noted
as taking part in Katherine's plots against her stepson and sister-in-law.
Not that the arrests stopped her. Destruction of her victims appears to
have become an obsession – indeed, she once said to Christian Ross that
she would do anything to get rid of Lady Balnagown – because even after
Christian had been apprehended, tried, and burned in late November,
Katherine was meeting Thomas MacKane and others in her house and
discussing fresh ways to poison the object of her hatred. Still, Thomas
was on the run and, having eluded capture under the October commission, was named in a second issued in January, 1578.[92] This seems to
have been successful, for we learn that on 22 July several of the
conspirators, including William MacGillivray, were tried, convicted,
and sentenced to death; that in September nine witches were tried

---

90 'Cassindonisch' = Gaelic *Cas an donais*, 'Devil's Foot'.
91 *Exchequer Rolls* 20.522–3.
92 *Exchequer Rolls* 20.525. *Calendar of Munro Writs*, no. 92. Laskie Loncart was in
   the same case, being named in both commissions.

and burned in Ross; and that on 28 November Thomas himself was burned in Dingwall.[93]

The net had closed in upon Katherine. Her father and brother were both questioned about their involvement in witchcraft[94] and Katherine herself, according to her dittay, came forward and made a declaration before two notaries that although she was rumoured to be a witch, she was willing to stand trial on that charge in order to clear her name, but was confident no one would actually accuse her judicially. The declaration made, however, Katherine then more or less admitted her guilt by fleeing into Caithness where she stayed for nine months with her uncle, the Earl, and it cost the Earl a great deal of persuasion before Robert Munro, her husband, was willing to take her back.

For nearly eleven years thereafter the affair fell quiet, like a dormant volcano. But in November, 1588 young Robert succeeded his father and early the following year, for reasons not openly stated, decided to apply for a commission to try a number of witches. It is not clear whether his stepmother's name was included among them. Young Robert, however, was unable to execute his commission at once because trouble broke out in the north. For about this same time, the Catholic Earls of Huntly, Errol, and Crawford, along with Lords Maxwell and Claud Hamilton, wrote to Philip II of Spain lamenting the failure of the recent Armada and offering him their assistance should he try again. Their letters were intercepted and passed on to James who thereupon dismissed Huntly as Captain of the Royal Guard, a post to which he had only just been appointed. Attributing his dismissal to the Chancellor, John Maitland, Huntly immediately gathered an army, intending to march on Edinburgh and recover his position. But James replied in kind and by mid-April had entered Aberdeen where he received the Catholic Earls' surrender.[95] As a result of these stirs, then, Katherine was able to obtain a formal suspension of young Robert's commission, adding to the document of suspension her own name and those of other suspects specified in the commission, as well as those of other people not therein specified. Nevertheless, despite all her efforts, she got no more than a postponement, and on 22 July, 1590 was obliged to be present in court to answer the long list of her alleged crimes. These she denied altogether. Several witnesses against her did not turn up, and the assize of

---

93 *CSPS* 10.365. *Calendar of Fearn*, 135. One of the men named in the commission of October was Coinneach Odhar. This was the name of the famous Brahan Seer, and opinion is divided about whether the two men are the same or not. See Sutherland: *Ravens and Black Rain*, 219–30 and Matheson: 'The historical Coinneach Odhar', 67–88.

94 *Calendar of Fearn*, 135–6.

95 The sequence of events can be followed in *CSPS* 10.1–58.

fifteen men from her immediate home area – principally Cromarty, Tain, and Dingwall – acquitted her on every point.

The verdict should not, perhaps, cause too much surprise. The identity of her pursuer, however, is a different matter; for he was none other than Hector Munro, her accomplice in at least some of the charges and a man who would be standing as panel in his own trial later that day. But the reason Hector had decided to prosecute his stepmother is simple: they had quarrelled. The disagreement went back to 1589 when, on 4 June, we find that Katherine had made an official complaint that Hector was seeking to dispossess her of lands in Foulis and had gone about this in two ways: first, by intimidating her tenants and servants with physical violence, and then by procuring a commission to have some of them arrested and tried for "witchecraft and utheris forgeit and feinyeit crymes allegeit committit be thame". In view of Hector's blatant misuse of his commission against "honnest wemen, swa repute and haldin thir mony yeiris bygane, spoted at na tyme with ony sic ungodlie practizeis", Katherine sought to have his commission cancelled, and to a certain extent she succeeded because, after an initial hearing before members of the Privy Council, the Lords decided to suspend the commission for the time being.[96]

In August, however, the boot was on the other foot, for on the 1st Lachlan MacIntosh and Hector Munro were obliged, on pain of 10,000 merks, to make sure that all necessary preparations for Katherine's trial should be completed by 28 October. In the meantime, Hector was to be accorded the right to use Katherine's income from her rents to pay all her expenses while she was kept in ward, beginning on 2 August, at the rate of forty shillings a day, until the date of her trial and its verdict.[97] But Hector continued to harass Katherine and her dependants and on 4 November (nearly a week after the trial should have begun, one notices) had to be told to stop on penalty of £2,000. This was Katherine's doing, so Hector counter-complained that although he had duly paid the forty shillings required of him until 27 October, Katherine's success in making him liable to pay £2,000 if he harmed either her or her tenants or servants meant that he could no longer safely make use of her rents to pay her maintenance, and therefore he asked the Council to relieve him of this obligation. These separate claims were given due attention and a compromise was reached. Katherine agreed to withdraw her demand for indemnity, and Hector agreed to continue payment of the forty shillings.[98]

Such, then, was the frame of mind in which stepmother and stepson faced each other across the courtroom in Edinburgh on 22 July. After her acquittal

96 *RPC* 4.392–3.
97 *Ibid.,* 404–5.
98 *Ibid.,* 431, 433–4.

came Hector's trial and he stood charged with three counts, none of which related to anything in Katherine's dittay, but all of which related to magic. The first tells us that in August, 1588 young Robert was ill and that Hector sent for three witches, one male and two female, to see if he could be cured. The change of heart is striking. Only ten years before, Hector had been happy to see his stepmother attempt to kill his brother; now he was apparently trying to save him. Everything had to be done in great secrecy. The witches duly arrived and stayed in a house belonging to one John Murray (who knew nothing about it and must have been away from home, because the witches stayed there for about five days). Even so they were nervous because if Robert Munro the laird had found out what they were doing, he would have had them arrested. The dittay says they cut some of Robert's hair and pared his fingernails and toenails, and so "socht be thair develisch meanis to haif cureit him of his seiknes"; but it is difficult to imagine, in view of his later action in asking for commissions to prosecute delated and suspect witches, that young Robert was privy to their magical attempt to cure him, or that they managed to gain entry to him to collect this material themselves. So one must presume someone else did that job for them. Their verdict on Robert's health was not encouraging. Hector had delayed too long in sending for them, they said, and they could do the patient no good; after which Hector "convoyit thame away, under sylence of nycht". The illness, however, did not prove fatal, for that November old Robert died and young Robert succeeded to the title.

But if Hector had had a change of heart towards his brother, it had not made him any less lethal: it merely changed the object of his malice. In January, 1589 he himself lay ill in the village of Alness,[99] and sent for a witch, Marion MacIngaroch, to come and cure him. When she arrived, she was carrying three stones which magically produced water, and Hector was given three draughts of it (presumably one from each stone). Marion then told him that if he was to be cured, someone would have to die in his place – a common enough magical condition – and that the person destined to be sacrificed for him was his kinsman, George Munro, Katherine's eldest son by Lord Foulis. Hector therefore sent for George (continuing to do so, indeed, every day for five days) and meanwhile refused to see anyone else, even though several friends came to wish him well. At last George arrived and, in accordance with Marion's prior instructions, Hector did no more than take George's right hand in his left and, after replying to George's initial question how he did that he was the better for George's coming, remained silent for the rest of the hour-long visit.

George then left and Marion, together with Christian Neill, Hector's

99 The village is in Ross on the north bank of the Cromarty Firth, between Dingwall and Invergordon.

foster-mother who had brought her daughter and young son with her, went out of the house at midnight and dug a shallow grave not far from the seashore. By the time they returned, however, Hector was having doubts: "Gif George should depairt suddanlie", he said, "the brute wald ryise [there would be a hue and cry], and all thair lyves wald be in danger". So he suggested that George's death be delayed for a while. Marion agreed he should live until 17 April, and then one or two of Hector's servants wrapped him in a blanket, took him furth of the house, and laid him in the trench, the turf which had been removed being placed on top of him and held down by staves. While Hector lay thus buried, the two women performed the following ritual three times. First Christian and her son ran a measured distance; then they returned to the grave where Marion was waiting and asked her which person (that is, Hector or George) did she choose; to which Marion replied that "Mr Hector wes hir schois to leif [live], and your brother Georg to die for yow". Finally, the ritual completed, Hector was taken home and put to bed.

The magic appeared to work, for Hector recovered, and as soon as he regained his health he went to stay with his uncle, taking Marion with him. Here she was treated exceptionally well ("as gif scho had bene your spous", the dittay says) and given the job of looking after sheep in a vain effort to conceal what may well have been a sexual liaison. But the resulting scandal was so great that the King, who was in Aberdeen between 18 and 26 April, heard of it and made it clear he wanted to see her. Hector, perhaps embarrassed, refused James's request until Katherine made it impossible for him to refuse further and he was obliged to take her to Aberdeen and present her to the King. James asked her questions and was shown the magical stones which had produced the draughts of water which had been given to Hector. The stones were confiscated and handed over to the Justice-Clerk, but apart from that nothing further seems to have happened to Marion.[100]

Finally, Hector was accused that the second part of his magical cure had worked, for in April, 1590 George Munro fell deadly sick and died on 3 June. Like his stepmother, Hector denied everything. Again witnesses for the prosecution failed to turn up and the assize, seven of whom had also passed judgement in Katherine's case, found Hector not guilty on every count. Both verdicts may have been a travesty of justice, but the assizers had to live with the results of their decisions, in a distant part of Scotland, far removed from Edinburgh, and one cannot in fairness blame them for their caution.

---

100 Indeed, she and Hector continued their association until 16 July, 1590 when he decided to put her aside. The imminence of his trial may help to explain why he did so.

6

Magic in League with Treason

K ing James's curiosity about Marion MacIngaroch seems to have been of a piece with his attitude towards witchcraft before the autumn of 1590. Like everyone else in Scotland, he would have been aware from his earliest years of the existence of *sìthean*, diviners, astrologers, palmists, physiognomists, alchemists, and operators of various kinds of magic including witchcraft, although it is difficult to tell how much credence he attached to them. His library seems to have contained only two books on the occult sciences (and one of those, Agrippa's *De Vanitate Scientiarum*, was the magician's repudiation of them), and, to judge by his astronomical poem *Sphaera* which warns of the dangers of astrological prophecy and magic, his tutor Buchanan was both wary of and hostile to them.[1] Members of the Court and of the gentry as a whole, as we have seen, were confident enough in the reality of preternatural powers to be willing to make use of them, should occasion require; but under different circumstances they were also prepared to laugh at practitioners of magic, just as people had always been able to make fun of priests and monks, and yet treat them with the utmost seriousness and reverence when solemnity was appropriate. Thus, we find that in c.1580 James may have seen a performance of Montgomerie's *Flyting* which contains scenes in which *sìthean* and witches are shown in a humorous light; and there is a possibility that James himself may have written a ribald comedy, *Philotus*, in which there is a series of comic conjurations and exorcisms.[2]

The King's curiosity continued even during the first flush of investigations of autumn 1590 when an extensive network of witches and magical operators had been uncovered in East Lothian, not far from the capital; for, on hearing that one of the male principals, John Fian, had so bewitched one of his rivals in love that the man used to fall into an hysterical madness and capering which lasted for one hour every day, he had the man brought before him so that he might witness the phenomenon for himself.[3] Similarly, when Geillis Duncan confessed that she

---

1 See Maxwell-Stuart: 'The fear of the King is death', 211 and the literature there cited.
2 On Montgomerie, see Simpson: 'The weird sisters wandering', 9, 10–11, 17. On *Philotus*, see Findlay: *History of Scottish Theatre*, 41–4. If James did not actually write the play, there is a very good chance he saw it, since it appears to have been written for performance at Court.
3 The man duly 'gave a great scritch and fell into a madness, sometime bending himselfe, and sometime capring so directly up that his head did touch the seeling of the Chamber, to the great admiration [astonishment] of his Maiestie and others then present', *Newes From Scotland*, 21. Whether this performance was genuine or feigned makes no difference to the King's motive for wanting to see it. He had heard that Fian could work magic upon another person, and wished to investigate the claim.

had played her pipe at a gathering of witches in the kirkyard of North Berwick the previous All Hallows Eve, James sent for her and had her play it for him.[4] To be sure, one of the King's motives in each case may have been curiosity, but curiosity is not in itself a fault, nor does it necessarily imply scepticism, and James's willingness both in 1590 and earlier to investigate certain notorious witches may equally well indicate a serious wish to find out at first hand, by 'experiment' (i.e. experience), what some witches actually did and were capable of doing.

There is no indication, however, contrary to what is now generally assumed, that he picked up knowledge of Continental theories of witchcraft during his six months in Scandinavia and brought them back to Scotland where they formed the basis of a new wave of persecution. The key features of these theories – transvection to the Sabbat, sexual orgies during the course of the Sabbat, reception of the Devil's mark, the Satanic pact, and shape-shifting – played scarcely any part in Scottish witchcraft either before or after James's Scandinavian visit, and indeed were little regarded in either Denmark or Norway.[5] So James's attitude towards Scottish magic and witchcraft seems to have depended largely, if not entirely, upon Scottish experience and Scottish beliefs and traditions, and what we see in the King is an intermittent curiosity in certain individuals who were alleged to operate magic, and a willingness to co-operate with both Parliament and the Kirk in their attempts to introduce effective control over a fairly wide range of behaviours which both authorities wished to designate undesirable. Of intention to persecute, however, there is no sign.

Nor is there any indication that the earlier events of 1590 involving witchcraft heightened his awareness of the subject in any significant way, or caused him any particular alarm. The presence of magic, both beneficent and malevolent, seems to have been as it were a background noise, present but not intrusive except when the occasional jarring note or unusual chord served to draw his attention to it; and with the novelty of a wife, a coronation, and what looked like armed rebellion from disaffected Catholic Earls in the north, James had many more pressing matters to occupy his attention.[6] But during

---

4 *Newes from Scotland*, 14.
5 See Maxwell-Stuart: 'The fear of the King is death', 211–13. As I have pointed out in that essay, the Satanic pact was known already in Scotland, but it is not until the seventeenth century that it plays any discernible role in the accusations brought against Scottish witches. One may also note that in any case, Scandinavia was not the only possible route along which Continental notions might reach Scotland. Both England and the Hanseatic ports could equally well have afforded such an outlet, as indeed could the Jesuits and seminary priests harboured by various Catholic families up and down Scotland.
6 Nor was the Kirk any more preoccupied with magic than it had been previously. When Robert Bruce preached in St. Giles during 1589 and 1590, for example, his sermons were devoted to the continuing presumed threat of Catholicism, and when he mentioned the Devil his context made it clear that he was referring to the activities of Scottish Catholics. See *Sermons*, 171, 202–3, 308, 317.

the autumn of that year, James discovered that while he had been furth of Scotland magic had been directed maliciously against both him and Queen Anne in more than one attempt to murder them. Thus magic became treason and James was directly involved.

The official narrative of events is fairly straightforward. Early in November the baillie depute of Tranent, David Seton, began to wonder why his servant, Geillis Duncan, spent every other night away from his house. Apparently she had suddenly acquired a remarkable ability to heal the sick and this made Seton suspicious that witchcraft might be involved. He therefore questioned her, both about her absences and about her new, almost miraculous powers, and when she refused to answer, he and some others tortured her and made the discovery of the Devil's mark upon her neck. At this point Geillis broke down and began to confess that she was a witch; whereupon she was lodged in prison and, during the course of further examinations, produced several other names, among which were Agnes Sampson, Agnes Thompson, John Fian *alias* Cunningham, George Mott's wife, Robert Grierson, and Janet Sandilands.[7]

Now, the first thing to note is that Seton had no authority to apply torture. His treatment of Geillis was therefore illegal and would have been overlooked (if indeed it was overlooked: but we have no record of his being reprimanded), only because her confessions led to the uncovering of a series of acts of treason. Secondly, none of these initial names belonged to anyone of any social significance. Agnes Sampson, for example, was a middle-aged woman from Nether Keith, a small village a few miles south of Haddington; John Fian was the schoolmaster at Prestonpans;[8] and Robert Grierson was the skipper of a boat. Thirdly, this group of names is the first of three, and each group is, of course, interconnected as those arrested provided their interrogators with a growing list of names, some already mentioned by others and thus confirmed by this later testimony, and some hitherto unmentioned – the usual 'ripple' phenomenon to be found in almost any large-scale prosecution of witches.

---

7 *Newes From Scotland*, 9–10. Her ordeal lasted at least until May the following year, for she was still being interrogated then in the presence of the King. See *JC26/2/16*. 'Sandilands' appears in the printed text of *Newes* as 'Bandilands', but this I take to be an error of transcription.

8 He is described as Dr. Fian, but the title was one commonly applied to schoolmasters. Schoolmasters were also frequently readers in their local kirk, and so it is possible that Fian filled this post as well. See Foster: *The Kirk Before the Covenants*, 192, 194. A late source says that Agnes Simson (sic) was 'a Matron of grave and settled behaviour', but this may or may not be reliable, Sanderson: *Compleat History*, 159–60. Spottiswood, too, described her as 'a woman, not of the base and ignorant sort of Witches, but matron-like, grave and settled in her answers, which were all to some purpose', *History of the Church of Scotland*, 383. Similar reservations, however, must apply.

Thus, Agnes Sampson and Geillis Duncan were acquainted with Barbara Napier, the wife of Archibald Douglas, a burgess of Edinburgh and brother to one of the city's legal establishment, and with Euphame MacCalyean, bastard daughter (later legitimised) of another advocate, Thomas MacCalyean, Lord Cliftonhall, a senator of the College of Justice, and wife of Patrick MacCalyean *alias* Moscrop, again a prominent advocate; and both Barbara and Euphame constitute the principals of our second group, that of the gentry. But the third group – if one man may be called a 'group' – is even more elevated; for running through the narrative is the name of the King's cousin, Francis Stewart, the Earl of Bothwell, the bane of James's life and a person whose sinister influence on contemporary Scottish politics is difficult to under-estimate. These three groupings serve to illustrate yet further a point which examination of earlier episodes of magic and witchcraft should have made clear already, that operative magic of one kind and another permeated Scottish society from top to bottom and continued to do so despite the Kirk's attempts to eradicate both the operation and the beliefs which made operation feasible.

Geillis and the others, then, revealed a number of startling facts. The storms which had greeted King James's initial efforts to set sail for Denmark in 1589 had been raised by magic. A number of witches, it seemed, including Fian, Agnes Sampson, and Robert Grierson met on a boat and put out to sea, "quhair Satan delyverit ane catt out of his hand to Robert Greirsoune, gevand the word to 'Cast the same in the see, hola!'"; and they (or rather Satan on their behalf) also created a mist on the occasion of the King's return to Scotland, aiming to drive the King's ship southwards and wreck him on the English coast.[9] These actions alone were treasonable but, just as Lady Foulis had tried to supplement magical murder with poison, so these East Lothian witches prepared more than a single way to kill the King.

One involved his picture. Someone stole a picture of the King, wrapped it in a long piece of white cloth or paper, and brought it to a large gathering of witches at Acheson's Haven.[10] Donald Robinson, one of the accused, described in his confession what happened next

Agnes Samson brought the pictour to the feild. She delyvered it to Barbara Naper. Fra Barbarie it was given to Eufame MacCaillon: fra Eufame to Meg Begtoune of Spilmurfurd. It passed through aught or

9 Dittay of John Fian (items 7 and 8), Pitcairn: *Criminal Trials* 1.2.211. Raising winds for destructive purposes was a common practice attributed to witches. Cf., for example, incidents off the west coast of Scotland in c.1589, Campell: *Witchcraft and Second Sight*, 27–30. The Queen, too, was to be stopped by a storm from coming to Scotland. See Agnes Sampson's dittay (item 40), Pitcairn: *op.cit.*, 236–7.

10 A small harbour about a mile west of Prestonpans.

nyne wemen. At last it came to Robin Grison: fra him to the devill. They spak all James the saxt amongis thame, handling the pictour. The devill was lyk ane man. Agnes Samson said thair wald be baith gold and silver and victuall gottin fra my lord Bothuel. Thair wer thair besyde the foresaids Catarine Wallace and Jonat Straton, Charles Wat in Garvat, quha offred to delyver the pictour bak to the theif againe to cummer [trouble] the King . . . Thair wer wemen of Leith and of the Pannis thair. He[11] delyvered the pictour to Gillies Duncane, and fra her to Jonat Straton, and receaved it from Catarine Wallace. They convened in the gloming [evening] and did thair turne in the night.[12]

It is interesting that someone should have stolen a picture of the King. From where was it stolen? Presumably from a house belonging to someone who was not part of the occult network of witches in East Lothian, otherwise there would have been no need to steal it, and there must always be the possibility that it came from the royal household. But one cannot speculate further on the identity of the thief. Agnes Sampson, as we have seen earlier, had a contact in the King's bedchamber, but he was not altogether reliable, and in any case there were others with aristocratic connections: Richard Graham, for example, a magician and personal acquaintance of Bothwell, whose name will appear ever more frequently in the narrative, and of course Bothwell himself.

This, however, was not the only incident involving an image of the King. Janet Straton confessed that on Lammas Eve [31 July], 1590 there was another meeting of about sixty witches in Prestonpans. "The purpos of thair conveining", she said, "wes to cummer and inchant a pictur of walx quhilk Anne Sampson brocht with her".[13] The image started with Agnes, passed widdershins round the circle, and when it had come back to Agnes she handed it to the Devil whom she had raised, who was there "standand in likness of a blak preist with blak claithis lik a hair mantill [a roughly woven cloak]".[14]

---

11 I.e. Donald Robinson.
12 *JC26/2/2*. The part I have omitted refers to details of payment and to a previous meeting between Robinson and the thief. Geillis Duncan was clear that the picture was wrapped in cloth, *JC 26/2/16*. One would expect participants to be able to distinguish between cloth and paper. Geillis also thought there were about forty people present, 'eight or ten principals and about threttie inferieurs', *JC26/2/15*.
13 *JC26/2/15*. Cf. *JC26/2/10*.
14 Cf. *stragulae villosae*, the mantles of shaggy frieze which Bishop Lesley noted were sometimes used by Highlanders, *De origine, moribus et rebus gestis Scotorum* (Rome 1578); and Nicolay D'Arfeville, 'Ceux qui habitent la partie Meridionale du Mont Grampus . . . portent comme les Irlandois . . . un habit longue jusques aux genoux, de la grosse laine a mode d'une soutane', *La navigation du Roi d'Ecosse, Jacques Cinquiesme du nom, autour de son royaume* (Paris 1583), Preface. Robert Grierson described the Devil as wearing a black gown and a skull bonnet, ill-favoured [that is, shabby or scruffy], *JC26/2/19. p.3*.

Agnes then said to the Devil, "Tak thair the pictur of James Stewart, Prince of Scotland, and I ask of yow, Maister Mahoun, that I may have this turne wrocht and done to wrak him for my lord Bothuillis sake". It is interesting to note the reference to the Devil's looking like a Catholic priest. When one reads these pre-trial papers, the jerkiness of the record makes it obvious that the separate sentences or groups of sentences have been put together from question-and-answer sessions with the questions omitted from the record. Envisaging the Devil as a 'black man' or a man 'clothed in black' is commonplace in witchcraft accounts. In this instance, however, there was an obvious desire on the part of at least one of the interrogators to make a confessional point and to suggest this specific clothing to the person being questioned. The thread of his intended reasoning is patent: Catholicism = Satan's own religion = treason against the King.

But neither picture nor wax image provided the only means whereby these witches sought James's death. The Devil, we are told, instructed several of them "to hing, roist, and drop ane taid [toad], and to lay the droppis of the taid, mixt with strang wasch [stale urine], ane edder-skyn, and the thing in the foirheid of a new-foillit foill [new-born foal], in his Hienes way, quhair his Maiestie wald gang inowre or outowre, or in ony passage quhair itt mycht drop upoun his Hienes heid or body, for his Hienes distructioune, that ane uther mycht haif rewlit in his Maiesties place, and the ward [government] mycht haif gane to the Dewill".[15] Clearly this arrangement implies that someone either among or known to their company had access to places where the King might be expected to come and go quite frequently. "Where his Majesty might go in over and out over" suggests a doorway, and we know that the threshold was a significant place for magical operations. Moreover, if the enchanted liquid was to drop on the King's head or body, a door-lintel would provide an ideal place to conceal the jar or phial in which it was contained. Access to one of the royal palaces, then, and the ability to arrange for the liquid to be put in position are strongly implied.

From the record of these several incidents, we gain (and are meant to gain)

---

15 Dittay of Barbara Napier, Pitcairn: *Criminal Trials* 1.2.245. Cf. *JC*26/2/19 and 15 where Agnes Sampson reports to the Devil that she has carried out his orders. *Newes From Scotland* gives an account of a similar but different operation which it attributes entirely to Agnes Sampson. 'She tooke a blacke Toade, and did hang the same up by the heels, three daies, and collected and gathered the venome as it dropped and fell from it in an Oister shell, and kept the same venome close covered, untill she should obtaine any parte or peece of foule linnen cloth, that had appertained to the Kings Maiestie', 16. Her aim was evidently to impregnate the cloth with the poison, after which it would 'put him to such extraordinary paines, as if he had beene lying upon sharp thornes and endes of Needles'. The aim here, however, seems to have been to cause pain rather than death, even though *Newes* gives it as an example of lethal intent.

the distinct impression that there existed in East Lothian a large group of witches, both male and female, who during 1589 and 1590 had been paid by someone (here named as the Earl of Bothwell) to cause the King's death by magic, and in accordance with their commission had tried to do so by more than one operation. Two main questions are raised by this: (a) since it appeared that large numbers of witches could be organised to assemble in various places to work this magic, did some kind of organisation actually exist, and if so, was it peculiar to East Lothian at this time, or is there evidence of some similar organisation anywhere else in Scotland? and (b) if there was indeed a genuine conspiracy against the King's life, was it really under Bothwell's direction, and if so, what did he hope to gain by it?

The sense that an organisation may have been real is strengthened in the recorded evidence by the account of a major convention of witches in the kirk of North Berwick on 31 October, 1589. According to Agnes Sampson's dittay, this is what happened.[16] The Devil in likeness of a man met her in the fields near Nether Keith between 5 and 6 pm on the 30th, and commanded her to be at North Berwick kirk the following night. Obedient to his orders, she went there, travelling on horseback with her son-in-law, John Coupar, and alighted in the kirkyard at about 11 pm, where perhaps a hundred people (six men, the rest women) had foregathered and were dancing around to the music of Geillis Duncan's 'trump'.[17] John Fian, his face concealed in some fashion, was leading them.[18] Then Fian blew upon the church doors and they opened. Once inside, he blew again on some large black candles which had been stuck around the pulpit and these caught alight. The participant witches gathered round, some standing, some sitting. Next, the Devil, wearing a black gown and a black hat, stood up in the pulpit and, much like a schoolteacher, called his register of those present, each person answering, "Here, Master", and there was a hubbub with people displaying signs of anger when the Devil called Robert Grierson by his real name instead of "Robert the Comptroller *alias* Rob the Rowar", as he should have done.[19]

Then the Devil asked them whether they had been his good servants, and to report what they had done since the last convention. This done, they opened two

---

16 Pitcairn: *Criminal Trials* 1.2.239–40. *JC26/2/12*, page 4. There are one or two verbal differences between these two accounts, but none of any particular significance.

17 I.e. a Jew's harp.

18 He is described as *mussellit* = 'muzzled'. This may mean he was wearing a mask, but could equally well imply that he simply had a scarf or a piece of cloth wrapped round his lower face.

19 Whether this implies that each person there had some kind of alias is not clear, but I have already pointed out (*supra*, pp. 30–1) that the possession of an alias did not necessarily imply that someone was a witch, since aliases were quite common in general society.

graves, two within and one outwith the kirk, and plundered the corpses for finger- and toe-joints and noses, which the Devil told them to keep until they were dry enough to be reduced to powder.[20] A final act of homage, the infamous kissing of his arse, was paid and then the meeting was over and everyone dispersed.

Now, while it is clear that this narrative contains preternatural elements the reader may wish to question, and that it has been built up from a series of interrogations which were intended as much to steer the answers towards some kind of preconceived notion of the kind of thing which ought to have happened, as to elicit a truthful and accurate account of what actually did happen, it is still insufficient to claim that everything here is false and that no such meeting can ever have taken place. To be sure, there are difficulties and inconsistencies. For example, Agnes says there were about a hundred people present; *Newes From Scotland* says two hundred; yet Agnes names only 38, to whom must be added the Devil;[21] and *Newes* depicts all the witches going to North Berwick by sea, "each one in a Riddle or Cive".

Taking such a convention seriously also means posing practical questions. How did so many women manage to leave home and travel fairly long distances at night without their husbands' or others in the household noticing their absence? In the dark October night, how did they see their way? Did they rely on moonlight – what if the sky should be covered by cloud? – or did they carry lanterns, in which case, did nobody notice so many twinkling lights converging upon North Berwick? How did these people actually gain access to the kirk, and who had been there beforehand to set the black candles round the pulpit? What was the effect on the neighbouring part of the town when, close to midnight on All Hallows Eve, a time notoriously traditional as that for the meeting of witches, the noise of a hundred or so people wafted across from the kirkyard and lights could be seen in the kirk itself? What was the minister doing? Did he not interfere, or at least complain to the kirk session afterwards? Who (if anyone) cleared away evidence from the kirk – the candles, the earth from the plundered graves, and so forth – that there had been an unauthorised meeting there? Above all, who was the Devil?

Such a list of practical problems, however, does not necessarily destroy the possibility that the convention was real enough. *Newes From Scotland*, one must remember, is a work of propaganda. It was published in London in 1591 and claims to be taken from a Scottish copy. No such copy exists (or has survived), but the pamphlet may well have been based on a first-hand account of the

---

20 The graveyard was situated on the east, south, and west of the kirk, Ferrier: *The North Berwick Story*, 20. Bessie Thomson, examined in presence of the King on 5 May, 1591 [mistakenly 1590 in the ms.], confessed that 'she wes present at the Rysing of the deid corpsis in the kirk and kirkyard of north beruik', *JC26/2/16*.

21 The English ambassador wrote to Lord Burghley in January, 1591 that 'there are more than forty apprehended and under trial and examination', *CSPS* 10.467.

examination of some of the witches in the presence of the King, written by James Carmichael, minister of Haddington.[22] Carmichael had a personal interest in painting James in a favourable light, since he had not long returned from exile in England whither he had been obliged to go because of his sympathy for the Ruthven raiders.[23] *Newes* therefore tends to emphasise the preternatural aspects of the witchcraft episode so that the King's courage in hazarding his person in the presence of powerful and malicious witches who had planned and practised such enormities against him may appear the more noble and admirable. It makes the political point that treason does not prosper, and drives home the moral that Satan's machinations will be uncovered and cannot prevail against the lawful magistrates who act as God's instruments of justice.

But *Newes* is also a work aimed at the general public, in the manner of dozens of other similar pamphlets, and is therefore written in such a way as to allure its intended audience. Thus, details of the ways in which both Agnes Sampson and John Fian were tortured depict the severity of temporal justice towards the wicked and so provide a picture of the torments of Hell they are doomed to suffer – a moral instruction for the reader. Anecdotes about the operations of witchcraft reveal the deep wickedness of the participants and thereby warn the reader against involving him or herself in magic of any kind; and a lengthy account of how one of John Fian's attempts to work love-magic went badly wrong and caused, not a young woman but a heifer to follow him, love-sick, everywhere provides both a touch of grim humour and also the lesson that magic is not even reliable. Indeed, as *Newes* explains, it was this very incident which led to Fian's downfall because it "made all men imagine that hee did woorke it by the Divell . . . and therupon, the name of the said Doctor Fien . . . began to grow so common among the people of Scotland, that he was secretlye nominated for a notable Cuniurer".[24]

22 Dunlap: 'King James and some witches', 43. It is not clear whether Carmichael's account was ever published. If it was, no copy seems to have survived.

23 See *Fasti* 1.369. The Ruthven incident took place in August, 1582 when James was held captive by a Protestant faction of his nobles to separate him from the Catholic Earl of Lennox. The raid created a deep impression on the King and made him liable to be hostile to anyone who may have supported it.

24 *Newes*, 23–4. The phrase 'among the people of Scotland' is perhaps a little odd if the pamphlet were directed to them in the first place, and may be a slight indication that *Newes* was actually written for an English audience and that there was, in fact, no Scottish original, at least in this form. One may also note that we are told that when Agnes Sampson was searched, the Devil's marks were found in her private parts. This is actually an extremely unusual detail in cases of Scottish witchcraft, where the marks are almost always to be found elsewhere – on the neck, the arms, or the shoulders. But the detail is very common in Continental demonologies, and one wonders therefore whether it was included in *Newes* because the private parts are where such marks are supposed to be found rather than because they actually were found there in Agnes Sampson's case. The anecdote about the heifer and John Fian is also suspicious, since it does not appear in Fian's dittay.

Nevertheless, the bias of *Newes* is no argument against its containing a kernel of accurate reportage. The numbers allegedly present in North Berwick have been exaggerated, but that does not mean to say the meeting never took place. If it was not by sieve that every witch travelled there, some may have done so by coracle, a common means of transport along the coast and fairly like a sieve in general shape.[25] The majority of those supposed to be present were women. One or two named by Agnes were married, but others may not have been and may have lived alone, while some may have come with the knowledge (and therefore approval) of their husbands or sons or guardians, as Agnes herself came with the active co-operation of her son-in-law. So it may not have been necessary for all, or perhaps any, of the women present to practise concealment from the man of their house.

As for the reaction of the people of North Berwick to such a misuse of their kirk, their minister, Thomas Greig, noted sadly that his parishioners were spiritually indifferent and often profaned the Sabbath by piping and dancing.[26] It is possible, therefore, that if a witches' convention had actually taken place within and outwith the kirk, the people of the town would not necessarily have been inclined to make a fuss.[27] Besides, the kirk was built on a tidal island, a fair distance out to sea along a promontory, while the manse stood in what at the time was open country. So both parishioners and minister were removed from the immediate neighbourhood of the kirk and may not have noticed that anything was amiss.[28] Prior access to the kirk could have been gained through the good offices of its reader – John Fian provides an example that a schoolmaster and thus perhaps a reader could also be a magician – and magic with lighting candles need have been no more than a conjuring trick. The early modern period saw many much more spectacular illusions.

Then, the Devil: he is described in Agnes's dittay as a man clothed in black, although the words 'gown' and 'hat' in the description are not as helpful as they might be. 'Gown' could refer to the distinctive form of garb worn by both

---

25 Hornell: *British Coracles and Irish Curraghs*, 297, 299–300. Cf. Agnes Sampson's confession that she had often been furth of Scotland in a riddle and that she and her companions frequently spent two days or even longer on board ships or unknown coasts, *JC*26/2/12, p. 5. We are also told that on a sea journey to North Berwick, 'sum wemen roued with airs', *JC*26/2/13, p. 2. This clearly indicates a normal ferrying craft.

26 *Fasti* 1.380.

27 It was a similar story in Tranent where the conspiracy was first uncovered. Alexander Forrester, the minister, was said in 1589 to be cold in doctrine and slack in discipline, and was reproved for the smallness of his congregations. See Seton: *History of the Family of Seton* 1.211, note 2. The difficulty met by the presbytery of Haddington in bringing Agnes Sampson to book in 1589–90 also suggests that the people of East Lothian were not vigorously hostile towards those accused of witchcraft, at this time.

28 Ferrier: *The North Berwick Story*, 18, 20.

clerics and lawyers, or to the loose garment worn by men both rich and poor indoors for comfort. But 'hat' is rather more specific; it suggests a member of the gentry or higher class, since poor men regularly wore a bonnet.[29] So if the North Berwick meeting did take place, the Devil was a man clearly able to exercise authority over the participants, although not so absolutely that they were prevented from making a voluble fuss when he breached an agreement on how one of their number was to be called. This man is unlikely to have been the Earl of Bothwell, as Margaret Murray suggested, if only because the records of confessions consistently speak of the two as separate individuals.[30] In any case, there is another candidate, Richard Graham, a well-known magician, someone frequently mentioned by the arrested witches as a key figure in their plots and magical operations, and the person who, according to the English ambassador, used to command Geillis Duncan to have the witches assemble.[31]

So, all things considered, it is possible that a meeting really did take place in the kirk of North Berwick. Apart from the detail of kissing Satan's arse, few of the characteristic features of a 'traditional' Sabbat appear in the narrative. There is no transvection, shape-shifting, feasting, or sexual orgy. The meeting is not presented to the reader as a conventional Sabbat.[32] It was, rather, one meeting among several, even if it was the largest and best-organised. But it was not the most important. *Newes* tells us that the Devil inveighed against James from the pulpit, but it was the meeting at Acheson's Haven which saw active operational magic directed against the King. Now, none of the other witchcraft episodes we have examined so far reveals any such organisation of witches' meetings. Three or four may be gathered together by one of the gentry or nobility for the purpose of working maleficent magic against one or more named individuals, as in the cases of Lady Foulis or William Leslie, but there is no evidence of any attempt to assemble witches in numbers as large as forty.[33] If, therefore, the North Berwick

29 Maxwell & Hutchison: *Scottish Costume*, 24, 26.
30 Murray: 'The 'Devil' of North Berwick', *SHR* 15 (1918), 318–20. *Newes* never even mentions Bothwell as art and part of the conspiracy, a curious but significant omission pointing to the influence Bothwell was still able to exercise in 1591 when the pamphlet was printed.
31 *CSPS* 10.502.
32 The picture of Satan in the pulpit, which accompanies *Newes*, is clearly not a representation of the man described in the pamphlet and the other evidence. But to show a man in a pulpit could not convey to the reader the immediate message that he was, in fact, the Devil. Indeed, he might even look like an ordinary minister. Hence the need for short-hand and visual impact.
33 One may perhaps discard 100 or 200 as the exaggerations of propaganda in contemporary records which are inimical to the witches. Interestingly enough, 'more than forty' is the figure quoted by the English ambassador writing to Burghley on 23 February, 1591, *CSPS* 10.467. On 7 December the previous year, this had been 'over thirty, and many others accused', *Ibid.*, 430.

incident actually happened, it was highly unusual, perhaps unique in Scottish witchcraft, and was summoned as part of the peculiar circumstances attendant upon this particular episode of magical treason.

The case of Richard Graham, a possible candidate for the role of Satan in these proceedings, bears further witness of an organised conspiracy. Graham was a practising magician who was on friendly terms with some remarkably powerful people; for, according to Bothwell himself, "I met with him once againe at the chancelours house, where in the presence of me and the chancelor, as we were ryding, he showed us a stick with nickes in yt all wrapped about with long heire, eyther of a man or a woman, and said yt was an enchanted stick".[34] What, one asks, was such a man doing in Maitland's house in the first place, by what amicability were the three of them able to go riding together, and why did Graham feel so at ease with the two nobles that he readily showed them what he claimed was an instrument of magic?[35] After his arrest, Graham sent a letter to the King. His chosen messenger to deliver it to James was William Schaw, Master of the King's Works, another not insignificant figure at Court.[36] Clearly, then, he was a man with important connections, but it is difficult to tell whether these were obtained because of his family or because he was a practitioner of magic well-known among the nobility.

Melville described him as a Westland man.[37] 'West', however, is a large designation and 'Graham' was a widespread family name. A remark by Barbara Napier, one of the arrested witches, may be worth noting. She wanted to get a golden ring enchanted and sent it to Richard Graham who was then in Fintry.[38] Now, it so happens that one of the most distinguished branches of the Graham name took its title from the lairdship there. The Grahams of Fintry were Catholics, closely allied to the Catholic Earls of Huntly and Crawford, and Sir David Graham, the sixth laird, was intimately involved in various Catholic plots both at home and abroad during the late 1580s and early 1590s. If, by any chance, Richard was related to this branch of the Grahams, it would help to explain his being at ease with some of the great names in Scotland. There is, however, no proving such a family connection.[39] Some of his acquaintance, on

34 *Calendar of Border Papers* 1.487.
35 There was a rumour that the Chancellor wore certain amulets about his neck and placed great confidence in their ability to protect him, Calderwood: *Historie of the Kirk* 5.148.
36 *JC26/2/17.*
37 *Memoirs,* 216.
38 *JC26/2/2.*
39 Fintry itself is about three miles NNE of Dundee. It had originally been part of an estate belonging to the Earls of Angus before it passed through marriage to the Grahams. It is interesting, therefore, to find that when the eighth Earl of Angus fell ill, the Countess sent for Richard Graham to come and cure him. Was this because he was well-known as a magician, or because of some remote family tie? The ninth Earl, one may note, was married to a Graham of Morphie in the Mearns.

the other hand, almost certainly got to know him because of his reputation and abilities. He raised the Devil in the Laird of Auchinleck's house, for example, and on another occasion in the house of Sir Lewis Bellenden who, we are informed, "was a lord of the session, council and exchequer . . . [who] by curiosity . . . dealt with a warlock, called Richard Graham, to raise the devil, who, having been raised in his own yard in the Canongate, he was thereby so terrified, that he took sickness and thereof died".[40]

The principal accusation against Graham was that he had conspired with the Earl of Bothwell to cause the King's death by magic. Its substance is set out most clearly in a letter written to Lord Burghley on 12 August, 1593 giving a report of Bothwell's trial:

> Certen metinges are specyfyed in the said depositions to have bene betwene thErle Bothwell and Greyme, and that therle Bothwell employd a man of his called Renian [= Ninian] Chirnsyde to procure more then xxtie metinges betwene his lordship and Greyme. The cheif pointes Greyme alledgeth were – that therle Bothwell should tell him that he was told in Italye that his King should favoure him well, and yet he should lose that love of him and be in dainger of his life by his kinge – wherin he requyred Greymes assistance to prevent yt. Wherupon Greyme had conference with other wytches (as he saith) amongst whome the conclusion was, that therle Bothwell should have a poison delyvered him, made of adders skynnes, tode skynnes, and the hipomanes in the forehead of a yong fole, all whiche being joyned by there arte together, should be such a poison as being laid where the kinge should comme, so as yt might dropp uppon his head, yt wold be a poison of such vehemencye, as should have presently cut him of. Another maner device for his destruction was this – to make his picture of waxe mingled with certen other thinges, which should have consumed and melted away in tyme, meanyng the King should consume as it did. A third mean to cut him of was – that he should be enchaunted to remayne in Denmarke, and not returne into Scotland.[41]

Chroniclers of events were, by and large, agreed that Bothwell had indeed conspired with Richard Graham[42] but Bothwell, as one might expect, poured scorn

---

40 Calderwood: *Historie of the Kirk* 5.148. The laird, John Boswell, was summoned before the Privy Council in March, 1591 to answer charges of consulting witches and practising magic himself, *RPC* 4.591. On Bellenden, see Scot: *Staggering State*, 130–1.

41 *Calendar of Border Papers* 1.486–7. This is a fairly accurate summary of the formal charge-sheet read aloud at Bothwell's trial, *JC26/2. Earl Bothwell Conspiracy.*

42 For example, Birrel: *Diary*, 25. Moysie: *Memoirs*, 85. *Historie of King James the Sext*, 242. A rumour at the time that the English ambassador had been an active member of the conspiracy never made headway because it was self-evident nonsense, *CSPS* 10.463.

on the idea, although he neither did nor could deny he both knew and had met him. His explanation of the acquaintance was that a friend of his (unnamed) had asked him to let Graham come and live within his bounds because he had been excommunicated (for what offence is not specified.) Bothwell's friend then asked the Earl to approach the King to see if he could obtain royal protection for Graham, an office Bothwell agreed to undertake, although he later said he had no opportunity to raise the matter with James. As a defence this is extraordinary. Who was the anonymous person so influential with Bothwell that he could ask him to get the King's protection for an excommunicate magician? What does it tell us about Bothwell that he should have said he would try? Why did the law-court choose to leave the name of this friend unspoken? It is a measure, once again, of the influence Graham was able to exert on his own behalf, and it says much about the favour with which at least some of the Scottish nobility regarded magic and its practitioners.

Since 11 November at least, Graham had been imprisoned in the Edinburgh tolbooth whence in April, 1591 he claimed that on more than one occasion while he was there Bothwell had sent him money, "persuading him to stand fast to the denial and to say that Bothwell had bene with him to enquyre whether his mother had bene bewitched or not, and for no other matter".[43] In his letter to the King, which William Schaw was meant to deliver, Graham set out a number of grievances. Unfortunately we do not have the original letter, only a summary, but the points contained therein are significant: (1) he was being kept under strict conditions in the Edinburgh tolbooth *against conditions made to him*; (2) those conditions were that he should have been lodged comfortably in Stirling Castle, with a servant to look after him; and (3) *he had kept his side of the bargain in saying what he was asked to say.*[44]

Some of this came out at the time, as Bothwell's defenders sought ways of trying to explain what had been going on. An anonymous letter addressed 'To the nobility' suggested that Graham had been suborned by the promise of a pardon and that he was only one among many who had been so manipulated. These people, said the letter, had been threatened with torture or bribed with the hope of a pardon to depone against the Earl, and eventually had admitted as much. "Even Grahame confessed that he had made the accusation bycaus it was aggreable unto the humeurs of some, and to save himself from torture and execution".[45] There is

---

43 *Exchequer Rolls* 22.160. *CSPS* 10.502.

44 *JC26/2/17.* My italics. Graham may have been fat. If so, this could indicate that he liked his food and would therefore have found the straitened conditions in Edinburgh particularly trying. See Dunlap: 'King James and some witches', 40–2.

45 *Warrender Papers* 2.159–60. Bothwell maintained at his trial that Graham had said nothing against him until he had entered into an agreement with certain people to testify against him in return for a comfortable imprisonment and a guarantee he would not be executed. Bothwell named some of these people as the Earl of Morton, the Chancellor, the King's advocate, Sir John Carmichael, and Sir George Hume, *Border Papers* 1.487.

also what appears to be a scribbled aide-memoire by Bothwell's advocates, expanding upon these points. Graham's evidence, it says, should not be admissible because (1) it is unsupported by other witnesses, (2) he was not sworn to tell the truth, (3) he had been subjected to threats, (4) he was a depraved individual whose evidence ought not to be believed for that reason, (5) he was a sorcerer who had renounced his faith in Christ and had been rebaptised by the Devil, (6) he had committed perjury, (7) he was a participant in the crimes which were being tried, (8) he was someone else's instrument, (9) he was inconstant and kept changing his story, (10) his life was full of faults and mischief and "not haldand the ryt fayth", (11) he was an accuser who should not be believed, and (12) the details of his depositions were different from those of other people.[46]

These claims and counter-claims give the strongest possible impression that something was indeed afoot. In about April, 1591 Barbara Napier, one of the accused, wrote to Bothwell, urging him "to stand fast, showing that his enemies had devised his dittay".[47] Several people read her letter before it finally reached the King, and yet James himself appears to have been in two minds about whether to believe Graham or Bothwell. He talked to the Queen to see what she thought about it; he wrote to his Chancellor, Maitland, that most of those witches who were not principals in the case seemed to be confused; and whereas, on the one hand, he was reluctant to be the means whereby "the Devil or any necromancer shall be found true in their answers", he also remarked that "the evidence against Bothwell for conspiring his death was so weak as the assize of the nobility would hardly be satisfied to declare him guilty".[48]

The situation which faced James was certainly very odd. He knew, as our previous survey of magic and witchcraft has made clear, that the Scottish nobility was perfectly prepared to employ magicians and to work alongside them whenever personal gain or revenge suggested this might be fruitful.

---

46 *JC*26/2/9.
47 *CSPS* 10.506. This was in spite of the fact that she was not altogether amicable towards him, having forbidden her daughter to be friendly with him, *JC*6/3, p.5, perhaps because Bothwell had an unsavoury reputation when it came to women. See *Records of the Synod of Lothian and Tweeddale*, 27 = 7 April, 1591. On the following paragraph, see Maxwell-Stuart: "The fear of the King is death", 218–19.
48 *CSPS* 10.502, 510, 504, 506, 511. The pressure to sway the King's mind was relentless. An anonymous note was pinned to the door of his chamber in May, 1591, advising him 'to examyne and chardge by tortours Mr John Graham and Glanorchye for conspiring the death of the King with the help and meanes of Bothwell', *Ibid.*, 519. 'John' is presumably a mistake for 'Richard'. The appearance of Sir Donald Campbell, Laird of Glenorchy, illustrates the way in which disparate individuals could be swept into this scandal for no reason other than the personal malice of whoever might care to denounce them. Glenorchy was in trouble later on, but for entirely different reasons.

There was therefore nothing exceptional about Bothwell's being accused either of consulting a magician or of using him to operate magic. Bothwell himself admitted to meeting Graham (although not as often as Graham claimed) and sending him to the Countess of Angus in order that he should magically cure the Earl of sickness. In spite of the fact that Bothwell, the Earl, and the Countess were all breaking the 1563 Witchcraft Act, however, it would not be the accusation of consorting with magicians and witches which was intended to do Bothwell damage: it was the treason of plotting the King's death, as well as that of the Queen.

Since we have only a summary of Graham's letter to the King, we cannot tell how much detail he put down on paper. But two points are worth noting: (a) he claimed he had made a bargain (with whom this document does not say) to give evidence in a case against Bothwell in return for comfortable lodgement in Stirling Castle; and (b) he chose to send this letter to the King. Why did he wish to avoid Edinburgh and stay in Stirling? The castle was a royal palace, of course, and James often stayed there, so Graham may well have felt that there he would have that protection he had asked Bothwell to obtain for him in earlier days. He was, after all, an excommunicate magician and the Kirk, as well as Bothwell himself, might seek to have him prosecuted for offences which, by law, carried the death penalty. But why tell the King he had made a bargain? Was there a veiled threat to retract his evidence unless his conditions were changed, and are we to infer from this that the bargain had been made with James himself? Or are we to understand that he was complaining to James that a bargain he had made with someone else was being ignored, in which case are we to infer that James was being warned, perhaps indirectly, that the evidence against Bothwell was tainted? Without the actual letter, we cannot tell. The former will assume that James had hatched a complex plot to rid himself of the Earl whose conduct during the summer of 1590 had veered, it is true, from outrageous to irritating; but could not much the same be said of certain other nobles, such as the Earl of Huntly? The second conjecture will suggest that someone else was trying to cause Bothwell's downfall, in which case one must ask *cui bono*, who would benefit? The phraseology of Barbara Napier's letter and of the anonymous letter to the nobility suggests that more than one person was involved.

These are questions to which we shall return, for there are further possible complications to consider. One of the points listed by Bothwell's advocates, for example, raises a question. No. 10 says that Graham did not hold the right faith. This is a peculiar phrase if it is simply intended to indicate that he was untrustworthy, and one also notes that he chose to send his letter to William Schaw for forwarding to the King. Now, Schaw is perhaps not the obvious choice for such a purpose. Why did not Graham send his letter to Maitland, since he was personally acquainted with him and Maitland was not on particularly good terms with Bothwell at the time? But Schaw was a Catholic, and one wonders whether "not holding the right faith" may be an indication that Graham was a Catholic, too. Certainly if he was related to Sir David Graham of Fintry, there is a fair chance that he was, for Sir David was a fervent Catholic, so much so that he was executed on 15 February, 1593, principally for his involvement in the affair of the Spanish blanks, a conspiracy to aid a Spanish attempt to land in Scotland and re-impose the Catholic faith by force of arms.[49]

There is also an interesting remark in one of Agnes Sampson's confessions to the effect that the Devil told her "that the ministeris wald destroy the King and all Scotland, but if he would use his counsall he sowld destroy thame".[50] The theological interpretation is obvious, but if the Devil were here a man rather than a spirit, the sentence opens itself to a political interpretation: the power of the Kirk is getting out of hand, and a living person professes himself able to advise James on the best way to bring it permanently under his control. Would this refer to a Protestant figure wishing to exalt the Crown over the Kirk, or to a Catholic whose aim might be to use James to destroy the Protestant establishment and thus open the way for a reintroduction of Catholicism to Scotland? James's tussle with the Kirk over bishops and relations between Church and State by now was long-standing and supports the former view; on the other hand, his well-known willingness to employ Catholics in his government and tolerate (not without impatience and occasional bouts of anger, it is true) rebellious behaviour from Catholic nobles in particular might have the result of encouraging someone to believe the latter. We shall therefore have to bear in mind the religious question as we try to disentangle what was going on at this time; and, indeed, the religious question raises its head from the very start with David Seton, the depute baillie of Tranent, whose suspicions and illegal torture of his servant Geillis Duncan led to the discovery of both the treason and the ramifications of witchcraft in East Lothian. The Setons of Tranent were Catholics, and the presbytery of Haddington had problems throughout the 1590s in getting Lord and Lady Seton to communicate according to Protestant forms.[51]

David Seton's wife was Katharine Moscrop; Katharine Moscrop was the sister of Patrick MacCalyean *alias* Moscrop; and Euphame MacCalyean was Patrick's wife. David Seton was therefore allied through marriage to some of the second 'group' of people who were accused of witchcraft in this case, the legal gentry of Edinburgh. Euphame MacCalyean was involved in a property dispute with her uncle, Henry MacCalyean, the subject of their lawsuit being

49 Mudie & Walker: *Mains Castle*, 11–12.
50 *JC*26/2/13, folio 5.
51 Seton: *History of the Family of Seton* 1.212–14.

lands which, at her conviction for witchcraft, were escheat to the Crown and given by the King to Sir James Sandilands, a gentleman of the bedchamber.[52] So there was a feud within the MacCalyean family to which David Seton belonged, and concerning which he must have had an opinion. Did David Seton, then, set off the accusations of witchcraft as part of a personal campaign within the context of this feud, hoping thereby to destroy an heiress whose escheated lands might then come to him as a legal officer involved in the case? This is the logic of a pattern which Louise Yeoman discerns in a series of similar cases in which the accused person is heir to property, or the parent of the sole heir, and is also involved in a quarrel with the person making the accusation. I do not dispute this general observation. On the other hand, I think it tangential rather than central to what we find in East Lothian. The main thrust of the arrests, interrogations, and trials in this concatenation of incidents is the treason directed against the King. Other evidence relating to magical activities serves only to indicate that the people involved were active witches, some of them long standing, and that the accusation of treasonable magic brought against them is thus the more likely to be both credible and true. So if Seton's investigations of his servant had produced a growing number of accused persons, one of whom turned out to be Euphame MacCalyean, he would no doubt have rejoiced at the opportunity this gave him of benefiting from a resolution of the family dispute. But this is a long way from saying he engineered a sub-plot, as it were, within the wider tragedy and used the treason trials as a cover for personal pursuit of financial gain.[53]

So let us turn to the question of evidence that Euphame MacCalyean and Barbara Napier were actually witches. The Crown seemed to have a good case against both. Barbara Napier, for example, was acquainted with the eighth Earl of Angus and his third wife, Jean Lyon, the daughter of Lord Glamis and widow of Robert Douglas of Lochleven. When Lady Angus was pregnant, Barbara asked Agnes Sampson to help stop her vomiting, and when Lady Angus owed Barbara some recompense but failed to pay it – it sounds as though relations between the two had cooled – Barbara again approached Agnes and gave her a ring to enchant, the object being, presumably, that when Lady Angus wore it, she would feel kindly disposed

---

52 A man of no small reputation, according to the *Historie of King James the Sext*, 265. By a curious coincidence, his second wife was a Barbara Napier. The issues involving these families have been discussed in detail in a number of unpublished lectures and conference papers by Louise Yeoman.

53 It is worthwhile pointing out that Seton himself had been the butt of maleficent magic. Geillis Duncan, in conjunction with two other witches, Bessie Thomson and Grey Meill, was accused of using magic to do him harm, *JC*26/2/13, folio 2, and Donald Robson confessed that John Cockburn had promised him £50 to destroy David Seton's goods, *JC*26/2/10, folio 1.

once more to Barbara.[54] On each occasion, it is notable that Barbara travelled furth of Edinburgh to meet Agnes, first in Dalkeith and then in Cameron, a small village in the east of Fife. She could not afford, it seems, to play the *grande dame* with Agnes and have the witch come to her. By contrast, Barbara was sent by Lady Angus to traffick on her behalf with Agnes, because she and the Earl had had a falling out and the Countess needed help.[55] Preparations were then set on foot to enchant the Earl to death by means of a picture or image, a magical operation which seems to have worked because the Earl died on 4 August, 1588. The purpose of Barbara's visit to Cameron was to make sure her husband, Archibald Douglas, who was then in the West country at the raid of Dumfries, would come home safely. Apparently there was an Archie Farquhar who Barbara feared might do him harm. Agnes's answer was to promise her a wax image which she was to put under the foot of Archie's bed and, this being duly delivered three or four days later, Barbara paid Agnes with a piece of linen cloth.[56] Barbara also consulted Richard Graham. As we have noted earlier, on one occasion she sent him a ring to enchant, and when her son was ill, she paid him to render assistance. "This was done in Johnne Ramsayis hous outwith the West-poirt of Edinburgh . . . att the quhilk tyme, sche inquyrit att the said Rychie Grahame, gif the King wald come hame or nocht",[57] which dates the occasion to the first half of 1589.

In addition to her involvement in the treason plot, then, Barbara was accused of seeking to kill by magic, relieve the discomforts of pregnancy, influence another person's feelings towards her, and protect her husband against malice – magical operations of which we have now seen several examples from other cases. Euphame MacCalyean, on the other hand, offers one or two fresh insights. Her dittay, much more extensive than Barbara's, contains 28 articles,[58] five of which refer to incidents connected with magical attempts to bewitch the King to death and prevent the Queen's arrival in Scotland, and one which simply accuses her of being a well-known witch. The assize convicted her on this last point and on two of the five which had her actively present during two of the East Lothian witches' conventions.

Thirteen of the remaining 22 articles, however, concern her marriage and personal life. From the very start of her marriage to Patrick MacCalyean,

---

54 Pitcairn: *Criminal Trials* 1.2.242–3. JC26/2/4, folio 1.
55 *JC26/2/14.*
56 *JC26/2/4,* folios 1 and 2. Douglas may have been in the West in the Spring or Summer of 1587 when King James himself went there at the head of a large army to quell disturbances in the Border country and to let the General Assembly see that he was responding to their complaints that there were attempts to revive Catholicism in the area.
57 Pitcairn: *Criminal Trials* 1.2.243.
58 Pitcairn: *op.cit. supra*, 1.2.249–56.

Euphame seems to have hated the union and done her best to get rid of her husband. First, she consulted Agnes Somerville in Dunfermline, "inquyring of hir, 'Gif sche knew ony wittie or skilfull wemene in the countrey, that will owthir caus your husband love yow, or ellis gett your will of him' ", and sent along two of Patrick's clean shirts to be enchanted by them. Apparently the shirts were returned, duly bewitched, and Patrick fell sick (item 4).[59] Next, having tried unsuccessfully to poison him,[60] she made life at home so unpleasant that he was forced to go abroad for a whole and seek peace and quiet in France. But Euphame was not satisfied, especially as he did not stay there permanently and so, "still invying his health and seiking to distroy him be Wichcraft", she sent her servant, Josias Coupar, to Catherine Campbell then living in the Canongate, an Irish woman well known to be a witch, along with Patrick's doublet: "quhilk dowblett the said Wich sprinklit with blude, and inchantit it with utheris sorcereis, and randerit itt agane to the said Josias your servand". All this was done very early in the morning before Patrick got up. The result was a serious illness, declared by the surgeons to be unnatural (that is, probably caused by magic), which lasted for several months (item 16). But even this was not sufficient, and Euphame consulted Catherine once again "anent the bewiching and slauchter of Patrik Moscrop, your husband,[61] quhairby ye mycht gett ane uther guidman; and consulting with hir, quhome ye sould marie" (item 3).

Whether Catherine duly advised her, or whether Euphame discovered the alternative for herself, her affection seems to have lighted upon Joseph Douglas, the Laird of Pumpherston, who was already betrothed to a young girl, Mary Sandilands. Euphame first tried to seduce him by love-magic, using an offer of marriage to her daughter as a cover for her activities, and as a token of her love and sincerity gave him a neck chain, two belt chains, a ring, and an emerald and other jewels (item 12). When this failed to make an impression, Euphame then sent her servant, Janet Drummond, armed with items of magic, to persuade Mary not to wed Joseph on the grounds that he was already betrothed to someone else and in any case was suffering from venereal disease (item 14); and when this did not work either, she consulted an old witch in the Canongate, Janet Cunningham *alias* Lady Bothwell, on the best way to poison Joseph (item 13),[62] and finally sent Janet Drummond once again to bewitch Mary with a view to preventing the

59 They had to be taken "over the water" to where the witches lived. Whether this means the witches lived north of Loch Leven or even further, north of the Tay, is not clear.
60 His face, neck, hands, and whole body broke out in red spots but because he was young, he was able to expel the poison before it killed him (item 5).
61 'Moscrop' was his alias.
62 Watson tries to connect Janet with John Fian *alias* Cunningham, and wonders if Janet got her alias because she had been a lover of the fourth Earl of Bothwell, *Bothwell and the Witches*, 186. Neither suggestion, however, is particularly credible or, indeed, necessary.

marriage from taking place (item 15).[63] Joseph Douglas, however, had kept the presents Euphame had sent him and as these were too valuable to abandon along with her hopes, on no fewer than seven occasions she sent Janet Drummond to Agnes Sampson to ask how they might be recovered. On one of these Agnes raised a spirit who could be heard but not seen, and the spirit gave response that the jewels would be delivered to Janet, although whether they ever were we do not know (item 16). It is a pity we have no further details of this incident because purely auditory cases of this type are noticeably less common than those which are visual or combine visual and auditory experience.[64] Was Agnes a skilled ventriloquist and if so, did she consciously or unconsciously project a spirit-voice; or did she fall into a trance and speak while possessed by a spirit?[65] This is the only occasion in the records on which Agnes is credited with an operation of this particular kind, although it is unlikely to have been unique in her methods of magical working.

Euphame's malice did not, unfortunately, stop at her husband, for she was accused of bewitching to death her nephew-in-law, a lad of seventeen, (item 9); her father-in-law (item 19); and a six-year old child, Lilias MacCalyean (item 22). This last shows how the slightest action might be re-interpreted once a person was suspect of witchcraft. Euphame had rubbed Lilias's face with a napkin one Saturday afternoon, and not long afterwards the child had fallen down at the entry to the close where Euphame lived, and died of her injuries. Her dittay also indicates the prominent role played by servants both in acting as go-betweens for their employers on errands to and from witches or victims, and also as subsequent witnesses for the Crown once charges of witchcraft had been laid. No one, it seems, was in any position to be a hero to his valet.[66]

---

63 Her plan did not succeed. The marriage contract was signed on 15 July, 1586. Euphame is also accused of using magic to kill two of Joseph's children (item 17). It is interesting that after Euphame was executed, the King chose to grant her escheated property to a member of the Sandilands family. Perhaps he considered it a form of poetic justice.

64 See further Green & McCreery: *Apparitions*, 80–90.

65 'Ventriloquist' is not meant to imply that Agnes was necessarily a fraud. Prophetic ventriloquism has a very ancient lineage, going right back to the ancient Greeks. A succinct early definition of its practitioners is given by the fifth-century AD exegete, Theodoret of Cyrrhene, who refers to them as 'people who operate by means of evil spirits. The Greeks used to call them 'those who prophesy from within themselves' ', *Question 29 on Leviticus* = Migne, *Patrologia Graeca* 80.349.

66 Nevertheless, it was not wise to cross Euphame. She conceived a deadly malice against Janet Cockburn who, for some reason unexplained, fetched Euphame's purse, belt, mirror, and some of her clothes from her bedroom and dumped them on a table. Patrick MacCalyean made as though to open Euphame's purse, and Euphame burst out to Janet, 'Weill, madin [young woman], haif ye lattin this be done? Ye sall repent itt fra youre hairt'; and so she did, for Euphame and an Irish witch scattered earth from a grave and enchanted powder over places where Janet was bound to walk, and Janet fell seriously ill from palpitations and shortness of breath (item 10). 'Madin' was a term used of a servant-girl.

Euphame's use of cloths and clothing belonging to her intended victim as a means whereby maleficent power could be transferred to him or her by a kind of magical infection reminds us of the intention lying behind Agnes's attempt to get hold of some of King James's linen, "as shirt, handkercher, napkin, or any other thing". Such cloths could be turned into potent carriers of malefice but did not actually have to belong to the intended victim. Touching them might be enough. Euphame, for example, consulted Agnes Sampson on the best way to attain revenge on John MacGill's wife. Again Janet Drummond acted as their go-between and brought Euphame from Agnes some enchanted objects which were then wrapped in a child's apron and neck-cloth and thrown in at the MacGills' window (item 20). Not all Euphame's servants were as complaisant as Janet, however, and some of them decided to reveal what Janet had done. In consequence, John MacGill made a complaint and Euphame had to instruct Janet to deny everything.

But something had gone wrong and Janet became troubled by frightening visions both day and night: "Scho vissiblie, in ane chalmer flwre of youris [on the floor of one of the rooms in your house], att twa eftir none, saw ane naikit man stand in the middis of the said chalmer, with ane quhyte scheit [white sheet] about him". Another servant, too, Janet Acheson, who had got up at midnight to draw herself a drink, saw a man behind her, clad only in a shirt which he was wearing upside down, the sleeves dangling by his legs and the tail over his head.[67] These sights are reminiscent of figures wearing only a shroud, which sometimes appear to those who have the second sight,[68] seen, as it were, in parody, as one might expect from the circumstances. In spite of these magical backlashes, however, a fresh attempt was made to bewitch MacGill's wife, Elizabeth Home. This time the objects consisted of an image made from a mixture of flour and clay, and a picture of Elizabeth embroidered upon what was presumably a representative rather than a full-length shroud, these two things being wrapped in an old black cap which Agnes enchanted, along with five strands of knotted threads (black, red, orange, yellow, and brown), which Euphame herself prepared. The whole package was then thrown in at the MacGills' kitchen window by Janet Drummond.

So Euphame had some skill in the magic arts and did not always need someone else to enchant objects for her and her dittay includes an unusual account of how she came by that skill. "Ye causit ane uther Wich", it says,

---

67 The dittay adds that Janet Acheson was troubled with urchins = hedgehogs. Pitcairn's note suggests that these may have been "imps of the Devil", and indeed the Scots *hurcheon* can be used figuratively of a mischievous child or slovenly individual.

68 For example, 'When a shroud is perceiv'd about one, it is a sure Prognostick of Death, the time is judged according to the height of it about the Person', Martin: *Description*, 302.

"quha duelt in Sanct Ninianis Raw, inaugwrat yow in the said craft, with the girth of ane grit bikar [the hoop of a large barrel], turnand the same oft owre your heid and nek, and oftimes round about your heid" (item 7). Again, this was seen by someone else, a child called Marion Love, who thereupon told her mother and father what she had witnessed. But Euphame found out and bewitched the two adults, causing them both physical pain and financial hardship (item 8). She appears to have left Marion alone, perhaps because Marion was a child and had merely told her parents. The others, however, seem to have spoken openly about the incident, and so maybe that is why they were punished.

This account is particularly interesting, partly because it is the only narrative of such a ceremony from this period, and partly because it implies the possibility that a person could be endowed with magical skills by ritual means. Four words or phrases are important to a proper understanding of the passage: (1) 'ye causit' indicates that Euphame asked or instructed the other witch to perform the ceremony; (2) 'ane uther Wich' implies that Euphame was a witch already, but this is the dittay's assumption anyway and so the phrase need not necessarily refer to Euphame's status at the time of the ritual; (3) 'inaugwrat' carries the sense of its Latin root, to consecrate a person chosen for a priesthood or some other office; and (4) 'craft', which at this period might refer to power and to magic as well as to skill in a particular art. We are therefore presented with the suggestion that Euphame wanted to acquire magical powers and asked an Edinburgh witch to perform a ceremony which would give them to her, although it is interesting that the word 'craft' suggests a system or collection of practical skills which may be taught, and so one wonders whether the rite with the hoop may have been a ritual preliminary to a lesson or series of lessons in which the Edinburgh witch as instructress passed on her knowledge of magic to Euphame as pupil or apprentice. Whether the ritual was one peculiar to this witch, her particular way of working – which would explain why Euphame approached her especially, and asked her to perform it – or whether she indulged in some mumbo-jumbo for a client she thought naive enough to be impressed by such a thing, is difficult to tell. Euphame, however, does not strike one as naive, so the former interpretation may be the more likely of the two.[69]

Now, unless one is going to argue that every piece of evidence presented to

---

69 The rite has its parallels. Rorie recorded an incident in which the iron rim of a
    large, disued washing-tub was wrapped with a straw rope. The rope was
    sprinkled with oil and set on fire, and then a sick child, thought to be suffering
    the effects of the evil eye, was passed through several times to disperse the
    bewitchment, *Folk Tradition*, 128–9. It must be noted, however, that the
    ceremony was observed in the nineteenth century, although of course its origins
    may have been earlier, and that its object was quite different from what Euphame
    had in mind.

the courts which tried Barbara and Euphame was fantasy, delivered out of fear or a desire to please or placate (an argument which is fruitless in view of the immense range of confirmatory evidence that people high and low throughout the whole of Europe at this time subscribed to the truth of magic and its claims, and practised its operations),[70] there can be little doubt that, like so many of their contemporaries, both Barbara and Euphame had performed, requested, and taken part in magical ceremonies and were therefore, by the terms of Scottish law, guilty of the crime of witchcraft. So the task of their assizes can scarcely have been to consider the theoretical question of whether such respectable women would have been prepared to engage in any or all the practices alleged against them, but whether they had actually done so; and this, on 8 May, 1591 they proceeded to do in the case of Barbara Napier.[71]

Barbara's proloquitors consisted of two professional advocates, John Moscrop and John Russell, and three members of her own family, but the two advocates were very reluctant to appear in her case and had to be forced to do so under threat of being put to the horn, that is, declared rebels or outlaws.[72] Indeed, so reluctant were they that when he did come to court, John Russell had to ask if he might see the dittay and be granted a postponement of the trial to give him time to read it. The court, however, refused his request, and so the two advocates settled down to the task of raising technical points against the form and wording of the dittay.[73] These preliminaries being finished, the court passed to choosing members of the assize and Barbara's proloquitors objected to three of them: David Seton, because he was a tenant of Lord Seton who was tangentially connected with matters alleged in Barbara's dittay; John Seton, brother of David Seton in Tranent, the *fons et origo* of this whole affair; and Joseph Douglas of Pumpherstone, who had

---

70 A point which does not suggest, either, that everything confessed by accused witches was necessarily true *au pied de la lettre*.

71 She had been released on bail, with her brother, William Napier, acting as cautioner, on 23 February, *Extracts*, 59. It may be this that misled Watson into thinking she was released after her trial, *Bothwell and the Witches*, 140.

72 Details of Barbara's defence are recorded in the High Court Minute Book, *JC6/ 3*. The family members who appeared for her were Andrew, William, and Alexander Napier.

73 A good example of their style of argument is the following: "The said barbara allegeis that for ony part of the dittay concerning the kingis maiestie scho offeris hir selff *suo motu* [of her own volition] to the knawledge of assyse. As to the rest of the dittay, [scho] allegeis that the samen is not relevant except sa far as concerns the kingis maiestie, because the act of parliament concerns only twa memberis, viz. consulteris of wichecraft and consulting . . . As to the secund, anent counsall, it is newir [never] affermit that I consultit with the saidis personis as wiches upoun ane matter of wichcraft *ad sumendum mali* [with a view to undertaking an evil act]. Naythar yit is it affermit that the saidis persounis the tyme of the consultatioun or att ony tyme before wer convict or declarit wichis, or sa commonlie haldin and repute".

been a hostile witness against both Barbara and Euphame MacCalyean. After further legal argument anent the dittay, it then came to the point where Barbara was asked to plead guilty or not guilty. She answered with "hir constant denyall of the haill dittay except the speiking of Anne Sampsoun for the help of the Lady Angus, Mistress Jeane Lyonnis, and the speiking with Rychard Grahame for the healthe of hir sone". In other words, she was willing to grant the lesser (though capital) charges of seeking help from a witch and a magician, but rejected completely the capital charge of treason.

It is scarcely surprising, then, that the assize found her guilty and that on 10 May she was sentenced to death in accordance with the law. In an effort to postpone execution, however, Barbara protested that she was pregnant, a claim which, if true, would mean a delay at least until after her child had been born. But complications intervened. For while the assize seems to have found her guilty of consultation, in accordance with her open admission in court, it had declared her not guilty of treason, and this verdict infuriated the King who thereupon issued a warrant of complaint on 14 May against members of the assize, accusing them of wilful error, for which they could be put on trial. Summonses were therefore sent out on 20, 25, and 27 May and the assize re-assembled on 9 June to have this charge heard in court.[74] Only a retraction of the verdict would be sufficient to appease the King's anger, so the assizers confessed to an ignorant rather than a wilful error, and thereby Barbara was duly convicted of treason.[75]

Why was the King so fierce for a full conviction? The fact of the matter is, he had been listening not only to Agnes Sampson, John Fian, Janet Straton, and the others, but also to Richard Graham and the Earl of Bothwell, and although he was in two minds about what to think, the weight of evidence was beginning to tell against Bothwell. On 17 April the Chancellor openly accused him of conspiring with Graham to kill the King by magic, and Bothwell was brought to Edinburgh Castle where he and Graham were confronted with each other – a standard practice when two alleged witches

---

74 Pitcairn: *Criminal Trials* 1.2.244–7. *CSPS* Appendix 2.591. *JC26/2/24*.

75 *JC49/7* records that she was executed on 8 May, the day of her trial. She was not sentenced until the 10th, but the mistake is understandable. It would not have taken long to ascertain whether or not she really was pregnant, and if she had been caught out in a lie, the sentence of the court would have been carried out soon thereafter. One should note that by her own admission Barbara had incurred the death penalty under the provisions of the 1563 Witchcraft Act, so a verdict of not guilty on the treason charges could not have saved her. The proceedings on 9 June were a legal matter involving her assize, and her presence would not have been required. There is, however, a problem with *JC49/7*, for an entry in the burgh records for 23 February, 1592 indicates that she had been kept in prison until then and was now to be released on bail, her brother William standing surety for her, *Extracts from the Records of the Burgh of Edinburgh*, 59. February, as it happens, is nine months after she had claimed to be pregnant. Are we to understand that her claim had been genuine?

had offered evidence against each other. By 5 May the King was saying on the one hand that the evidence against Bothwell was too weak to guarantee his conviction, and yet the English ambassador had formed the impression that James was convinced of Bothwell's guilt, perhaps because Bothwell's servant, Ninian Chirnside, whom he had used on several occasions to fetch Richard Graham to meet him, had been talking about his role in the affair. On 8 May Barbara Napier's assize acquitted her of the charges of treason against her, and on 9 May Bothwell was imprisoned on charges of treasonable conspiracy with witches among whom, of course, it was alleged Barbara had played an important part.[76] It is small wonder, therefore, that the King, whose nerves must have been affected by the whole business with which he had been living since the previous November, exploded in exasperation. Whatever he may have thought of the quality of the evidence of minor players in this drama, and whatever reservations he may have had about Graham's role in it, he must have known that Bothwell was perfectly capable not only of dabbling in magic but also of conspiring against him, since his behaviour both before and after James's visit to Scandinavia was unstable and sometimes frightening.[77]

But if the King was indeed hesitant at this point, there came fresh evidence to clinch the case against Bothwell. On 14 June, James granted private audience to a witch from Redden, a small place near the bank of the River Tweed about a mile from the English border and four miles north-east of Kelso. She told James that Graham was altogether right and that Bothwell was indeed guilty of trying to bewitch James to death. She also admitted being present when the King's image was being roasted in Agnes Sampson's house, and heard Agnes say there were important people involved in the conspiracy, as well as poor folk such as themselves, naming Euphame MacCalyean and Barbara Napier in particular, "bot expressit not ther proper names".[78] For-

---

76 *CSPS* 10.502. Maxwell-Stuart: 'The fear of the King is death', 219. *CSPS* Appendix 2.590–1. In the light of the accumulation of evidence with which he was faced over a period of several months, James's belief that the charges of treason against Barbara were justly brought should be given proper weight, and it is frivolous to suggest that he pursued Barbara out of mere vindictiveness. Prosecuting an assize for wilfully bringing in an improper verdict was not something James had invented. It was a charge which had been available under Scottish law since the fifteenth century. See Walker: *A Legal History of Scotland* 3. 472–3.

77 See, for example, Watson: *Bothwell and the Witches*, 60–7, 75–84.

78 *CSPS* 10.531. *JC*26/2/11. That last is a curious addition. One is reminded of the meeting in North Berwick where the witches became angry because the Devil had used Robert Grierson's real name instead of his alias. We are told that the woman had recently been in England. Several witches connected with the East Lothian affair had fled thither, and David Seton had been given the task of fetching them back. Since the deponer admits to having been part of that conspiracy, it is possible she was one of the fugitives, returned to Scotland either of her own free will or under inducement.

tuitous or engineered, her intervention appears to have steered the King into making up his mind that Bothwell's protestations of innocence were not to be trusted. He would not have so many kings in this realm, he remarked with a degree of understandable bitterness at the rumour that certain people were saying they would deliver Bothwell from prison, and on 19 June he took measures to circumvent them. Bothwell should indeed be released, but on terms the King dictated, and he should be granted his liberty on condition that it was spent in exile abroad. The English ambassador was impressed. "Thus Bothwell has found the King's mind more resolute than he or others looked for", he remarked in a latter to Burghley.[79] Bothwell, however, took matters into his own hands. On the 21st he learned of the King's decision, broke out of the castle, and fled to Caithness, only to be declared traitor and his possessions escheated to the Crown, the King's declaration thereanent, issued on 25 June, drawing attention to Bothwell's former rebellious attempts to interfere with Scotland's government and James's clemency towards him after the Earl had been convicted of treason by an assize.[80] During the next two years his behaviour became wilder and less predictable as he and James circled each other round Scotland, like two wrestlers testing each other's weakness and looking for a chance to make the final fall. But the Earl was unable to resist the growing pressure to bring him to trial and at last, on 10 August, 1593, he faced an assize of his peers.[81]

The dittay drawn up against him gives a very clear picture of his alleged dealings with Richard Graham.[82] Six meetings between them are recorded in detail, and others are said to have taken place at various times in Crichton, Syntoun, and Kelso. But a similar pattern seems to have been observed at each of the six key meetings. Bothwell would send his servant, Ninian Chirnside, to fetch Graham from wherever Graham happened to be staying at the time – the man appears to have led a peripatetic existence, at least during this

---

79 *CSPS* 10.531, 533. On 21 May James had taken the trouble to consult the presbytery of Edinburgh on two questions: (1) Did the Bible make consulting witches an offence equal to that of actually being a witch? and (2) Was it allowable for the King to punish the one offence differently from the other? The presbytery replied that the two offences were equally heinous, and that his Majesty could not ignore God's law and dispense with the divinely ordained punishment, *CH2/121/1*.

80 See Pitcairn: *Criminal Trials* 1.2.259, 268–75, 278–81, 287–9, 291, 293–7. *JC27/32*.

81 Bothwell's most harebrained scheme included an attempt to seize James in person while the King was at Holyrood on 27 and 28 December, 1591. See Melville: *Memoirs*, 397–401. *Historie of King James the Sext*, 243–5. Cf. Watson: *Bothwell and the Witches*, 77–84. Bothwell's proloquitors for the trial were Thomas Craig, John Preston, and John Russell, the advocate who had been so reluctant to appear for Barbara Napier.

82 *JC26/2*: Earl of Bothwell, Conspiracy.

period[83] – and would then either ask about the state of his relationship with the King, or complain that there was no improvement therein, or would inquire about the best persons and means to implement the conspiracy against James's life. Graham would then consult his spirit and give response.[84]

It is interesting to note that Graham claimed to be attended by such a spirit and that he does not seem to have undertaken any reply to Bothwell's questions without first consulting it. Indeed, on one occasion when the two men met in a glen near Crichton and Bothwell asked the perfectly simple question, "Gif he knew ony wemen to be craftit and meit for the executioun of the said purpois" (that is, killing the King by magic), Graham refused to answer at once "bot delayit for ane certane space quhill [until] he raisit the spreit be his devillishe incantatiounes, prayeris, and invocatioun . . . be making of ane triangle".[85] It sounds rather like Alison Pearson's relationship with 'Thomas Reid', and we may well interpret Graham's spirit as some form of guide. On the other hand, he maintained that *sithean* really did exist and that spirits could materialise and thus be seen, although they were not tangible;[86] and since he seems to have summoned his spirit by ritual magic, perhaps a closer parallel is Sir William Stewart who summoned 'Obirion', or Janet Boyman invoking *sithean* or other spirits by her 'elreth' well.

The dittay also suggests that Bothwell knew Agnes Sampson, for when he and Graham met on the third recorded occasion, in Sir James Newton's

83 He had *entrée* into several houses in the south-east and south-west of Scotland. John Provand, Thomas Law, John Wood in Monkland, Sir James Newton, Alexander Johnston, and John Barron are all recorded as being willing to receive him. Of these, John Provand is perhaps the best known. A wealthy merchant and burgess of Edinburgh, he was an ally of the Earl of Morton and was suspected of being the Earl's accomplice in poisoning the Earl of Atholl in 1579. See Lynch: *Edinburgh and the Reformation*, 158. See also *RPC* 4.181, 415, 493, 704. *RMS* (1580–93), no. 1730.

84 Graham informed the King that he had a familiar spirit which showed him many things, Melville: *Memoirs*, 396.

85 The triangle is reminiscent of one of Aleister Crowley's invocations in the desert beyond Tangiers. He drew a circle – the normal means whereby the invoking magician is kept safe from the entities he is summoning to appear – and beside it a triangle within which the evoked spirit was to be confined. See J.O. Fuller: *The Magical Dilemma of Victor Neuburg* (Mandrake 1990), 137. That there was felt to be a degree of potential danger in this practice of invocation can be seen from the observation in Bothwell's dittay that "in the raising of the spreit [Graham] conjurit him that he sould nocht trouble the air, the walter, nor the erd". Modern ceremonial magicians, in similar vein, dismiss evoked spirits with a command that in departing to their rightful place of abode, they do no harm to any living creature. Graham, incidentally, was not always concerned with recommending the means of ritual murder. He was also said to have provided Bothwell with a drug or herb intended to make James favour the Earl, if Bothwell should succeed in touching the King's face with it, Melville: *Memoirs*, 397.

86 The context suggests he was talking to the King, Melville: *loc.cit. supra*.

house, Bothwell complained that Graham was not doing enough to help him and said that "thair was ane wyfe quha assuret him that in caiss the king was not cuttit away, his hienes wald not faill to causs cutt him away"; and the dittay adds that this woman was known to be Agnes Sampson. We are also told that "the said Anny Sampson declarit the samyn secreitlie to the said umquhile [late] Richerd grahame the tyme scho was keipit in the abbay of halyeruidhous". Now, Agnes was interrogated both on and before 5 December, 1590 in the presence of the King, and we know that James was in Holyrood on the 4th.[87] So it looks as though she was kept under guard in the palace while these interrogations were being pursued. If Graham really did gain access to her at this time, and was able to have any kind of private converse with her, no matter how brief, it suggests either that he had remarkable contacts within the administration – one thinks of his apparent amity with the Chancellor as well as with Bothwell – or that he was permitted to visit her in the hope of inducing her to reveal secrets about the conspiracy, which he could then pass on to his controllers; or that he was willing to bribe a guard or two and run the personal risk of being caught communicating with a prisoner lodged under the King's own roof. Whichever may be true, one has the distinct sense of a genuine conspiracy and of strings being pulled by a person or persons unidentifiable. One also notes that as late as mid-December, by which time large numbers of witches in East Lothian had been arrested and put to question, Graham seems to have been at liberty to move about Edinburgh and enter a royal palace, although it cannot have been long thereafter that he too was arrested and kept in the Tolbooth.[88]

Bothwell's acquittal, of course, was more or less a foregone conclusion, for both assize and court (not to mention the city itself) were packed with his friends and allies.[89] The trial lasted for about nine hours, from 1 pm until 10, and so announcement of the verdict was postponed until the following morning. But James had no cause to think that would be an end of the matter. Even before the trial, Bothwell had tried to intimidate the King by entering Holyrood, armed with a sword and pistol, and bursting into the King's chamber. James, naturally enough, was frightened and turned to flee with the words, "Frauncis, thou will doo me no yll". Bothwell pretended

---

87 *JC26/2/12*. *CSPS* Appendix 2. 585. *RPC* 4.551. She was executed on 16 January the following year, according to the records of the burgh of Edinburgh, *Extracts*, 334, or 27 January according to *JC49/7*.

88 Unless, of course, one is going to argue that he was released from imprisonment in order to pay this visit to Agnes Sampson. There are several Nisbetts who feature in these episodes. Bessie Nisbett was one of Euphame MacCalyean's servants; a James Nisbett was one of the gaolers in the Tolbooth; and Bothwell had a servant called David Nisbett. Whether there was any connection between any of these is a matter for speculation.

89 The following paragraph is based on *Border Papers* 1.485–9.

humility by kneeling down and offering the King his sword, and then the Earl and Countess of Atholl who were party to this theatre came in and added their voices to Bothwell's plea for pardon. Pardon for what? asked the King. For bursting into your house like this, said Bothwell.[90] But both sides knew what the other meant, and therefore it is not surprising to find that during the night of 10–11 August, James made arrangements to leave Holyrood secretly and go first to Falkland and thence to his friends in the north. Bothwell, however, was forewarned and took steps to prevent the King's escape, and an extremely uneasy stalemate ensued.

That there was a conspiracy to kill the King by magic, it seems impossible to doubt. A review of earlier decades in the century has shown that people regarded this as a perfectly acceptable way of trying to commit murder and that they were quite prepared to hire others to do it for them, and to participate in the requisite operations. So there is nothing at all unusual in the charge which Bothwell had to face. But was he, in spite of the verdict, actually guilty? The prosecution, and therefore the defence, seems to have centred around Graham's depositions. If these were untrue, the case against Bothwell would be much more difficult to sustain. Indeed, the implication of the dittay and of Bothwell's recorded speech in his own defence alleges that the confessions of the other witches could not be trusted: "who being often examyned, said still they never knewe any thing by thErle Bothwell, but as a noble man, neyther had they ever any conference with him as Greyme alledged".[91] Several respectable men from Edinburgh, reported Carey to Lord Burghley, had deponed "that Richard Greyme said to theme that he must eyther accuse the Erle Bothwell falselye, or els endure such tormentes as no man were able to abyde. His owne brother came in, and before the court was deposed that he had many tymes protested to him that he was forced to accuse thErle Bothwell for feare of maymynge with the bootes and other tortures".[92] In other words, the whole accusation was a conspiracy against Bothwell himself, engineered by his enemies, of whom the Earl named the Chancellor, Sir John Carmichael, and Sir George Hume. It is a mirror image

90 See *SCM* 2.67. Eight people were arrested as a result of this escapade and hanged the next day.

91 *Border Papers* 1.487. In a self-justifying letter to one of the leading ministers of the Kirk, Patrick Galloway, written on 12 April, 1593, Bothwell sought to blame Graham: "for of all that was subornit to speik so sklanderosly of me only ane viz. Riche Grahame went to deith with constant affirmatioun aganis me, and yit I laik not attentick instrumentis [trustworthy documents] to prove that at sindry tymis eftir his imprisonment he confessit that he was forcit to sklander me upon hoip of his awin lyff", *Warrender Papers* 2.203. Bothwell then goes on to name the Chancellor, Sir George Hume, and Sir John Carmichael as the *éminences grises* of the enterprise against him. Cf. his other reported letter to the presbytery of Edinburgh, Calderwood: *Historie* 5.150–6.

92 *Loc. cit.supra*, 488.

of the Chancellor's own complaint, made on 17 April, 1591, that Bothwell had conspired with Richard Graham, and perhaps it is worth noting that when Graham was burned in February or March, 1592[93] – remarkably late for one of the key figures in the alleged treason plot – the English ambassador's informant, Roger Aston, observed that everything Graham had said about Bothwell was true.[94]

But one should also note the opinion of Bothwell's wife. On 30 April, 1591 just before her husband was due to come to trial for the first time on these charges, she wrote to her nephew, Lord John Hamilton, begging him to uphold the family honour by being present in court, "quhair your lordship may sie his lordship tried honestlie" – in other words, make sure Bothwell was acquitted. The whole conspiracy, she said, was a malicious, ungodly invention "be ane reprobat persoun quhais saull is alredy gevin over in the hands of the Devil and body to the fyres torment", and she asked Hamilton to ensure that neither she nor her children might suffer as a result of his not turning up at the trial.[95] The letter smells of fear. Lady Bothwell's unspoken but patent dread seems to be that Hamilton may stay away because he believes her husband to be guilty – hence her repeated emphasis on Graham's lying malice – and that unless the whole nobility presents a united front at the trial, her husband will be found guilty by his assize and, as a result, her honour and the welfare of her children will be badly affected. Behind the nervous, almost frantic plea lurks the greatest fear of all, that the charges against her husband were actually true.

The waters, however, are muddied because it is said that torture was used and not just threatened in several instances during the course of investigations into the plot. David Seton, depute baillie of Tranent, allegedly tortured Geillis Duncan with a series of dreadful torments which he had no legal authority to employ, in order to get her to confess that she was a witch; Agnes Sampson too is said to have received "such torture as hath bene lately provided for witches in that country"; and we are told that John Fian was severely tortured on at least two separate occasions.[96] Nevertheless, none of this can be allowed to pass without comment. The source of all three allegations of

---

93 Birrel says the last day of February = 29th (1592 being a leap year), *Diary*, 27. So does Calderwood: *Historie* 5.148. Roger Aston, however, dates the execution to 7 March, *CSPS* 10.652. Order had been taken for the execution on 24 February, *Ibid.*, 649. Perhaps this accounts for Birrel's mistake, although one might think that so public an event should have been readily datable.

94 *CSPS* Appendix 2.603.

95 GD406/1/56. It is interesting that the Countess should have thought that Graham had already been executed, but her letter was sent from Kelso and she may not have been *au courant* with every detail of the affair, especially as her husband was absent most of the time.

96 *Newes From Scotland*, 9, 12–13, 18–19, 27–8.

torture is the pamphlet, *Newes From Scotland* which, as I have observed before, is a work of propaganda almost certainly compiled for the English market,[97] intended to impress its readers with a picture of James as a perceptive individual, rigorous in his weeding out the tares from God's kingdom; to divert with a series of entertaining vignettes; and to preach a moral lesson, that crime will be found out and does not pay. One therefore needs confirmation from other sources that the tortures described herein were actually used on the persons who are said to have suffered them.

There was no general statute in Scottish law which permitted the use of torture, even under carefully delineated circumstances. Whenever its application was required, a commission had to be sought and issued, its provisions applying only within the limits therein defined; and in the sixteenth century these commissions were very few. One (1567) related to treason, the murder of King Henry at Kirk o' Field; one (1579) to two men accused of perjury; one (1591) to rioters in Edinburgh; and one (1591) related to witches. By this last, two named advocates, two ministers of the Kirk, and two other laymen were granted authority to put to torture any persons accused or delated of witchcraft coming before them for further investigation, should these accused wilfully refuse to declare the truth of those matters about which they were being questioned.[98] This commission was issued on 26 October, by which time Agnes Sampson and John Fian had long been dead. So unless one is going to argue that there was an earlier commission to torture, which has not survived in the records, or that James was prepared to have these people tortured illegally when he could easily have issued a commission to make their torture legal, there is at least a possibility that neither Agnes nor Fian was tortured at all.[99] Intimidation, brutal treatment,

97 One cannot envisage a Scottish author's writing "that country", for example, when he meant his own.

98 *RPC* 4.680. The other commissions are mentioned by Walker: *A Legal History of Scotland* 3.434–5, who inadvisedly observes that 'torture seems to have been principally used on alleged witches', since the evidence for that is extremely tenuous, in spite of his list of instruments of torture. Three other instances of torture in 1588 are offered by the index to *RPC* 4 (pp. 250, 263, 291), but the first two refer to ill-treatment, not torture, and in the third the torture, if actually torture, was clearly illegal. One may also note that in 1542, Lord Glamis had his sentence of forfeiture reduced because his confession of guilt had been obtained under threat of torture, *APS* 2.422; and that on 13 July, 1598 three men from Edinburgh stood trial for illegally torturing Margaret Gardner to make her confess she had stolen some money, Pitcairn: *Criminal Trials* 2.44–6.

99 This is not to say, of course, that they may not have been very badly treated. But if the word 'torture' is to retain any meaning in a legal context, it must be understood as the judicial and legal application of instruments designed and intended to inflict pain on the the human body in order to elicit information or to confirm information already gained. Still, torture does seem to have been applied during the course of the investigations, for we are told that Robert Grierson, one of the principal witches, died on 15 April, 1591 'as it is thought be the extremyty of the tortours applyed to him', *CSPS* 10.502.

and the dreadful example of Euphame MacCalyean's death – she was burned alive instead of being strangled first – may well have proved sufficient to induce many of those arrested and accused in this case to say what they knew and perhaps also what they thought they knew; and one should also make the point that statements elicited under ill-treatment or even torture are not therefore necessarily bound to be untrue. They may contain untruths, exaggerations, and fantasies, but their entire contents cannot be put to one side simply because of the way they were obtained. So Agnes Sampson, John Fian, Barbara Napier, Euphame MacCalyean, and indeed Richard Graham too, not to mention the others who added to and confirmed their testimonies, could easily have been telling, if not all, at least a part of the truth.

If, then, we are not entitled to dismiss out of hand the entire narrative of treasonable conspiracy against the King, and if the claim that the conspiracy, consisting largely of various attempts to kill him by magical means, is not inconsistent with evidences of earlier, similar attempts against other individuals, three principal questions arise: (a) why would anyone wish to kill the King and Queen in 1590? (b) if the murders had succeeded, who would have come to the throne? and (c) who was the person (or perhaps who were the persons) behind the conspiracy?

The inclusion of Queen Anne in any murderous plans seems to have been fortuitous: James was the actual target. Had the magical storms destroyed his ship, it is likely they would have destroyed hers, too; but that would have been by the by. Killing the King through enchanted poison or his wax image occupied most of the witches' attention and energies. While James was absent in Scandinavia he took his Chancellor, Maitland, with him, leaving behind a Council of Regency in which the Duke of Lennox, Lord John Hamilton, and the Earl of Bothwell occupied the principal chairs.[100] During that time, Maitland made himself remarkably unpopular with the Scottish nobility because of what it saw as his arrogance, especially his rumoured desire to diminish the nobles' influence at Court and to remove them from the Privy Council altogether. But Scotland itself was relatively quiet, and even Bothwell made some apparent effort to win new friends by reconciling himself with the Kirk after having been at odds with it for a while.[101] At the same time, however, he was associating with the Catholic Earls of Huntly and Arran, and coming to the support of the Catholic Graham of Fintry when Graham fell foul of the General Assembly. In other words, he was clearly trying to establish some claim of obligation with both sides of the Scottish religious divide.

During the early months of 1590, as we have seen,[102] rumours of Catholic

---

100 *RPC* 4.422–7, 429–30.
101 Melville: *Memoirs*, 372–3. *Historie of King James the Sext*, 242. *CSPS* 10.192.
102 Supra, p. 109.

plots abounded in Edinburgh, and it was even said that when King James and Maitland returned from Denmark, they would be seized and (in an ominous phrase) put out of the way.[103] In March, therefore, the General Assembly, full of nervous fears, set about passing anti-Catholic acts and stimulating the Privy Council to enforce existing legislation against Jesuits and seminary priests, and to set up thirty-one commissions to see it administered throughout the whole of Scotland.[104] So the early months of 1590, while the King and Maitland were absent, saw political tranquillity and religious agitation in almost equal measure. It was not long, however, before the bitterest feud of this period, between the Earls of Huntly and Moray, gathered pace and strength for a violent confrontation. Both sides, in fact, used the summer and autumn of the year to make their preparations, and then in December the boil finally burst and the north-east of Scotland found itself in a virtual state of war.[105]

So the important considerations relating to late 1589 and 1590 are (a) the King's absence from Scotland, (b) the strong rumours of a possible Catholic coup d'état, and (c) the Huntly-Moray feud. If King James had died at any time between September, 1589 when he set out for Denmark and November, 1590 when the investigations into the witchcraft conspiracy got under way, the near certainty is that Scotland would have been plunged into civil war for there was no immediate, obvious successor to the Crown. The leading contenders, the Lennox-Stewarts and the Hamiltons, would have fought each other; the war might well have become a religious as well as a political struggle; and England might not have sat idle upon the sidelines. So no one person can be singled out as the obvious beneficiary of James's premature death. But this is not to say that someone may not have believed he could emerge victorious from the chaos. Only a few months before the King left for Denmark, Bothwell had been involved in a rebellion against him in the south, while the Catholic earls made insurrection in the north. Then suddenly, as it were, in the autumn he was made one of the principal members of the Council of Regency, equal in importance, as he could well have seen it, with the two main claimants to the Scottish Crown. This appointment must have been immensely gratifying, a recognition of kinship with James which, as Brown points out, was something Bothwell had wanted since 1585 and which now, "coming within months of his rebellion . . . represented a considerable breakthrough for him".[106] Did it also, perhaps, give him ideas well above his actual station? Only someone given to fantasy, it is true, would be likely to think so, but Bothwell had

103 *CSPS* 10.854–7.
104 *RPC* 4.463–7.
105 Brown: *Bloodfeud in Scotland*, 144–52. Lee: *John Maitland*, 208–18.
106 *Bloodfeud in Scotland*, 151.

already given and would continue increasingly to give indications that his grip on reality was far from stable.

Let us examine the plot in the light of this hypothesis. Bothwell decided to kill the King by magic and then take his chance of seeing the Lennox-Stewarts and Hamiltons fight each other to a standstill until the factions were willing to unite under a man belonging directly to neither house but with some notion (however remote) of a claim to royal blood, who might be seen either as a compromise ruler or as the acceptable power behind the throne. Magical assassination had its attractions. It would not be easy, for example, to establish with any legal certainty the identity of any directing hand at the back of those who performed the actual operations, and with any luck no one would take the trouble to do so, being content with the fact that the King had died an unnatural death and that the magical perpetrators were under lock and key. Bothwell knew Richard Graham. He may have been introduced to him by Maitland, with whom he was on fairly good terms at this time,[107] or he may have known him anyway, since Graham appears to have been quite well connected. Graham also knew several witches in East Lothian – we are told he had been a witch for twenty years, so he had had plenty of opportunity to get to know them[108] – including, of course, Agnes Sampson who had already been in trouble with Haddington presbytery in 1589 and 1590. So Graham organised groups of established witches to enchant an image of the King and to prepare magical poison (*veneficium*). This last was to be placed above a door in one of the royal palaces, most probably that of the King's bedchamber, and for this part of the conspiracy a reliable contact was needed. Agnes Sampson seems to have thought she had such a contact in John Kers, one of the King's gentlemen, and there was talk of obtaining some of the King's linen to spread the poisonous magic further. This, however, came to nothing.[109]

Some kind of organisation existed among these witches, probably created for the occasion of the conspiracy so that Graham could exercise greater control over their treasonable activities. It would be both inefficient and dangerous to have disparate groups working on their own without someone's having overall knowledge of what they were doing; and in order to emphasise

---

107 *CSPS* 10.137.

108 *JC6/3*. p.5.

109 The English ambassador wrote to Burghley on 7 December, 1590 anent this getting of the King's shirt that 'in this, Lord Claud and other noblemen are evil spoken of', *CSPS* 10.430. Clearly the Court was alive with rumour and speculation on this very point. But if no one agreed or managed to steal any of the royal linen, someone may have been successful in stealing a portrait of the King, although this is mentioned only once. Agnes also knew a person called Rankin who was to have been given the task of casting the poison in front of the King, presumably a reference to smearing an appropriate threshold as opposed to a lintel, *JC26/2/19*, p.1.

that control and to create a sense of camaraderie among the co-conspirators, for whom it would have been both thrilling and comforting to know that they were part of a grand design, a greater whole, Graham arranged a meeting for everyone involved in the kirk at North Berwick.[110] It is possible he played the part of the Devil, too. On the other hand, one of the witches seems to have distinguished between them when she confessed that on their way to North Berwick in a rowing-boat, Graham was with them and that she and Graham drank to each other in white wine which the Devil had fetched out of the bottom of the boat.[111]

But then came potential disaster. The conspiracy was revealed by accident. David Seton's suspicions about Geillis Duncan's nocturnal activities and his brutal treatment of her led to the uncovering of the network which Graham had carefully constructed. Moreover, as was perhaps inevitable, investigation turned up Bothwell's name and as soon as that happened the Earl needed to cover his tracks and extricate himself from a dangerous situation. Throwing the blame on Graham was easy. The man was an excommunicate, a known magician, and a consorter with witches. Surely no one would believe such a person, and in any case his testimony could be ruled inadmissible in court. Such indeed, as we have seen, was the line taken by Bothwell's proloquitors. Bothwell's enemies then made a mistake. They offered Graham immunity from execution and a comfortable imprisonment under what seemed to be royal protection in Stirling Castle in return for his willingness to testify against the Earl. But this played into Bothwell's hands, since he was able to claim – and did – that Graham's confessions could be disregarded on the ground that he had been suborned by the Earl's known enemies into giving false information.[112]

The inclusion of Maitland as chief of these instigators was a strong card for Bothwell to play. Maitland knew Graham personally. What more convincing than that he should make his friend (or acquaintance) an offer? What is more, Maitland was extremely unpopular, especially among the rest of the nobles who might well feel they had to present a united front against so serious an accusation against one of their number, made by the disreputable combination

---

110 Organisation seems to have been his forte. We are told, for example, that he arranged meetings for Geillis Duncan, *CSPS*10.502.

111 *JC*26/2/13, p. 2. The Devil was certainly not Bothwell, as Margaret Murray suggested, "The Devil of North Berwick", 320–21. Apart from anything else, it would have been far too dangerous for him to have involved himself so personally in the conduct of the plot, and there was no need at all for him to have done so.

112 The concentration by the defence upon Graham's information is interesting. Several of the other witches named Bothwell in their confessions, but their testimony seems to have been ignored in Bothwell's eagerness to discredit the one person whose evidence might carry enough weight to convince people of the Earl's guilt.

of Maitland and a reprobate magician. It looked like a case of personal malice directed against Bothwell. Certainly this is the line taken by Stene, a member of the King's household, in a political satire, *Robe Stene's Dream*, written in 1591 or early 1592.[113] Here, Maitland is represented as Lawrence the fox, greedy for money, hostile to the Stewarts, and eager to advance the Hamiltons to the Crown. Bothwell appears as one of King James's faithful dogs:

> The grewhound, quhome thow maist estemid
> To be thy kinsman and thy freind,
> Salbe accusit of socerie,
> Of murthor and adulterie . . .
> Off tressone and leismaiestie;
> All salbe provin sufficientlie[114] –

and the King is reproached for his credulousness:

> "Bot Samsone or sum Riche Grahame,
> To your perditioun skaith and schame,
> Hes yow bewitchit and bund yow to him [Maitland],
> For udir wayis how could ye luve him?[115]

So Maitland provided an admirable diversion from the uncomfortable feeling evident among many of Bothwell's contemporaries, not least the King himself, that Graham may well have been telling no more than the truth.

There is one further point to be considered. A thread of Catholicism runs through the story. The Devil at North Berwick, we are told, was dressed like a Catholic priest;[116] the Seton family was Catholic; there is a possibility that if Richard Graham belonged to the Grahams of Fintry, he too was a Catholic; Bothwell had been an active ally of the northern Catholic earls during their attempted coup in the Spring of 1589; rumours of another Catholic uprising flooded Edinburgh throughout the early months of 1590; and even while he was on the run, Bothwell flirted with the Kirk, but maintained his contacts with Catholics on the Continent to such an extent that the Jesuit, William Crichton, thought he had actually converted;[117] and when the Catholic earls rebelled a second time in 1594, Bothwell was on their side yet again.

113 In the poem, Agnes Sampson is referred to in the past tense and Richard Graham in the present, *Dream*, p.20. Hence, it must have been composed between February, 1591 and February, 1592.
114 *Dream*, pp.12–13.
115 *Ibid.*, p.20. On Bothwell's feud with Maitland, see further Brown: *Bloodfeud in Scotland*, 127–30. On Stene, see Lee: *John Maitland*, 225 and note.
116 We are also told he thought the ministers of the Kirk were bringing Scotland to ruin, *JC26/2/12*, p.5 and *JC26/2/13*, p.2.
117 Watson: *Bothwell and the Witches*, 102. King James remarked in 1594 that 'a Bothwell and a Papist shall now be one'.

Now, no one would wish to suggest that Bothwell was anything but self-interested throughout the whole of his career, never mind the witchcraft episode. His support for the Catholic earls was dictated at least as much by personal considerations of political advantage as by anything else, just as his courting of the Kirk during the most awkward moments of his pending trials for treason and witchcraft owed much to his hopes of securing the moral support of that powerful body. Nevertheless if the hypothesis that he wanted to create a political chaos in Scotland by killing the King so that he himself might emerge with some particular personal advantage is at all feasible, one can see why he might turn to Catholics and use them as his instruments. What better way to protect himself against being "cut away" by the King, as the Italian seer had warned him, than by cutting James away first? What better way of gaining by that deed than by appearing to have a foot in both Catholic and Protestant camps while the consequent civil war raged in Scotland? What more seductive way of getting Catholic support for his murderous scheme than to persuade a priest and a magician (unless Graham alone had played the part of the Devil) that out of the chaos of the King's death might emerge the chance of a Catholic monarch? Hence, perhaps, Euphame MacCalyean's mysterious remark that in the event of the King's death, Scotland should not lack a king.[118] Clearly some, if not all, of the leading conspirators had someone in mind for the Crown.

This suggestion assumes that the witches' confessions, *separatim et conjunctim*, were broadly representing the truth. If this is so, it means that there really was a plot to kill the King by magical means. Hence, we can exclude James as a contriver of the conspiracy, since the notion of James's devising a genuine plot to have himself killed, merely with a view to discrediting Bothwell, is simply not credible; and one has to remember that the *mentalité* of the time allowed the possibility that such a magic might work. Nor can Maitland be seen as a candidate for villain, as Bothwell and his adherents would have liked to persuade people. Had Maitland organised a real conspiracy, he would have run the same risk of discovery as Bothwell himself, but unlike Bothwell could not have relied on noble support in the event of his coming to trial. The only person unbalanced enough to think he might get away with such a treason seems to have been Bothwell, brooding for months over the prophecy of "ane man of science in Italie or alinanyie [Germany] that his prince sould caus execute him and . . . he feirit his lyfe sould be taine be him".[119] In the cold light of political history, of course, this sounds like fantasy. But Bothwell's whole career is an illustration of someone not acting

118 *JC*26/2/2, p.2.
119 *JC*26/2: Earl of Bothwell, Conspiracy.

according to the rational dictates of political history. Here, rather, was a man
governed (if that is the right word) by emotional self-interest, and such a
ruling passion may provide a chink through which fantasy may enter political
calculation and wreak all kinds of havoc.[120]

---

120 A number of people died for this fantasy. In addition to Graham himself, for
     example, we know that Fian, Sampson, and MacCalyean were executed, since the
     atendant costs have been preserved, *Extracts from the Records of the Burgh of
     Edinburgh*, 333–4. Janet Straton, however, may still have been alive on 10 September,
     1595, although by 30 October, 1596 she was dead. See *infra*, pp. 197–8.

7

The Final Years of the Century

What had King James learned about witchcraft from this experience? One fruit of the magical conspiracy against him was his *Daemonologie*, published in Edinburgh in 1597, but clearly written (or at least planned) much earlier, possibly as early as 1591 while the investigations and executions were in full spate.[1] After lamenting "the fearefull aboundinge at this time in this countrie, of these detestable slaves of the Devill, the Witches or enchaunters", James says the intention of his book is twofold: (a) to prove the reality of witches and witchcraft against the doubts expressed by sceptics, 'scepticism' here being a reference to Reginald Scot whose book, *The Discoverie of Witchcraft*, expressing certain doubts about aspects of maleficent magic, had been published in 1584; and (b) to show what severe punishment witches and other magical operators merit. He recommends that the reader consult further Bodin, Hyperius, Hemmingsen, Agrippa, and Wier,[2] and then proceeds to the text of the book itself which is divided into three sections: one on magic, one on witchcraft, and one on ghosts and related spirits.

Magic, he says, differs from witchcraft in as much as magic is necromancy (that is, conjuration of spirits), and is practised largely by the learned whose motivation is intellectual curiosity. Witchcraft, on the other hand, tends to involve sorcery and the use of charms by "daft wives" [silly women], as James calls them, who wish to appear learned but are, in fact, moved either by greed for material things or by the desire for revenge. Intellectual curiosity often

---

1 See Dunlap: 'King James and some witches', 43. It was published by Robert Waldegrave, an English printer who specialised, while he lived in London, in publishing Puritan works, among which should be included the *Marprelate Tracts*. He came to Edinburgh in 1590 and was appointed the King's Printer on 9 October that year. See Van Eerde: 'Robert Waldegrave', *Renaissance Quarterly* 34 (1981), 44–6, 57, 65, 68.

2 Jean Bodin (1530–1596), French political philosopher. His *Démonomanie des sorciers* was published in 1580. Hyperius = Andreas Gerhard (1511–1564), German Protestant theologian. An English translation of his *True tryall and examination of mans owne selfe* appeared in 1587. Niels Hemmingsen (1513–1600), Danish Protestant theologian, published *Admonitio de superstitionibus magicis vitandis* in 1575. Heinrich Cornelius Agrippa von Nettesheim (1486–1535), German occultist and physician, completed his *De Occulta Philosophia* in 1510 but did not publish it until 1533. Johann Wier (1515–1588), German Protestant physician, published two books on magic and witchcraft: *De praestigiis daemonum* (1563) and *De lamiis* (1577). The appearance of this bibliography in James's introduction is no guarantee he had read it, nor would he have had to do so in order to write his treatise.

begins its descent into magic by practising judicial astrology, and whereas many perfectly respectable people use charms because they are too ignorant to know any better, anyone who conjures spirits cannot plead the same excuse and is therefore worthy of being punished even more severely than a witch. Scripture proves the reality of witchcraft and no one is immune from its effects. Those whose Christian faith is weak are most susceptible to the workings of Satan through witches, and magistrates must therefore be diligent in prosecuting this type of offender. If they are not, the witches will prevail against them.

Such arguments are unexceptional and can be found in dozens of similar demonologies both longer and more replete with learning. What makes James's *Daemonologie* interesting is the evidence it gives of forming a personal document written out of a very particular set of circumstances. I have suggested earlier, for example, that the Scottish Kirk saw magical operations in general and witchcraft in particular as art and part of certain aspects of Catholic belief and practice. James illustrates this on several occasions in his text. Those who conjure evil spirits, he says sarcastically, cannot do without two things – an assistant and holy water, "whereby the Devill mocks the Papists"; and even then, the conjured spirit will not appear until "after manie circumstances, long praiers, and much muttering and murmuring of the conjurers, like a Papist priest dispatching a hunting Masse".[3] He compares the supposed ability of the Devil to contract witches' bodies into so small a shape that they can enter through tiny vents or crevices into a house to "the little transubstantiat god in the Papistes Masse", and says he does not believe either.[4] Catholic Scotland, he maintains, was full of superstitious credence in ghosts and spirits and *sithean*, and "that mist of errours [i.e. Catholicism] overshadowed the Devill to walke the more familiarlie amongst them, and as it were by barnelie [childish] and effraying terrours, to mock and accuse their barnelie errores".[5]

When it comes to exorcising evil spirits, however, James has a little more difficulty in sustaining this patronising tone, though he does his best. He dismisses the use of holy water, the sign of the cross, and the use of God's

---

3 *Daemonologie*, 17–18. Mathew mentions this aspect of the treatise, but misses the tone and the relationship between Catholicism and magic in the eyes of the Kirk, *James I*, 77–8.

4 *Daemonologie*, 40.

5 *Op.cit. supra*, 54, 65. Cf. "That fourth kinde of spirites, which . . . amongst us was called the *Phairie* . . . or our good neighboures, was one of the sortes of illusiones that was rifest in the time of *Papistrie*", 73–4. Cf. also the belief that intercourse between spirits and women can produce monstrous offspring, which James says is most common in wild parts of the world such as Lapland, Finland, or Orkney and Shetland, *Ibid.*, 69. Again, he says that he himself does not credit this particular belief.

name as "vaine thinges that were alike fashious and feckles to recite", and says it is doubtful whether Catholics "or anie not professing the onelie true Religion" can really cure someone possessed by spirits. This, he says, is either because many of the cases cited by Catholics are counterfeit, "which wyle the Clergie inventes for confirming of their rotten Religion", or because the Devil is happy to cease tormenting the demoniac for a short period so that he may obtain thereby "the perpetual hurt of the soules of so many that by these false miracles may be induced or confirmed in the profession of that erroneous Religion". If, on the other hand, Catholics use Protestant methods of exorcism, they may be genuinely successful.[6]

But it is in the echoes of the 1590 conspiracy, which sound within the book, that we can detect more tellingly the notes of James's personal experience. Many recent witches, he says, have not been melancholics but "rich and worldly-wise, some of them fatte or corpulent in their bodies, and most part of them altogether given over to the pleasures of the flesh".[7] A manuscript of the *Daemonologie* has in the margins at this point the initials EM, RG, and BN, and Dunlap has argued that these are meant to accompany particular phrases in the text and can be identified with specific people. Thus EM = "rich and worldly-wise" = Euphame MacCalyean; RG = "fat or corpulent" = Richard Graham; and BN = "given over to the pleasures of the flesh" = Barbara Napier.[8] Witches often confess to convening in a church where they meet the Devil who occupies the pulpit, and worship him with the *osculum infame*.[9] It is the reference to the Devil in the pulpit which reminds one of North Berwick. May princes mitigate the sentence of death which ought to be passed on witches? No, they should not.[10] The question and answer are reminiscent of James's exchange with the Edinburgh presbytery in 1591. Is the evidence of witches against someone accused of witchcraft admissible in court? "In my opinion", comes the answer, "in a mater of treason against the Prince, barnes [children] or wives or never so diffamed persons may of our law serve for sufficient witnesses and proofes."[11] Satan can and does visit witches in prison. It is a very general statement, but one is reminded that the Devil visited John Fian while he was in ward, angry that Fian had repented of his former service to him.[12] Even James's remarks about

---

6 *Ibid.*, 70–3.
7 *Ibid.*, 30.
8 'King James and some witches', 40–2.
9 *Daemonologie*, 37.
10 *Op.cit. supra*, 78.
11 *Ibid.*, 79.
12 *Newes From Scotland*, 25–6. In a discussion on magicians as students under the Devil's instruction, James calls them 'capped creatures', 52. 'Capped' seems to imply they had been to university and received a degree. Since the context of the remark is the Devil's visiting witches in prison, is this a reference to John Fian's possible status?

the manner in which witches make pictures of wax or clay, or compound extraordinary poisons, take on a particular resonance in this context; and the flat assertion that "the consulters, trusters in, over-seers, interteiners or sturrers up of these craftes-folkes, are equallie guiltie with themselves that are the practisers" is reminiscent of the blanket condemnation of the 1563 Witchcraft Act.[13] There is also a Scottish flavour (although one does not wish to claim any more for it than that) to his references to turning the riddle, seeing or conjuring fairies, and his contemptuous use of the word 'ethnicks' to describe people who foresee in a dream-like state the death of others.[14] One is reminded of how much James despised Highlanders.

It does seem, therefore, that James's composition of the *Daemonologie* was stimulated by a personal experience which had taught him, more vividly than any book could do, what witches did, or tried to do, or believed they were capable of doing; and it is clear that however dismissive he may have tried to be of some of their claims and practices, *au fond* he was or had become a believer. For although he refers to tricks, illusions, and ignorance, and gives examples of each, he also maintains that Scripture which says that witches and witchcraft are real cannot be denied, that maleficent magic can be effective, and that those in charge of administering the law must exercise that law rigorously against these servants of Satan. He also mentions or describes certain features of witchcraft, which are taken to be typical of Continental demonology: the diabolical pact, renunciation of baptism and reception of Satan's mark, and floating an accused witch to see if he or she sinks or floats.[15] These notions, it is often said, James introduced into Scotland. The Satanic pact, however, was certainly known there as early as 1552, and although *Newes From Scotland* says that David Seton found the Devil's marks upon Geillis Duncan, and that in Scotland "it hath latelye beene found that the Devill . . . dooth lick them with his tung in some privy part of their bodie before hee dooth receive them to be his servants", its credentials as an accurate report of Scottish witches and their examinations in 1590–1 are not altogether reliable.[16]

---

13 *Daemonologie*, 44, 78.
14 *Op.cit. supra*, 31, 73–4, 80, 75.
15 *Ibid.*, 19, 23, 32–4, 80–1.
16 (Pact), *Catechism of John Hamilton*, 50. (Mark), *Newes*, 9, 12. John Fian, however, according to his dittay, was marked by the Devil's rod, the Devil appearing to him twice, clad in white, Pitcairn: *Criminal Trials* 1.2.210 (items 1 and 2); and Agnes Sampson was marked on her right knee, *Ibid.*, 235 (item 33). The appearance of a spirit clad in white is repeated in *JC*26/2/10 where the deponer (a female) says that about thirty years previously there came to her an old man "claid in quhyte, quha eftir diverss speichis haid with hir schew furth a buik he had in his hand, and caussit hir to suer that sche suld taik hir to the mercement of God, and forsaik the foull theife and all his warkis to keip hir fra temptatioun". It becomes clear later in the document that she had not at first taken the apparition to be evil, no doubt because he was wearing white and spoke of God's mercy and avoidance of the Devil. Her interrogators, however, have evidently changed her mind.

As for the renouncing of baptism and floating, these play scarcely any part in Scottish witchcraft in the sixteenth century, and floating hardly at all even in the seventeenth. Indeed, renouncing baptism, receiving the mark, and making a pact tend to become common in Scottish witchcraft only after the rise of the Covenanters. So James should not be blamed for something he almost certainly did not do.

The magical treason of 1589–90, however, has so dominated discussion of Scottish witchcraft in general and the century's final decade in particular that it is easy to forget what other kinds of magic the principals were working, and how many magical operations were taking place (or alleged to be so doing) outwith the capital. John Fian, for example, did not only attend the meetings at North Berwick and Acheson's Haven. He was given to falling into ecstasies and trances, "lyand be the space of twa or thre houris deid, his spreit tane, and sufferit him selff to be careit and transportit to mony montanes, as thocht throw all the warld". He was able to tell people how long they would live, and how they would die. He bewitched William Hutson in Windygoull by sending an evil spirit to possess him. He opened locks in the houses of both David Seton and Seton's mother. He raised winds and mists at sea. He also travelled on horseback from Tranent to Prestonpans with another man, and lit their way by conjuring up five candles, four on the horse's head and one on his companion's staff.[17] Apart from this last, there is nothing to surprise one about his apparent magical gifts and activities, for we have met them all before, and had Fian not been part of the treason-plot, it is possible he would never have appeared in front of a court.[18]

Agnes Sampson is perhaps a slightly different case in that the presbytery of Haddington wanted to question her about her magical activities but, as we have seen, the ministers had great difficulty in getting her to take any notice; so she may have felt confident in evading their repeated summonses either because she had powerful protection or because she thought herself immune from such investigation, having practised her arts in the area without apparent difficulty for so many years. A large number of other women accused of witchcraft, who had carried out their magical operations for as long or even longer, must surely have felt a similar confidence, and their arrest and interrogation may therefore have come as something of a surprise or shock.

17 Pitcairn: *op.cit. supra*, 1.2.210 (items 17 and 18); 211 (item 5); 212 (item 12); 211–12 (item 10); 211 (items 7 and 8); 212 (items 16 and 11).
18 One item in his dittay may seem to contradict this. It says he received commands from Satan to deny God and all true religion, and to persuade as many people as he could to join the Devil's service, *JC6/3*. It is difficult to tell, however, whether this damning item would have appeared in his dittay had he not been accused of treason and tortured so severely, since such explicit accusations do not seem to occur in the other witchcraft dittays of this period.

The items of Agnes's dittay indicate that she was principally a healer and had the gift of being able to foretell whether a sick person would live or die.[19] Her most famous exhibition of magical powers, however, does not appear in her dittay. The King had expressed disbelief at some of the things she was telling him and so, "taking his Maiestie a little aside, she declared unto him the verye woordes which passed between the Kings Maiestie and his Queene at Upslo in Norway the first night of their mariage, with their answere eache to other: whereat the Kinges Maiestie wondered greatlye, and swore by the living God, that he beleeved that all the Divels in hell could not have discovered the same".[20] It was, to some extent, a turning-point, for thereafter, we are told, the King gave her greater credence than before. But in fact this is one instance when Agnes need not have relied upon magic for her information. She may have had contacts in Copenhagen, for Geillis Duncan confessed that she and some of the other witches met someone from "Coppenhowin" – the manuscript is damaged at this point, so we do not know who it was – in the middle of the Firth of Forth and had a lengthy conversation with her.[21] We also know that Agnes knew John Kers, one of the King's gentlemen, and if he had been on duty on the night in question, he would probably have heard snatches of conversation from the royal bed, and could then have relayed these to Agnes. There is also the intriguing possibility that Agnes herself may have been in Copenhagen during the King's visit. Hence her cryptic remark, which we have noted before, that "now the king is going to [manuscript damaged] his wyf, but I sall be thair befor them".[22]

Her methods of divination and curing, some of which she said she had learned from her father,[23] included examination of a sick man's shirt (by which she declared "that the seiknes that he had was ane elf-schot"); incantation, which may mean what it says, or may refer to her recitations of 'charms' which, from the examples given, turn out to have been Christian prayers; and occasionally by means of an attendant spirit. The most extraordinary example of this last occurred during an episode when she was summoned to cure the elderly Lady

---

19 See Pitcairn: 1.2.230–41. There are 53 items listed there. Of these, 19 refer to healing and 12 to divination of sickness and death = 58%. Five more refer to her meeting other witches, three to acts of revenge, and four to her meeting the Devil. The rest are disparate acts of magic such as foretelling a storm, providing enchanted powder to assist in a childbirth, or enchanting a ring to conjure affection between the giver and the receiver.

20 *Newes From Scotland*, 15.

21 JC26/2/13, p.1.

22 JC26/2/3, p.2. Cf. JC26/2/12. p.5 where she says she had more than once been furth of Scotland and on foreign shores for as long as two days. It would take longer than two days to get to Denmark, of course, but the confession indicates that Agnes was accustomed to going abroad.

23 Pitcairn: *Criminal Trials* 1.2.232 (item 15).

Edmestoun.[24] On arrival at the house, she promised Lady Edmestoun's daughters that she would tell them that night whether their mother would mend or not, and arranged to meet them later in the garden. Then she herself went into the garden and summoned up her spirit with the cry "Eloa!"[25] The spirit appeared in the form of a black dog which jumped over the wall. In answer to Agnes's question whether Lady Edmestoun would live or die, he said her days were past. Then he asked where Lady Edmestoun's daughters were, and when Agnes said that they would come into the garden by and by, the spirit told her that one of them was in danger and that he intended to take the woman with him. Agnes roundly declared that he should do no such thing; whereupon the spirit departed, "yowling", and disappeared into a well or a stream;[26] one thinks immediately of the spirits who endowed with magical attributes those wells and streams to which people went on pilgrimage in defiance of the Kirk's displeasure and repeated bans.

In due time, Lady Edmestoun's daughters came to keep their appointment with Agnes. Suddenly, the spirit re-appeared and began to draw one of them towards the water and would have drowned her therein, "war nocht the said Agnes and the rest of the gentilwemen gatt ane grip of hir, and with all thir forceis drew hir abak agane". The spirit then vanished and Agnes told the women their mother would not recover, after all. But the tussle with the spirit had so frightened the woman he had tried to drown that she fainted and had to be carried to her bed where she lay "frenettik" for three or four days and "crippill" for a further eleven weeks.

Agnes's other encounter with the spirit had not been so disconcerting. On that occasion, too, he appeared to her in the likeness of a dog and answered all her questions (item 34), but this time she seems to have been in control, because when "sche chargeit him to depart on the law he lewis one [according to the law by which he is bound] . . . with thay wordis is conjurit and passis away". In other words, it looks as though Agnes was not quite in the same case as Elizabeth Dunlop, Alison Pearson, or any of the others who relied on a spirit-guide to answer their questions. Spirits such as those seemed to appear of their own volition and in more or less pleasing guise. 'Conjurit', however, suggests that Agnes's method was to invoke a spirit and seek responses from him,[27] and if that

---

24 *Op.cit. supra*, 235–6 (item 38). 'Lady Edmestoun' may have been Helen, widow of Henry Haitlie the younger of Mellerstain, and second wife of William Home whom she married in January, 1577. Agnes admitted to the truth of this episode in her dittay, *JC26/2/4*, p.1.

25 Pitcairn has mistranscribed this as *Elva*, but *JC26/2/12*, p.2 quite clearly writes *eloa*.

26 The text has 'wall' which may refer to either. It does not mean 'wall' in the English sense. The word for that is 'dyke'.

27 Her cry of 'Eloa', for example, may actually have been 'Eloy' or some similar spirit-name. *Eloy* appears in ceremonies of conjuration of spirits in contemporary grimoires (books of spells and magical instructions).

were so, the episode in the garden illustrates very clearly how dangerous such a practice could be; for Agnes was quite clearly not in control of the situation. As the dittay says, "sche chargeit the Dewill . . . quha come in owir the dyke . . . and come sa neir to hir that sche was effrayit", and if this interpretation is correct, the passage is very significant, for it will be the only occasion in the Scottish records of this period on which the fear of an invoking magician is recorded.

Agnes Sampson and John Fian were not the only witches James chose to meet and question. Others connected with the treason conspiracy were examined by him or in his presence, and before ever this plot came to light he had sent for and talked to Marion MacIngaroch.[28] But can we assume (as is often done), that 1590–1 represents a turning-point in Scotland's official relationship with witchcraft and that henceforth a wave of persecution started, fuelled by the King himself? The evidence does not altogether support this view. In March and May, 1590 the presbytery of St. Andrews set on foot inquiries into two suspect witches, one in Abdie, the other in Crail, and answered in the affirmative a query from the minister of Lathrisk whether "anie woman may bere witnes in the sklander of witchcraft". In March, 1591 the King and Council learned that John Boswell of Auchinleck, who had not only frequently consulted witches but had himself practised magic, was refusing to answer a summons to answer the charges: so they denounced him rebel. In April, there were witches (we do not know how many) awaiting trial in the tolbooths of Haddington and Edinburgh, and on 26 October a commission was issued to six persons including the Provost of Edinburgh to inquire further into all cases of witchcraft and bring the accused to trial, "the personis wilfull or refuseand to declair the veritie to be putt to tortour, or sic uther punishment . . . as may move thame to utter the trueth". Clearly the commission was intended for Edinburgh and the affected parts of East Lothian, and its rigour was surely dictated by the persistent fear that the magical conspiracy against the King's life had not yet been fully cauterised.[29]

But outwith Edinburgh and the environs of the capital there does not seem to be a great deal of evidence that the authorities were made more nervous or

---

28 He had also listened to the woman from Lübeck, rumoured to be a witch; to Janet Kennedy, the witch from Redden; and he had been particularly anxious to speak to a Scottish witch who had fled into England, presumably when news of the conspiracy broke, but had been arrested and brought back to Berwick in February, 1591. *CSPS* 10.457, 460.

29 *St. Andrews Presbytery Records*, 31r, 33v, 39v. *CSPS* 10.591. *Synod Records of Lothian and Tweeddale*, 27. *Extracts from the Records of the Burgh of Edinburgh*, 38. Pitcairn: *Criminal Trials* 1.2.261–2. We also learn that one witch was burned in Dundee, *Burgh Treasurer's Accounts*, 1591; and that two witches were fetched from Dalkeith and Colinton into Edinburgh for trial, *Treasurer's Accounts* 1.631, 634.

vigilant with respect to witchcraft than they had been before the conspiracy broke. What we do have are indications that the ministers of the Kirk were endeavouring to maintain a respect for justice and equity in such cases. On 7 October, 1591, for example, the presbytery of Haddington raised a point before the synod: "Thair be certain persones within the parochin of Trenent quha ar sclanderit and dilatit of witchecraft and as yit nather ar condemnit nor clensit of the samin, desyring thairfore . . . the resolution of this assemble, quhidder gif sick [such] persones aucht to be resavit to the table of the Lord or not".[30] A technical point, of course, and the synod replied that they should not be allowed communion: but the fact that Haddington felt any doubts on the question indicates an absence of persecutory zeal which, considering the presbytery's somewhat awkward position as the principal representative of the Kirk's authority in the midst of what appeared to be Satan's favoured domain in Scotland, says a great deal for the local ministers' wish to be scrupulously just.

A similar example can be found further afield in Stirling where, on 5 October, the presbytery began to hear a case of slander by Walter Adie and Elizabeth Airch, his wife, against Christian Gib whom they accused of being a witch and a thief.[31] Walter turned up to the session and said he would abide by what he and Elizabeth had averred; his wife, however, did not appear. At the next meeting of the presbytery on the 19th, neither of them appeared and the ministers ordained that Walter must come on 2 November with his charges against Christian Gib committed to writing and his witnesses prepared and ready to testify, otherwise he himself would be found guilty of slander. On the 2nd, both Christian and her husband, John Adie, brought with them a legal document requiring Walter Adie to produce his accusations in writing, but Walter withdrew his charges and that should have been that.[32]

The affair, however, was not yet over. At the last visitation of Glendoven parish, said Walter, the commissioners had discovered that Isobel Murray, a suspected witch, "was ressavit in the said John adeis houss quhair scho remainit all nycht and spak with the said Cristane gib beand thane lyand seik". So Christian might be guilty of the crime of consulting a witch, even though Walter's charge that she herself was a witch was now dismissed as slander. This fresh charge came before the presbytery on 8 February the following year, but Christian (or her husband) had not been idle meantime, and now produced a letter from James Graham, justice in Kincardine, testifying that Isobel Murray had never been convicted of witchcraft in his

30 *Synod Records of Lothian and Tweeddale*, 35.
31 *CH2/722/2.*
32 The similarity of the men's surnames suggests that they may have been related and that perhaps it was a family quarrel or feud which had sparked off the accusation.

court. Faced with this apparent proof that Walter's charge of consultation, too, was slander, the ministers issued orders that he present and explain himself at the next meeting of the presbytery; but when this arrived, on the 15th, Walter did not appear and the ministers, having inquired whether Isobel Murray had been convicted of witchcraft in any other court, apart from that of James Graham, and found that she had not, "absolve the said Cristane from witchcraft and of consulting with the said Issobell Murray as ane wich, and decernis [instructs] and ordanis the said walter adie to restoir the said Cristane gib to hir gude fame publicclie in the kirk of Glendoven in tyme of sermond".

So at a time when the capital and parts of East Lothian were still feeling the effects of a treason-conspiracy, it seems that alleged witches both within and outwith the periphery of that particular convulsion could still rely on the careful diligence of at least some presbyteries to winkle out the truth of the charges brought to their notice; and this is the more worthy of notice when one considers that 1592 was a year fraught with other political and religious problems. The North-East of Scotland was alive with feuds and in February the Earl of Moray was killed by men belonging to the Earl of Huntly. The murder caused outrage in both Edinburgh and the Kirk (for Moray had been a Protestant and Huntly was a Catholic), but the King, while putting on an appearance of indignation, was actually indifferent and dragged his feet over punishing the culprits. At first he gathered an army, since now he had two renegade earls to pursue, Huntly as well as Bothwell, but then he postponed his march north for nearly a month, and in that interval the Kirk became very exercised. The Chancellor, Maitland, already unpopular with the nobles, found that common opinion, too, was surging against him and by the end of March he was forced to leave the Court. But by June he was back, persuading the King to accept a piece of legislation, 'the Golden Act', which restored to the Kirk a degree of control over a wide range of affairs, which it had lost in 1584. The Kirk was delighted and appointed commissioners to travel about the kingdom "to tak diligent inquisitioun of papistis, jesuitis, and all sic as trafficquis and travellis in ony thing contrair the trew religioun . . . as alswa with pouer to thame to inquire the names suspectit and dilaitit of wichecraft, or seikand responssis or help of thame".[33] He hoped – and presumably so did James – that this would stop, or at least modify, the Kirk's continual demand that the King punish Huntly for Moray's murder. The King, however, did little or nothing even though the North-East was engaged in scarcely less than a civil war, and the Kirk became ever more fearful of what it perceived as a Catholic threat. Indeed, in November it decreed a week-long fast for various

---

33 Ives: *The Bonny Earl of Murray*, 38–41, 49–60. MacDonald: *The Jacobean Kirk*, 46–9. *CSPS* 10.753–4.

reasons including "a fearful defection of a great number of all Estates to Papistrie, and Atheism; specially of the Nobilitie, through the resorting and trafficking of Jesuits, Seminarie-Priests and other Papists, without execution of any Law against them".[34] It was, to be sure, an old song but one the Kirk repeated with ever-increasing fervour.

Then, at the beginning of 1593, these fears received what appeared to be a startling confirmation in the Affair of the Spanish Blanks. A Scottish Jesuit named Ker was arrested on his way into the country and found to be carrying blank sheets of paper signed by Huntly, Errol, and other prominent Catholics. Under torture, Ker admitted there was a plot to bring Spanish troops into Scotland, and so immediately both Kirk and King reacted. James denounced the Catholic earls as rebels and moved north with an army, entering Aberdeen on 12 February; but Huntly simply retreated into the fastnesses of his domain, and although there was much official sound and fury, little was done in practice and the civil war continued. A second royal expedition in the autumn of 1594, however, was somewhat more successful. Huntly demonstrated his power by defeating the King's young lieutenant, the Earl of Argyll, but did not choose or dare to outface the King himself and in the Spring of 1595 went into what proved to be temporary exile abroad. Bothwell, who had been an active player in this balletic skirmishing, fled first to Caithness and then escaped to Italy. He never returned to Scotland. The Kirk, for its part, issued excommunications and, perhaps satisfied that the King at long last seemed to be taking his rebellious Catholics seriously, co-operated with him by relaxing its mood of open contentiousness.[35]

Throughout this nervous, indeed neurotic, period there seems to have been little preoccupation with witchcraft. On 27 April, 1593 the presbytery of Glasgow "ordenis that anent the impietie of the witches and thair late conspiracie, the samin be proponit in the nixt Generall Assemblie to be set furth in print, that the samin may be divulgat and maid notorious to the haill inhabitantis in this cuntrey" – although if this did result in a published account, it does not seem to have survived – and on 19 May, Katherine Muirhead was burned in Edinburgh after confessing to various points of witchcraft.[36] On 3 April, 1594 the presbytery of Dunbar was instructed to investigate further charges of witchcraft against Janet Lyndsay, but at the October meeting of the synod it was reported that "eftir hir apprehensioun, nane accusing hir, the justice sett hir at libertie upon caution [on bail]". The

---

34 Calderwood: *History*, 271–2. Cf. *Ibid.*, 272–3, 274–5.
35 MacDonald: *The Jacobean Kirk*, 51–9. See also Pitcarin: *Criminal Trials* 1.2.317–35.
36 *Registers of the Presbytery of Glasgow*, 59. Birrel: *Diary*, 30. The minister at Pittenweem was ordered by his presbytery to look into the case of Janet Loquhour, suspect of witchcraft, *St. Andrews Presbytery Records*, 49r.

synod, however, was not satisfied with this and ordered fresh inquiries to be made.[37] Its persistence is a little unusual. Perhaps the ministers had got wind of rumours which have not been recorded, or perhaps they were suspicious that Dunbar had been misled by Haddington under whose advice it had acted in this case, since Haddington had a reputation with the synod of being slack when it came to witches.

May, June, and July saw a case of slander pursued by the presbytery of Dalkeith.[38] John Lydell accused Janet Unes of being a witch, saying that "he saw hir and xi or xii wiches rosting the picture of hir awin husband", and Janet retorted by accusing him of slander. Lydell promised to supply witnesses, including Janet's own husband, and added further details to his charges which included a famous name. "Agnes Samsone, witch, lay in the bed with her, quhilk sche denyid. He also affirmed that ane litil lass lay with hir and Annie Samsone in Keith, and the lass was fleyit [fled] out of hir wit, quhilk also sche denyied". The mention of 'Keith' identifies this Agnes Sampson as the witch of the treason case. There is no need to suppose any lesbianism in this passage. People at the time commonly shared beds. Janet's denials are directed towards the dangerous accusation that she had been associating with a known witch, not that she had been having sexual relations with a woman.[39]

Such associations, whether suspect or real, were potentially dangerous, as we have seen before. In September, Agnes Smith, a wet-nurse, was brought before the kirk session of Elgin on charges of "conferring with ane woman callit Janet Cuming suspect of vitchcraft". Agnes admitted that she had indeed spoken to Janet and asked her help for the sick child she was presently nursing. Janet agreed to give it and came three times to the house of Agnes's employer with water in a jug. Then Agnes, under instructions from Janet, went to the kirkyard and in complete silence took a handful of earth from a child's grave, brought it back to the house, and mixed it with the water. Next, the two women washed the sick child with the water and, this being done, Agnes carried the water (now contaminated, as it were, with the child's disease) to a running stream and threw it therein "that nane suld hurt thairby".

---

37 *Synod Records of Lothian and Tweeddale*, 76. The case was taken up again in April and October, 1595, *Ibid.*, 90, 98. As in the case of Agnes Sampson, however, Haddington seemed to drag its feet. Janet is not mentioned again by the synod after October, 1595.The second session of its meeting in 1594 instructed Dunbar to investigate and proceed against Maly Fell, another woman suspect of witchcraft, *Ibid.*, 77. Her name does not appear again in the records.
38 *CH2*/424/1: 45r-47v.
39 There was another case of slander in Aberdeen, discussed by the provost, baillies, and council on 14 August. Isobel Abercrombie, a servant, called Christian Kyntoir a witch-carling and a vagabond-carling. It was decided that in view of Isobel's previous bad record, she should be confined in a kind of bridle for three hours and then banished, *Extracts from the Council Register of Aberdeen* 2.93.

Finally, she came back to the house and helped Janet to escape over the back wall of the yard.[40]

These two years, then, during which Edinburgh and the North-East were particularly concerned with apparent threats of Catholic invasion and armed rebellion at home, produced only seven cases of witchcraft in the records, of which three were said to merit further inquiry (the result not being known), two were cases of slander, one was an execution, and one likely to be proved as a case of consultation and participatory magic. Four come from the capital and its environs, one from Fife, and two from the North-East. Evidently the tensions of the time did not produce any immediate instinct to set about persecuting operators of magic.

It is the same story during 1595 and 1596, although each of those years did produce one scandalous revelation about magic and its use by the landed classes. The first refers to the West of Scotland. On 4 February, 1592 John Campbell of Ardkinglass instigated the murder of John Campbell of Calder, and in June 1593 was formally accused of the crime. By May, 1594 he had been arrested and had confessed to his part in the murder, a confession later corroborated by Margaret Campbell, widow of John Campbell of Cabrachan, who was questioned by the authorities regarding her late husband's part in yet another murder, that of the Laird of Cadell. Her interrogation took place on 5 October, 1596, and what follows is the substance of that deposition.[41]

In July, 1592 Ardkinglass sent for Margaret and told her there was a rumour going about that he had murdered Calder. He then remarked that the witches of Lorn[42] were wiser than those of Argyll, and asked Margaret if she would try to persuade them to influence the Earl of Argyll to be favourable towards him: to which Margaret replied "that sic turns could not be done without she maid the witches to knaw the haill veritie of the caus". At first Ardkinglass was worried by this request, but after some hesitation he told her the background to the murders of both Cadell and Calder, confessing his part in each, but holding back certain details. "Then Ardkinglass said to the Deponer, Now I have reveilit to you all things concerning this matter and my

---

40 *Records of Elgin* 2.39. Cf. the case of Isobel Thomson *alias* Preinak, brought before the same kirk session on 8 December, 1596, *op.cit.*, 44–5. She was accused of charming one child by washing it with iron ore and cinders from the smithy; speaking words over another to stop its vomiting; concocting mixtures of honey, oil, and vinegar which the mothers refused to use; and washing a child with a black cloth. Various other mixtures appear in the details of her record, made of entirely harmless ingredients, but received with suspicion by many of the women who, one must presume, had sent for her in the first place.

41 *Highland Papers* 1.159–75. See also Maclean-Bristol: *Murder Under Trust*, 98–115.

42 Lorn is a district in Argyllshire, bounded on one side by Loch Linnhe. Margaret lived in Lismore which is an island in the district of Lorn.

man Gillipatrick Oig has schewn to me that all witchcraft is to be practised in the beginning of every quarter;[43] and now the first begining of the harvest quarter approtches and thairefore I desyre you to haif and get me intelligence of my own estate and quhat favor I may look for at my Lord [Argyll's] hands". So Margaret went home and sent one of her servants, armed with suitable gifts, to one of the local witches and asked her to reveal what would become of Ardkinglass and his associates. The witch replied that they would all go to Edinburgh where Ardkinglass and one of his men, MacCùil, should be imprisoned: "Yet [they] suld be releivit again and cum hame safely, quhilk she tuik upon hir; bot she wald not tak in hand to safe them any langer, and forder declairit that although MacCouil wald escheip for a lang tyme yeit, that at the last he wald pay for it".

Apparently satisfied by this reply, Ardkinglass showed himself willing to consult and use witches more frequently. Two or three days before his arrest, indeed, Margaret brought two of them, Euphric NicNeacail and Dugald MacGuaire, "and the said Nickeoll tuik upon hir to convert my Lord's angir and to mak him to favor Ardkinglass"; and as proof that the woman knew what she was doing, Margaret told her interrogators that Euphric had learned her charms from Old MacKellar of Cruachan who in turn had learned them from the monks of Inchcolm.[44] Just so, apparently, MacGuaire offered to teach Margaret how to enchant Ardkinglass and his company so that no weapon should have power to hurt them, "The quhilk inshantment", she said, "wes receivit be thame all except Ardkinglass himself". One wonders why Ardkinglass did not accept Margaret's offer.

Margaret also confessed that her husband often used to consult witches, especially when he went on a journey, and that she herself had been present when several of them promised to make the Earl of Argyll friendly towards him. She named four of them: Katharine NicClarty and Nic a'chléirich in Blairgowrie; Euphric NicNeacail in Lismore; and Christian, daughter of MacCùil in Lismore. She also noted for her interrogators' benefit that "the messengir that passit frae hir to the witch of Morvene is ane woman of Lismore callit Mary mhoir NicMhol mhoir MacCùil MacNeil,[45] quha . . . is not ane witch, but sche will see things to cum be sum second sight". Margaret herself consulted a witch with a view to pacifying by magic the hostility of the Laird of Lochnell towards her. The woman declared "that thair wes syndrie of

43 He is referring to the ancient quarter-days of Scotland, namely, Candlemas (2 February), Beltane (1 or 3 May), Lammas (1 August), and Hallowmas (1 November).

44 Inchcolm is an island in the Firth of Forth just to the south-west of Aberdour. Its abbey was founded by Alexander I in 1123.

45 Big Mary, daughter of Big MacNicol (?) who was the son of Cùil who was the son of Neil. The secretary who recorded these details made several mistakes, which makes it difficult on occasion to follow what he meant.

hir neibors quhom sche knew to be perfit in witchcraft, and that they assistit hir in thair works to releif MacCouil then out of ward". Every day, we are told, these women – and four are named – practised witchcraft to benefit MacCùil, and Margaret maintained that, as a result, if Argyll and all his allies were to face MacCùil on a field of battle, they would not prevail against him, "for he wes abel to resist thame by women".

Three principal assumptions about magic are easily discerned in these confessions: (a) that magic can be used to win the favour of someone presently hostile to you; (b) that witches can accurately divine the future; and (c) that magic can invest someone with protection against his enemies. The first two we have met before in evidence from the East of Scotland, and it is useful to see that expectations of magic were more or less the same in the West. That being so, one wonders how far (c) was to be found in the east as well, especially perhaps in the North-East where civil strife was common and liable to break out at a moment's notice. But it is the way in which the existence of a large number of witches is taken for granted that is perhaps most noticeable. One must bear in mind that Margaret was giving evidence, not in a case of prosecution of witches, but in a case of ordinary murder, and yet the authorities give no sign of wishing to prosecute the perpetrators of these magical operations. It is the murders which occupy their interest and attention.[46]

It is also worth noting that some of the witches' magical formulae had come down from Catholic sources – indeed, from a highly respectable Catholic venue in the East – and this serves as a reminder that the Kirk's apparent assumption that some Catholic practices and magic were interlinked had acual experience to lend it a certain weight. But the Kirk could not afford to be smug, for in September, 1593 Ardkinglass asked Margaret whether the witches she employed used to name God or Christ in their operations and was told that they did. Whereupon he produced the remarkable piece of information "that he had ane man callit Patrick MacQueine, a minister,[47] quhae wes a far better inshanter nor any of thame, and usit not in his prectizes to name God; and Patricks work of witchcraft and inshaintment wes verie oft hinderit and steyit be the rest of the witches becaus in thair work theye namit God" – perhaps because, according to Patrick's claim, he had seven devils attending him who acted as his servants.[48] Nor was Patrick alone,

46 It is also worth noting the penultimate sentence of Margaret's deposition which says that it was "freely maid and givin up be hir but [without] onie kind of tortor, interogators, or cumpulsion".

47 He was minister in Rothesay in 1589 and was transferred to Monzie, a parish in central Perthshire, in 1595. See *Fasti* 4.39, 279.

48 This may mean no more, of course, than similar claims made by other magical practitioners who had spirit-guides of one kind or another, which were interpreted by the written records as evil spirits or devils. But one must also be prepared to acknowledge that Patrick's claim could have been an idle boast, intended to impress a potential client.

if one may believe him, for he claimed he had other ministers, "companionis with him in his craft". To find that one Protestant minister actively practised magic is interesting in itself. To be presented with the possibility of several suggests that magic had not altogether retreated before the organised scrutiny of the reformed Kirk, and that even in places where reformed parishes and presbyteries had been established, magical beliefs and practices were still sometimes able to flourish, and to flourish in relative safety.[49]

The scandal of 1596 involved John Stewart, Master of Orkney, who was brought before a court on 24 June and, according to the first item of his dittay, charged with consulting Alison Balfour, a witch, throughout the last three months of 1593 and the first of 1594 "how thay micht haif bewichit the said Patrick Erll of Orknay his brother, and bereif him of life be Sorcerie and Wichcraft".[50] This was by no means the only such charge brought against him, but it is the only one involving magic, and it seems a confession was extorted from Alison by the most brutal use of torture not only upon herself, but upon her 81-year-old husband, her son, and her daughter.[51] Once the torture had ceased, however, and again at the point of her execution, Alison withdrew everything she had said, maintaining she had confessed "pairtlie to eschew ane gretar torment and puneischement, and upoun promeis of hir lyffe". It is very doubtful whether this application of torture was legal at all. A commission to investigate witches, empowering the holders thereof to torture anyone wilfully refusing to declare what she or he knew, had been issued in October, 1591, but that was limited to Edinburgh and East Lothian and had been granted for the specific purpose of uncovering the treason-plot of 1590; and indeed it is important to remember, as Walker reminds us, that such commissions were not "granted generally or for longer space than required for that particular affair for which they were granted".[52] In the absence of such a commission in Alison's case, therefore, we may take it that she, like Geillis Duncan, was tortured by someone almost certainly acting *ultra vires* on the presumption that his station in life would protect him from judicial punish-

---

49 One may also note John Napier of Merchiston who was a respected member of the General Assembly, and yet had a local reputation of being a magician in league with the powers of darkness. He was supposed to be attended by a spirit in the form of a black cock, and there is a document in his own hand contracting with Robert Logan of Restalrig to find hidden treasure in Robert's house of Fast Castle. See *History of the Napiers*, 89–90. In general, however, it is true to say that witches still tended to need a degree of luck to escape prosecution. During 1595, an unknown number was burned in June, *CSPS* Appendix 2.684; three of those who had assisted Bothwell in 1590 and had fled to Caithness were finally sent back to Edinburgh in October, *CSPS* 12.43, *CSPS* Appendix 2.697; and a witch was burned in Aberdeen, *SCM* 5.63.
50 *JC2/3*, pp. 41–7. Pitcairn: *Criminal Trials* 1.2.373–7.
51 See Anderson: *Black Patie*, 49–50, 156–7.
52 *RPC* 4.680. Walker: *Legal History of Scotland* 3.416.

ment, and that his victim's confession would be thought sufficiently important to warrant officialdom's winking at the way it was obtained.

One small point, however, is troublesome. Lady Bellenden suffered from persistent colic and asked Alison to send her a piece of wax from which she might make an emplaster to ease her discomfort. Now, while it is perfectly possible that such a request may have been entirely innocent, one wonders why Lady Bellenden sent outwith her own household for something as commonplace as wax. Enchanted wax, on the other hand, could be obtained only from a magical healer. Perhaps Alison, in vehemently denying she was a witch, distinguished between healing magic and witchcraft, just as Margaret Campbell's Mary Mhór had the gift of second sight, but was not a witch.[53]

The rest of the year contained no such notorious cases, although the ones which do appear are not without their significance. In January, Margaret Crawford, a midwife and a widow from Denny, was arrested "as ane wiche or ane abusar of the pepill (as is alledgit)" – an interesting distinction which seems calculated to make sure she would be prosecuted under the terms of the 1563 Witchcraft Act.[54] But it turns out that Margaret was a Catholic, and as the presbytery of Stirling was currently engaged in a long drawn-out struggle with one or two of the local prominent Catholic landowners, there may have been a touch of animus behind its apparent determination to bring her to court.[55] The ministers, however, found it difficult to get witnesses to come to meetings of the presbytery to give evidence against her, several being absent on 19 and 28 January, but eventually on 25 February they thought they had enough to warrant their approaching the Sheriff of Stirling and asking him to obtain a commission to put her on trial before a judiciary court.[56]

Then at the end of the year appear two cases of alleged magical murder. On 30 October, Alison Jolly from Fala, not far from Edinburgh, was accused of instigating the death of Isobel Hepburn in May, 1595/6 by sorcery and witchcraft, having hired a notorious witch, Janet Straton, to perform the requisite malefice or venefice.[57]

53 It is the kind of distinction one can see elsewhere, in a Mexican tradition heavily influenced over a long period of time by European. See Reyes Garza: 'Del amores y de otros males', *Estudios de Historia Novohispana* 16 (1996), 83–99.
54 *CH2/722/2*. Denny is a parish in south-east Stirlingshire.
55 On 8 December, the presbytery decreed a fast to remove idolatry and idolators (i.e. Catholics) furth of Scotland, *CH2/722/3*.
56 The presbytery had less success when it summoned John Thomson and his wife Christian Bennet on 20 April 'to answer for wichcraft in turning of ane riddell that therby thay myt get knawlege of sum clathes thay wanted', *CH2/722/3*. John and Christian simply ignored their summons and we hear no more about them.
57 Pitcairn: *Criminal Trials* 1.2.397–9. In one place the *Book of Adjournal* records her death as taking place in 1596, and in a second place allocates it to 1595. The latter date appears twice in Alison's dittay. In the second case, Alison would not have been brought to trial for sixteen months after Isobel's death, and in the first case, four, but there is no telling when she was arrested or how long she may have been in prison.

A Janet Straton had been one of the principals in the treason-trials of 1590–1, and as Alison's Janet was living in Lauderdale at the time of their consultations, there is a chance that the two Janets were one and the same. If this were so, it would be a remarkable indication that not everyone concerned in the treason-plot was executed, not even someone who had played a major part in its magical operations. Alison was found not guilty. Christian Stewart, however, who was tried on 27 November for killing Patrick Ruthven "be casting of Wichecraft upoune him with a black clout", was found guilty by her assize and executed.[58]

Four years, then, during which eastern and north-eastern Scotland were suffering the upheavals caused by political and religious strife, produced only eighteen recorded cases of witchcraft brought to official scrutiny, of which the majority turned out to be investigations without any apparent judicial resolution, with two people being released, and three being executed. The number is scarcely excessive over a four-year period and cannot be said to constitute a 'hunt'. But tensions within the kingdom were growing, if anything, worse and the outburst of prosecutions for witchcraft in 1597 was noticeably greater than that of any previous year, except for the treason period of 1590–1. Hence it has often been referred to as a time of witch-hunting. The designation, however, has little to recommend it.

Part of the tension of the period may be sought in the actions of Andrew Melville who, throughout the 1590s, made every effort to remould the Kirk along stricter Presbyterian lines, undermine and reduce the power of the King in ecclesiastical matters, and create an ecclesiastical organisation free from civil control. "There are two Kings and two kingdoms in Scotland", he told James to his face, "and in Christ's kingdom, the Church, you, the head of state, are neither a king nor a lord, but only a member."[59] Such an encroachment upon royal authority, threatened from more than one quarter and with increasing boldness, not to say verbal brutality,[60] divided Protestants

---

58 Pitcairn: *Criminal Trials* 1.2.399–400. MacKenzie referred to Alison's case in connection with the legal position of testimony offered by other confessing witches, and pointed out that because the only such witness against Alison was Janet Straton – MacKenzie calls her 'Hepburn' by mistake – the assize did not accept her evidence as sufficient, *Laws and Customs* 2.94. The reference to a black clout in Christian's case reminds one of Isobel Thomson in Elgin (*supra*, note 40), who washed a child with a black cloth as part of a curing process. A charge of witchcraft against Janet Gawie on 16 December was abandoned because an assize was not summoned, presumably because the prosecution had collapsed beforehand. The case is interesting because the main pursuer was a woman. Pitcairn: *Criminal Trials* 2.1. (This misprints Janet's name as 'Grawie'.)
59 See Maxwell-Stuart: 'Witchcraft and the Kirk in Aberdeenshire', 11.
60 David Black, for example, one of Melville's most enthusiastic supporters, had to be summoned before the Privy Council in November, 1596 to explain a sermon in which he had not only denounced the King and Council together but had branded all kings as offspring of the Devil. See Graham: *The Uses of Reform*, 207–9.

in Scotland at the very time they needed to be unified against the real and supposed perils of Catholic counter-measures, and as St. Andrews was the centre of Melville's activities (though it, like so many other places in Scotland, was divided into pro- and anti-Melvillian camps), it is not surprising to find that after anti-episcopal rioting in Edinburgh in December, and a meeting of the General Assembly in Perth in February, 1597 which was persuaded, not without difficulty, to grant the King extended powers in ecclesiastical matters, the King paid a visit to St. Andrews in July and, among other disciplinary measures, deprived Melville of his rectorship of the university, a notable blow to the minister's prestige.[61]

It is worth noting that while St. Andrews was convulsed by this quarrel with the King, the presbytery seemed noticeably to increase its interest in alleged witches. In May, the presbytery learned that one David Yeman, a witch, had been arrested but had been allowed out of ward by the baillies of Pittenweem to visit a sick youth. A good many people, it appears, had been in the habit of consulting him, principally to ask for cures, to seek ways of lifting bewitchment, or to have the source of bewitchment identified to them. Investigations into these allegations by representatives of the presbytery uncovered a network of recommendation and consultation, and by the end of June the ministers had received the names of at least six other witches. The consulters, the presbytery decided, were "to be debarrit from the benefeitis of the kirk whill [until] they schew teakonis of repentance, and [were] to be refarrit to the discretioun of thair severall sessionis".[62]

From an entry in the record for 7 July, we learn that some witches had been burned in St. Andrews. We do not know how many they were or when the executions took place, but the King was in the town from the 6th to the 13th, as Robert Bowes reported to Lord Burghley, "in the examination of informations exhibited against sundry principal officers and preachers in the University there and for the trial and punishment of witches . . . The number of witches exceed; many are condemned and executed chiefly for their revolt

---

61 See MacDonald: *The Jacobean Kirk*, 78–82. A General Assembly held in Dundee in May, 1597 with the King in attendance, in the words of James Melville, 'transferrit the haill power of the . . . Assemblie into the hands of the King and his Ecclesiastic Counsall'. Quoted by MacDonald, 81. At an earlier session of the Assembly on 9 March, a list of pressing concerns was drawn up for the King's attention, which included, 'To advyce with his Majestie, if the carieing of profest witches from towne to towne, to try witchcraft in uthers, be laufull ordinar tryall of witchcraft or nocht'. James's reply reminded the ministers that this was a matter for the Privy Council to decide upon advice; in other words, the secular not the ecclesiastical power would make the necessary ruling. The Assembly, however, retorted by saying that because civil magistrates had been setting some convicted witches at liberty, in future magistrates who did this would be subject to ecclesiastical censure, *BUK* 937–9.

62 *St. Andrews Presbytery Records*, 80r-v.

from God and dedicating themselves and services to the devil, by especial sacrament (as they term it) in receiving the devil's mark set in their flesh and in secret part as has been confessed by and seen in many and wherein many of several sorts are accused. They profess sundry fantastical fats to have been executed by them, all which shall (as I think) be published, as I forbear to trouble you therewith".[63] This is a somewhat curious notice. Seven witches is hardly an 'exceeding' number; the word 'sacrament' does not appear in any witchcraft dittay as a description of receiving the Devil's mark; Scottish witches at this time did not receive such marks in their privities; and the accusations alleged against the witches named or referred to in St. Andrews presbytery records contain nothing in the least 'fantastical'. It is always possible, of course, that details were produced in court which do not feature in these records, but Bowes's references to such things and to a forthcoming possible publication sound much more like the alleged operations of 1590–1 and the production of *Newes From Scotland*, and one cannot help surmising that, in the absence of factual evidence from St. Andrews, Bowes may simply have assumed that the incidents in Fife were of the same order as their notorious predecessors, and reported them as such. Nevertheless, some witches do seem to have been executed in St. Andrews, and it is a pity we do not know whether this happened prior to or during the King's visit. The former might suggest that the presbytery was making a political point: witches are essentially ecclesiastical business, therefore executing them is a matter for the Kirk's direction of the civil judiciary. The latter, on the other hand, might suggest that the King wished to emphasise to an arm of the Kirk, in an area where his authority had been vigorously questioned, that the trial and execution of witches were affairs for the state, regardless of any preliminary part played by kirk sessions or presbyteries.[64]

Once the King had gone, investigation of witches in Fife dropped back to what one might call normal levels. A number of women from Largo were examined in August; the presbytery ordered a public fast "because of goddis jugementis presentlie strykinge be pestilence and famine, as also of the discoverie of the gryt empyre of the deivill in this countrey be witchecraft"; and in October a witch from Pittenweem, Fritte Guttar, was being examined, along with Thomas Martin who was accused of consulting her.[65] But perhaps the most notable feature of the second half of the year in Fife was the allegation by certain residents of Pittenweem that their minister, Nicol Dalgleish, had deliberately withheld "certein deapositiounes of personnes suspected of witchcraft", an allegation he denied but one whose reverberations

63 *CSPS* 13.56.
64 It is noteworthy that the reports of his being in St. Andrews link his disciplinary actions against certain ecclesiastics and the examination and trial of witches.
65 *St. Andrews Presbytery Records*, 82r-v, 84v, 86r-v.

continued from July until October.[66] Graham wonders whether Dalgelish may not have had "reservations about the nature of witchcraft accusations and the trials which resulted",[67] a possibility, of course, but perhaps it is worth remembering that from 1584 until 1588 Dalgleish had been chaplain to the Earl of Angus, leaving his post in August of that year when the Earl died of witchcraft (as was widely alleged at the time).[68] Such close proximity to such a death could have convinced Dalgleish that there was nothing in the allegations – hence a presumed scepticism later on in 1597; but it may have had just the opposite effect and persuaded him of the dangers of magic and consultation of its operators.

Reading the presbytery records for this year makes one or two points clear: (a) a majority of the alleged witchcraft activity at this time seems to centre upon Pittenweem; (b) Dalgleish's indignation at the suggestion he had withheld records was accepted as genuine by the presbytery; and (c) several witnesses from Pittenweem declared that the minister had not kept back any depositions. The likelihood is, therefore, that the accusation against Dalgleish was malicious, and that the rounding up of witches and their consulters in Pittenweem in particular owed something to Dalgleish's diligence in the task.[69]

These conclusions, however, apply only to local matters. A much wider and more important question is raised by another event from this same summer. Did the King's visit to Fife stimulate a wave of persecution across Scotland? Some documents give the impression that there is reason to believe so. "The King has been lately pestered", wrote the English ambassador on 15 August, "and many ways troubled in the examination of the witches which swarm in exceeding number and (as is credibly reported) in many thousands. McKolme Anderson confesses that he and other witches practised to have drowned the King in his passage over the water at Dundee at the late General Assembly of the Church there, and the life of the Prince [Henry] has been likewise sought by the witches, as is acknowledged by some of them. All others I refer to the report and sufficiency of this bearer."[70] Nevertheless, one has one's doubts about this passage. Again there is exaggeration of numbers, and one wonders whether Bowes was merely trying to tell an entertaining anecdote, to give Lord Burghley the impression that Lowland Scotland was in the grip of a diabolical infection, or whether

---

66 *Op.cit. supra*, 81v, 84v, 86v. It looks as though the depositions had turned up by the end of December, *Ibid.*, 88r.
67 *The Uses of Reform*, 306.
68 *Fasti* 1.99–100. Spottiswood: *History*, 372.
69 On 13 July, 1598 he was still pursuing consulters, and on this occasion delay was the fault of the presbytery, not the minister, *St. Andrews Presbytery Records*, 93r.
70 *CSPS* 13.73.

he had simply based his remarks on rumour and faulty information. That this last is probably the truth seems to be indicated by a notorious series of events described by Spottiswood:

> This Summer there was a great business for the triall of Witches; amongst others one *Margaret Atkin* being apprehnded upon suspicion, and threatned with torture, did confesse her self guilty. Being examined touching her associates in that trade, she named a few, and perceiving her delations finde credit, made offer to detect all of that sort, and to purge the Countrey of them, so that [on condition that] she might have her life granted: for the reason of her knowledge she said, *That they had a secret mark, all of that sort, in their eyes, whereby she could surely tell, how soon she lookt upon any whether they were witches or not*; and in this she was so readily believed, that for the space of 3 or 4 months she was carried from town to town to make discoveries in that kinde. Many were brought to question by her delations, especially at *Glasgow*, where divers innocent women, through the credulity of the Minister M. *John Cowper*, were condemned and put to death. In the end she was found to be a meer deceiver (for the same persons that the one day she had declared guilty, the next day being presented in another habit, she cleansed) and sent back to *Fife*, where first she was apprehended. At her triall she affirmed all to be false that she had confessed, either of her self or others, and persisted in this to her death: which made many forthink their too great forwardness that way, and moved the King to recall the Commissions given out against such persons, discharging all proceedings against them, except in case of voluntary confession, till a solid order should be taken by the Estates, touching the form that should be kept in their triall.[71]

So many of these prosecutions and their hideous results being based upon fraud, however, the presbytery of St. Andrews, from whose jurisdiction Margaret Atkin had sprung, was quick to alert the King to these miscarriages of justice, resolving on 1 September that "a supplication [was] to be maid to his maiestie for repressing of the horable abuse by carying a witch about, and Master Robert Wilichie ordainit to request magis[tratis] of Sanctandros to

---

71 *History*, 448. John Cowper had been a minister at St. Mungo's from 28 February, 1587, before which he had been attached to St. Giles in Edinburgh, *Fasti* 3.460. Patrick Anderson's near-contemporary *History of Scotland* mentions large numbers of witches, men and women, especially in Atholl, and a Sabbat there, held in May, at which 2,300 were present. But he explicitly relies on the flawed testimony of Margaret Atkin for these details. See Chambers: *Domestic Annals* 1.291. Some witches were, indeed, arrested in Atholl but in March, 1598 we find the Earl and Countess in trouble with the Privy Council for their delay in having these witches sent for trial, *RPC* 5.448.

stay the samew thair".[72] In consequence, on 12 August the Privy Council revoked those commissions it had already granted, while making clear that fresh commissions could and would be issued, and it directed that proclamation be made "at the mercat croceis of the heid burrowis of this realme and uthiris placeis neidfull", reminding people that those who consulted witches were as guilty under the law as the witches themselves.[73] Both Kirk and state, therefore, had been made aware of possible abuses in the system of investigation into witchcraft, and it is noticeable that when they knew about it, they sought to correct it.

Not that the state had always to rely upon the Kirk to let it know something was wrong. For in July, Janet Finlayson brought a complaint against the baillies of Burntisland, alleging that they were taking advantage of just such a commission to enrich themselves with the goods and property of those people they succeeded in getting condemned for witchcraft. The baillies had arrested her, said Janet, and brought her to trial where she was found innocent; and yet, notwithstanding this judgement, the baillies not only tried to suppress the record of her trial, along with its verdict, but "continewing in thair haitrent and malice aganis hir, intendis still to trouble hir for that caus, and of new to putt hir to ane assise, and swa fra ane assise to ane uther, ay and quhill [until], be sum indirect meane, sho be convict of that quhairof sho is maist innocent". The baillies failing to come before the Council to answer these charges, and Janet appearing in person to press them, the Lords decided in Janet's favour and issued an order that the baillies desist in future from all proceedings against her.[74]

In short, then, the King's visit to St. Andrews in July enabled him to make a point about ecclesiastical authority by suspending Andrew Melville from his rectorship, and may also have allowed him to underline that point by his being present at the trial of some witches who were found guilty and executed. If their trial and execution were not used by the King for this purpose, however, they may well have been used by the Kirk with the aim of making its own particular point in the tussle for supreme authority in which Kirk and state were then engaged. The sudden increase in prosecutions for witchcraft across the central belt from Fife to Glasgow owes everything to the fraud of one woman (understandably terrified by the prospect of torture and death) and the

---

72 *St. Andrews Presbytery Records*, 82v.
73 *RPC* 5.409–10. Since 5 February, 1596 requests for judiciary commissions had had to be presented first to the King's secretary and then to the Privy Council for consideration before they could be granted, *Ibid.*, 268.
74 *RPC* 5.405–6. The same complaint was made by Margaret Hay on 16 November against James Bellenden of Pittendreich near Edinburgh, and the Lords decided to suspend Bellenden's commission, *Ibid.*, 495. Janet Smyth from Burntisland, however, was not so fortunate, being condemned on charges of witchcraft and almost certainly executed. See Ross: *Aberdour and Inchcolme*, 343–4.

complaisance of a Westland clergyman. This increase has nothing to do with King James himself, and the moment he and the other responsible figures of both Kirk and state found out what was going on, they put a stop to it. So although one may discern the possible beginnings of a 'hunt' during the summer of 1597 – and the absence of reliable figures makes assessment of how reasonable it would be to use such a term problematical – any such outbreak seems to have been nipped in the bud before it could get seriously under way.[75]

The other principal outbreak of witchcraft prosecutions that year occurred largely during February and March in Aberdeenshire and is often described as a 'hunt' or a 'craze' inspired by James's *Daemonologie* and fed by hysteria. I have indicated elsewhere that the King's book almost certainly did no such thing, since it was probably published in the autumn of 1597, too late to stimulate emotions in the North-East of Scotland,[76] and so it remains to see whether the indictments threatened or brought against nearly sixty people constituted anything resembling a 'hunt'.

The panels involved may be divided into three groups: (a) a family from Aberdeen itself, consisting of Janet Wishart, her husband John Leis, her son, three daughters, and the husband of one of the daughters; (b) a disparate group of women consisting of individuals from various townships within a seven- or eight-mile radius of each other, and some twenty or so miles south-east of Aberdeen, all of whom were accused of meeting on Hallowe'en, 1596 in the countryside between Lumphanan and Craiglug; and (c) another disparate set of individuals coming from the locality of Foveran, Logie Buchan, and the kirktoun of Slains.[77] Janet Wishart, the matriarch of the

---

75 But I have suggested that the events of the summer may have stimulated James to send his *Daemonologie*, written some six years before, to his official printer. See Maxwell-Stuart: 'Witchcraft and the Kirk in Aberdeenshire', 13.

76 *Loc.cit. supra.*

77 This account of the Aberdeenshire episode is based on my article cited *supra*, note 75. The toun was a very small community. A kirktoun had a kirk or a chapel as its focal point; the fermtoun had perhaps up to a dozen households working jointly upon a farm; and fishertouns strung out their dwelling-places in stumpy rows beside the seashore. When touns became too big for the comfort or liking of their inhabitants, they split and thus formed new, though proximate, communities. Even burghs, whether royal or not, were likely to be small. For example, it has been calculated that in 1500 only 1.6% of the population lived in towns with more than 10,000 inhabitants, although this had nearly doubled by the end of the century. Even so, the probability is that nearly everyone in both town and country would have had the common experience of living in intimacy with his or her neighbours, a condition which could easily turn to violence, verbal or physical, if patience at last wore out; and indeed the interplay of these tensions forms a constant theme of witchcraft accusations and provides the leitmotiv, as it were, which underlies their various accounts of good will or malefice. See Whyte: *Scotland Before the Industrial Revolution*, 132–3, 172. Larner: *Enemies of God*, 48–9. Houston: *Population History*, 20.

first group, was accused of a variety of acts of magic, most of them malefices, in 31 articles ranging over a period of 24 years, and one of her daughters, Janet Leis, also had a history of operative magic, including several malefices, going back 20 years. Between the two of them, indeed, they were accused of inflicting illness and consequent death on both people and animals, raising winds, reducing people to beggary, bewitching corn and seed, and foretelling the future. Similar accusations were brought against all the other panels – although it must be said that many of them were also alleged to have worked love-magic and cured the sick – but because the principal features of all their dittays are substantially the same as those of earlier cases we have already examined, there is no point in rehearsing them here in any detail.

Still, there are one or two features of these Aberdeenshire dittays which are worth mentioning briefly. Thomas Leis, Janet Wishart's son, was unable to marry his mistress, Elspeth Reid, because neither his mother nor his father would permit it. So at Christmastide, 1596 he suggested to her that they go away together to Moray and there he would marry her. At first Elspeth was reluctant, since she did not know how they would make a living; but at last she asked Thomas what he wanted her to do and he answered that "thair is ane hill betuixt this and Mwrray, and at the fute thairof thow suld gar [make] ane man ryse and plene appeir to hir, in ony lyiknes scho pleisit; and that thow suld speik the man first thi selff, that scho suld nocht feir, and becum that manis servand, and do as he commandit hir, and scho suld newir want".[78] In other words, Elspeth was to consult a *sith* and rely on his good will to provide sufficient means whereon she and Thomas could live. Elspeth's reaction, we are told, was a suspicion that Thomas might be asking her to raise an evil spirit – understandable, perhaps, in the light of Thomas's later conviction and execution – and so she made the sign of the cross. Elspeth, then, was a Catholic. Is this why Janet Wishart and John Leis were opposed to their son's marrying her?

Thomas, however, was not the only alleged witch to reveal knowledge of *sithean*, for the dittay of Andrew Man gives a remarkable account of his intimate dealings with them.[79] About sixty years before his trial, the Queen of the *sithean* came to his mother's house and there gave birth to a child. Andrew then received the Queen's promise that he would have the gift of foreknowledge and be able to cure almost any kind of illness; and sure enough, we find that many of the items on his dittay refer to his curing both people and animals.[80] Her gift may have been

---

78 *SCM* 1.98.
79 *Op.cit. supra*, 119–22.
80 His methods consisted of a mixture of prayers, magical charms, and sprinkling water (which the dittay records as 'baptising'). On one occasion, he passed a patient nine times through a circle of unwashed wool and then transferred his illness to a cat which was passed nine times backwards through the same circle. See items 3 and 5.

granted in return for his having sexual intercourse with her, for they had several children whom he later saw but whose upbringing was clearly none of his affair.[81] Andrew gives descriptions of the *sithean* which are more or less the same as those provided by Robert Kirk a hundred years later: "The elphis hes schapes and claythis lyk men, and . . . will have fair coverit taiblis, and . . . are bot schaddowis, bot ar starker nor [more vigorous than] men, and . . . have playing and dansing quhen they pleas . . . They will apeir to have candlis, and licht, and swordis, quhilk wilbe nothing els bot deed gress and strayes [straws]".[82] On certain days in the year the *sithean* go riding out on the earth upon white horses ('hackneys'), and the spirits of famous men – Andrew names James IV and Thomas the Rhymer – consort with them. It is all reminiscent of Elizabeth Dunlop's testimony.

But the most notable parts of Andrew's testimony are those which contain his somewhat unorthodox religious views which are linked with his references to an attendant spirit called "Christsonday". This was not a name given by Andrew himself. Marion Grant, from the parish of Methlick in the northeast of Aberdeenshire, was also accused of having a spirit ("the Devill thy maister") called Christsonday, with whom she danced and had sexual intercourse,[83] and in both cases the spirit might appar as a man or a stag. But Andrew's spirit did more than simply appear. It told him of nature's secrets – "thow affermis the crawis will bring a stane from one cuntrie [district] to ane uther, to gar thair birdis clek [to make their young hatch], quhilk intelligence thow hes of Christsonday" – and revealed that 1598 would be a difficult year, but that the next fourteen would be good ones.[84] Christsonday was able to know all this, said Andrew, because he was an angel clad in white clothes – Andrew's interrogator recorded this as "the Devill, thy maister", of course – and God's son-in-law, and "at the day of judgement, the fyre will burne the watter and the earth, and mak all plain, and . . . Christsonday wilbe cassin in the fyre becaus he dissavis [deceives] warlingis men . . . [and] at the day of judgement Christsonday wilbe nottar [secretary], to accuse everie man; and ilk man will hawe his awin dittay, wretin in his awin buik to accuse him self".[85]

81　Cf. another of the accused witches, Isobel Strachan from Dyce, who said that she learned her magical skills from her mother who learned them from a *sith* who had sexual intercourse with her, *SCM* 1.177 (item 2).

82　Items 9 and 13.

83　*SCM* 1.170–1 (items 1 and 3).

84　Items 14 and 12.

85　Items 7, 12, and 15. Christsonday was raised by Andrew's saying *Benedicite* ('Bless you'), but dismissed with ceremonial magic. Andrew had to tuck a dog into his left armpit, muzzle the dog with his right hand, and say the word 'Maikpeblis', (item 7). This ritual seems to be peculiar to Andrew, but he was clearly a man capable of adapting both religion and magic to his own requirements. Dogs were capable of seeing *taibhsean*, apparitions of the dead, Sutherland: *Ravens and Black Rain*, 34–5, 48. Christsonday's appearance in white clothing reminds one of the spirit which visited one of the confessing witches from the North Berwick episode, *JC26/2/10*.

Andrew was brought to trial on 20 January, 1598 and convicted by the unanimous voice of his assize "in nyn or ten poyntis of witchcraft and sorcerie, contenit in his dittay", as the record says. It is a pity we do not know the points on which he was acquitted, since there were fifteen items altogether, but the only marginal note "provin" in the record appears beside the article which accuses him of curing Alexander Fordyce by passing him through a circle of unwashed wool. Assuming that the assize would also have condemned him for his admissions about Christsonday, however, is not altogether safe. Certainly the identification made by the court between Christsonday and the Devil could have suggested a diabolical pact, but if one may judge by the decisions of other assizes in other cases, the assizers could as easily have made up their minds they did not believe a word of it and so have found him innocent in those points.

Two of the women tried in March and April, 1597 and found guilty may have been practising murder as well as magic. Bessie Thom, it was said, was asked by Elspeth Jack to make a quantity of slaik[86] which she then fed to her husband who quickly fell ill and died. It sounds like a contract for murder, and indeed the dittay specifically refers to it as "murthour and bevitching".[87] She was also said to have killed Patrick Coull, her own husband, by similar means, and even if one puts aside the suggestion of deliberate poisoning, the incidents are a reminder of the dangers inherent in the making and administration of herbal drinks in the type of magical operation known as *veneficium*, which might kill by accident instead of cure or bewitch.[88]

Margaret Clerk *alias* Bane, who came to court on 25 March, 1597 and was convicted of ten out of sixteen points on her dittay, seems to have been a remarkable woman. She was a midwife, much in demand, with the ability to foretell future events, informing James Braibner, for example, that while he was coming to see her, his wife had given birth to a son, and correctly prophesying that a man who had called her "witch carling" would fall into water and drown.[89] What makes her especially interesting, however, is the information that she had had a reputation as a witch for the past thirty years and had been hauled into court in Kincardine the previous June to answer a list of charges which included witchcraft, sorcery, and murder. But she had bribed the clerk and some other members of the court to get the long dittay reduced to only two points, and when these came to trial she persuaded Lady

---

86 An unctuous concoction of some kind.
87 *SCM* 1.166 (item 2).
88 Cf. Katharine Gerard who was accused of poisoning two women by sending them parts of a leaf to eat, *op.cit. supra*, 175. 'Leaf' here may refer to a segment of fruit. The last item on her dittay baldly accuses her of "the devilische murthering of thy awin husband", without any additional reference to witchcraft.
89 *SCM* 1.156–61. These two items are nos. 8 and 15.

Auchlossan to bribe the assize to bring in a verdict of not guilty of these.[90] It is a useful reminder that corruption was possible (in every trial, of course, not simply those for witchcraft), although the evidence for it is rare and assizers were obliged by law to reveal in open court any bribes, gifts, or solicitations which had been made to them.[91] One may note, however, that on this second occasion Margaret did not escape justice and indeed confessed to this very point of her dittay.

But here we are led once more to the question, how much of the evidence against these women and men was obtained by torture? We know that Isobel Richie was tortured before her trial on 24 April, 1597 because item 6 on her dittay records that "thow confessit, being tormentit, etc.", but one cannot be sure whether any of the other panels suffered the same, since there is no mention in their records of any such application – an *argumentum negativum* whose value is hard to assess. What one can say, however, is that the commissions issued for the trials of Janet Wishart and her family, Isobel Cockie, Andrew Man, and nine other persons, contain no mention of permission to extract evidence by torture,[92] and so one is left with the possibility either that it was used illegally on Isobel Richie – a circumstance we have come across before – or that for some unexplained reason the record chose to note its use in this one item of a single dittay, but not in any of the others.

Finally, we should note that the trials were much more complex than is usually allowed. At least eleven of the accused were found not guilty; others were examined before they came to trial and found to be honest and respectable, or guilty of nothing except being the subject of gossip, or suspect without there being sufficient evidence to warrant their remittance to trial; and in the cases of three who were brought to court and acquitted, the principal witness against them was later arrested and charged with malicious prosecution.[93] So the notion of a 'hunt', with its attendant symptoms of

---

90 Item 14. It appears from item 13 that she had been indicted for witchcraft at every justice court held during the previous thirty years, but had always refused, or at least failed, to appear.

91 *APS* 2.23, an Act of 1436. By an Act of 1540, judges who took bribes were to lose their office, *Ibid.*, 374. Bribery was not the only inhibitor of justice, of course. Katharine MacFerries' assize may have been weighted against her because it contained at least four men who could have been personally hostile towards her. See Maxwell-Stuart: 'Witchcraft and the Kirk in Aberdeenshire', 8. David Roy consulted a witch on the best way to deflower his daughter, and when the magic did not work, he took her by force. For these offences he was brought to trial on 21 February, 1601 but was acquitted by his assize. This caused a scandal and the assizers were hauled before the Privy Council on 21 May to explain their wilful verdict, *RPC* 6. 241–2.

92 *SCM* 1.83–4, 117–18, 184–5. Cf. *Aberdeen Council Letters*, 70–1.

93 *SCM* 1.138–9.

emotional imbalance and deliberate purpose, seems ill-suited to what was going on in Aberdeenshire during the last months of 1596 and the early months of 1597.

Still, the matter is not quite as simple as that. The Kirk was involved in all these cases, but most witchcraft prosecutions seem to have made their way to the criminal court via kirk or presbytery sessions, and so its initial involvement is neither unusual nor sinister. But one does need to bear in mind the violence of the division between King and Kirk during the period when these trials were being prepared and brought before their assizers, a division which may be illustrated by the cries which reached James's ears on 17 December, 1596 as he sat in the Edinburgh Tolbooth: "God and the King" and its hostile counterpart "God and the Kirk".[94] David Black, who had been high-handedly rude to James in November and was a champion of ecclesiastical absolutism, was tried before the Privy Council, found guilty of sedition, and packed off to a parish in the presbytery of Arbroath. The Catholic Earls of Huntly and Errol and other prominent Catholics, on the other hand, continued, it seemed, to receive the King's support despite frequent attempts by the Kirk to have them brought under Protestant control.[95] Thus, relations between the two powers continued to see-saw until the summer of 1597 when the King at last managed to establish his authority over the Kirk. As MacDonald puts it, "what happened from December 1596 until midway through the following year was a concentrated demonstration of royal anger at the events surrounding the trial of David Black and of James's determination that such a thing would not happen again".[96]

One may argue, therefore, that these prosecutions from Aberdeenshire served a similar purpose to those later on in Fife. They acted as vehicles for a political message between Kirk and state, and it is perhaps a moot point whether the Kirk in the North-East was made peculiarly vigilant by the tensions of the moment, and thus became more diligent in noting episodes of operative magic; or whether some ministers took advantage of a situation in which more panels than usual named other people who were, in their turn, arrested, and so gathered before the court a larger than normal number of suspects for trial.

Fife and Aberdeenshire account for the majority of witchcraft cases during this year. Elsewhere there were a few, but not in numbers out of the ordinary. On 27 April, the kirk session in Elgin heard that Agnes Smyth, a wet-nurse, had been delated by a confessing and executed witch, Janet Cumming, in connection with an act of healing magic upon a child, performed by Elspeth

94 Birrel: *Diary*, 39.
95 See MacDonald: *The Jacobean Kirk*, 62–72.
96 *Op.cit. supra*, 82.

Corsour at the behest of Agnes Smyth. It was the second time Agnes had been before the ministers anent this matter, the first being in 1594, and it is clear that all she had done was to send for magical healers when the child she was nursing fell ill.[97] It is also clear that the kirk session had done little or nothing about Agnes when the episode first came to their notice, so we must conclude that they were moved to act in 1597 either because of Janet Cumming's delation, or because the atmosphere infecting Aberdeenshire had spread as far as Elgin. A man, John Naughtie, was accused of witchcraft in May, and in July John Fairer accused John Laing of doing him an evil turn, while Fairer himself was accused by Andrew Spank of malefice.[98] It is unusual to find such a quarrel occurring between men, and yet Elgin provides another case in August when Robert Malleis complained that Andrew Dick had slandered him as a witch, a complaint which Andrew admitted was justified.[99] One or more of these cases is likely to have come to court, for it was reported on 27 May that "the minister producit the commissioun fra his Majestie purchast [obtained] aganis vitches and counsalaris with thame".[100]

Late summer and early autumn saw eight arrests reported to the presbytery of Stirling, along with evidence of irregularities in Falkirk which are clearly to be associated with the earlier activities of Margaret Atkin from Fife; and on 12 November, four women were put on trial in Edinburgh, principally for "geving thame selffis out for Witcheis, and to understand that thai had craft of Sorcerie, abill to haif curit diverse grit diseissis and seiknesses; quhilk be na naturall meanis of phisik, or uther lawfull and Godlie wayes, thay war abill to performe".[101] The note of scepticism should not be misunderstood. Some of these women were claiming to be able to cure such intractable disorders as leprosy and epilepsy, so it is hardly surprising that their dittays should have sounded more than one note of disbelief. Besides, there were other reasons for the court to be suspicious.

Christian Livingstone, for example, one of the four, seems to have practised conscious deception on Thomas Guthrie, a baker from Haddington, who

---

97 *Records of Elgin* 2.49–50. A similar case came before the ministers on 25 May, *Ibid.*, 51.
98 *Op.cit. supra*, 50, 54. Fairer also alleged that Laing's mother had the reputation of being a witch.
99 *Ibid.*, 56. Cf. the earlier slander which happened during a quarrel when George Warrand called Andrew Hoissak's wife a witch "that passit in the likness of ane bee", *Ibid.*, 55.
100 *Ibid.*, 52.
101 (Stirling) *CH2/722/3*: 27 July, 31 August, 7 September, 5 October. One wonders whether there is a similar instance in the case of Patrick Herring and his wife who were delated by a witch from Stirling, *Extracts from the Records of the Burgh of Stirling* 1.86. Herring did not turn up for his trial on 19 October, and was declared outlaw. (Edinburgh) Pitcairn: *Criminal Trials* 2.25–9. Quotation from p. 29.

came to see her because he was bewitched and wanted her to raise the magic from him. Christian took him and his wife down the outside stair of his house, dug out a hole in the earth, and produced from it a small bag made of black cloth, in which were several white pebbles and woollen threads of different colours, together with human hair and fingernail clippings. These, she said, throwing them to Guthrie's wife, must be burned: and so they were. It turned out, however, according to Christian's own confession, that she herself had laid the witchcraft there and had merely pretended to Guthrie and his wife that it had been hidden by someone else. The reason behind this episode is not explained, but since magical operators were usually paid to perform their craft, it is not difficult to suggest that this may have been at least one of Christian's motives.[102] But Christian and another of the four, Christian Sadler, appear to have worked from time to time as a pair. They promised to cure Robert Baillie's wife of bewitchment by giving her a herbal bath and a drink made of worts seethed in butter, neither of which, however, seems to have done any good. They also undertook to relieve Andrew Pennycuik of a bewitchment he said had been laid on him by Janet Stewart. Their method was to kill a red cockerel, mix its blood with flour, make a bannock therewith, and give it to Andrew to eat. In addition, they took his shirt, dipped it in the well at the back of his house, and then "Cristian Saidler put [it] upoun him, wat as it was, being very evill at eise, and gaif him to understand that he wold get his health be this meanis". The dittay makes it plain that in this particular instance the two women were definitely in cahoots, because when Andrew came to Sadler with his problem, she sent for Livingstone, "and at hir cuming the said Cristian [Sadler] desyrit hir to gif her selff furth for a wyise wyffe and a woman of skill".

Janet Stewart, the witch named by Andrew as responsible for his sickness, lived in Edinburgh in the Canongate. She too worked shirt-magic (but seems to have done it properly) and cured several people by passing them thrice through a circle made of green woodbind which she afterwards cut into nine pieces and burned – a magical practice she claimed to have learned, along with the rest of her cures, from an Italian called "Johne Damiet, ane notorious knawin Enchanter and Sorcerer".[103] Janet also professed to cure epilepsy by hanging a stone round the patient's neck five nights in a row, "quhilk stane scho affermit scho gat fra the Lady Crawfurd", and said she could heal leprosy with a salve whose principal, or only, ingredient was quicksilver – a cure she said she had been taught by her father. He should certainly have warned her it was not to be ingested, for when she administered it in a drink to Robert

---

102 She also confessed that her own daughter had been taken by the *sithean*, and that she had correctly foretold the birth of a son to Guthrie and his wife.
103 Giovanni Damietta, as one supposes his name would have been, is not otherwise known.

Hunter, the poor man died within the next twelve hours. Janet, then, depending as she did largely upon magical remedies she got from others, may have been naive rather than malicious and she must have had sufficient faith in their efficacy, for it seems she was ready to take on a pupil of her own. Bessie Aitkin, the fourth woman on trial, had been one of Janet's patients, one of those who passed through the woodbind circle. This method Bessie picked up and then used herself in the treatment of several clients, not to mention a number of herbal salves and herbal drinks whose composition she said she had learned from Janet.[104] The four women were found guilty and sentenced to death. Bessie, however, pleaded she was pregnant and thereby managed to escape execution, because we find that on 15 August the following year her sentence was commuted to banishment.[105]

Why was there an increase in the number of prosecutions for witchcraft in 1597? I have already suggested that those in Aberdeenshire and Fife may have been influenced by the power-struggle between the King and the Kirk.[106] Others from Edinburgh, Perth, and Glasgow, however, may perhaps be attributed to the malign influence of Margaret Atkin, for even as late as 15 February, 1598 John Morrison admitted to the presbytery of Glasgow that he had offended God, the Kirk, and the local minister, John Couper, by "spreading of the infamous libell contenit in the depositioun of umquhill [the late] Margaret Aiken ane notabill witche aganis the said Mr Johnne be sindrie copeis thairof in diverse partis of this cuntrey".[107] This, however, was only the latest of a series of reactions against the Glasgow clergy, which had been going on since at least the autumn of the previous year; and when we read that on 23 November, 1597 Perth was applying for a commission to try Janet Robertson "long imprisoned" for witchcraft, we may legitimately ask whether or not she too was a victim of Margaret's long summer of identifications throughout the central belt of Scotland.[108]

The final years of James's permanent residence in Scotland saw little in the way of witchcraft prosecutions. An unspecified number of witches was imprisoned in the Edinburgh tolbooth in May, 1598; there were three executions in Perth during September; Janet Allane was burned alive in Burntisland, a highly

---

104 In addition to the patients named in her dittay, see also a kirk session minute of 16 June, 1597 naming Archibald Tait, *South Leith Records*, 2.

105 Pitcairn: *Criminal Trials* 2.52–3.

106 One cannot attribute all trials or executions in the North to these events, of course. An unspecified number of witches was burned in Inverurie in 1597, and it is difficult to tell whether these had anything to do with similar hearings in Aberdeen or not, Davidson: *Inverurie and the Earldom of the Garioch*, 152.

107 *Registers of the Presbytery of Glasgow*, 90.

108 *Op.cit. supra*, 89. Lawson: *Book of Perth*, 229. It may be worth noting here that Kitty Rankine, the famous witch of Abergeldie, is almost certainly fictitious. See Wyness: *More Spots From the Leopard*, 1–5.

unusual form of execution which is not explained in the record; and St. Andrews presbytery heard evidence during the summer against one Patrick Stewart *alias* Pracker who was judged to be properly suspect of "abusing and deceaving of the people, superstitioun, scharming, [and] professing of thoses thingis that giff they be done and practisit indeid is witchcraft".[109] St. Andrews also received a request on 26 October from the Laird of Lothackar to pass judgement upon Alison Pirie who had confessed to having consulted Geillis Gray, a suspect witch. The presbytery, however, deferred its answer until it had more information and ordered every minister "mak intimatioun of thair parochineris giff they had anything aganis the said Alesoun and Geillis". On 30 November, the Laird came in person to the presbytery session and sought its decision, but he cannot have been satisfied with what the ministers told him, because on 22 February, 1599 we read that the Laird had meanwhile kidnapped Geillis Gray, taken her back to Lothackar, "and thair tortureit hir quhairby now scho is become impotent and may not labour for hir living as sho wes wont".[110] It is a shocking case of brutal high-handedness which helps to illustrate the illegality of David Seton's torturing of Geillis Duncan in 1590.

It is self-evident, then, that the number of recorded prosecutions dropped dramatically after 1597 and it is probably no coincidence that by 1598 James had clearly established a firmer royal control over the Kirk.[111] Even the Gowrie conspiracy of August, 1600, when James appeared to have been kidnapped by the Earl of Gowrie and his brother and to be in actual danger of his life, did not precipitate the kind of tensions which Bothwell's conspiracy caused at the beginning of the decade. The difference between the two, of course, is obvious. No magic was used by the Gowries, so neither Kirk nor state felt itself threatened by preternatural powers. So with relations thus regulated, King James disappeared to London in the Spring of 1603, leaving scarcely a ripple of magical trials behind him. Hugh and George Methven failed to appear before the Priviy Council in 1601 to answer charges of theft, reset of theft, witchcraft, and sorcery and were therefore put to the horn on 2 July; far away in Shetland, on 6 and 7 August, 1602 Nicol in Calysetter and Janet Archibald, having been

---

109 (Edinburgh) *Extracts from the Records of the Burgh of Edinburgh*, 220. *Treasurer's Accounts* 2.115. Official accounts often fail to give numbers. Cf. the arrest of some witches in Aberdeenshire in March, 1599, *Records of the Burgh of Aberdeen*, 71. (Perth) Lawson: *Book of Perth*, 229. (Burntisland) Ross: *Aberdour and Inchcolme*, 344. (St. Andrews) *St. Andrews Presbytery Records* 93r (13 July and 3 August). Anent consulters of witches, the ministers ordained that they should do the same penance as adulterers, and for the same length of time, *Ibid.* (20 July). On 31 July the following year, the presbytery decided that the deposition and confession of Isobel Flick from Pittenweem did not come under this act, apparently because they were slanderous, and so she was ordered to make public repentance for that offence, *Ibid.*, 106v-107r.

110 *Op.cit. supra*, 95r, 96v.

111 See MacDonald: *The Jacobean Kirk*, 92–100.

accused of divining by using the shears and riddle, were ordered to clear themselves by means of the saxter oath, testimony offered on their behalf by six respectable neighbours; and in Edinburgh, James Reid came to trial "for ane cowmone Sorcerer, charmer, and abuser of Godis peopill, be geving him selff out to haill all kynd of seiknes".[112]

Reid's case illustrates one last time several themes of the magic we have often come across before. He cured Sara Bothwell with south-running water, and John Christie by putting three silk threads around his waist. But he was also persuaded to operate malefice by John Christie's daughter, Janet. She asked him to help her destroy David Libberton, a baker; so with the assistance of the Devil, they enchanted nine pieces of raw meat and laid one underneath his mill door and the other eight beneath the door of his stable and, to make sure his corn was ruined, enchanted nine stones and threw these into Libberton's fields. Then Reid, Janet, and Janet's mother made a wax image of Libberton and, after it had been enchanted by the Devil, roasted it over a fire. Reid, we are told, learned his craft directly from the Devil "quha gaif him thrie penneis at ane tyme, and a peice creische [grease or fat] out of his bag at ane uther tyme". The Devil appeared to Reid on several occasions over a period of thirteen years, sometimes in the shape of a man, sometimes in that of a horse, and seems to have played a large part not only in Reid's instruction in magic but also in its practical applications. One cannot but think, therefore, that 'the Devil' may have been the court's interpretation of an attendant spirit or spirit-guide such as seems to have been a not uncommon feature of Scottish operative magic during this century.

The picture of magic which emerges is one which has little in common with the witchcraft portrayed by demonologists of the period. The Devil meets his servants more frequently as individuals than in company, and even on those relatively few occasions when they gather at a Sabbat, the witches dance and play music rather than feast and indulge in sexual intercourse. Shape-changing is most uncommon; journeys are taken by horse or riddle/boat, not by transvection through the air; the pact is scarcely mentioned, although one might allow that it is implicit in any relationship the magical operator may choose to have with the Devil; and the Devil's mark, when given, is almost always discovered upon the witch's neck or shoulder or arm or hand. People are not proven witch by swimming but by personal confession or the accumulation of testimonies offered first to a kirk session and then to a court of law. If they are brought before an assize, they have the legal right to be represented by friends or an advocate, and the assizes which hear the evidence quite frequently acquit the

---

112 *RPC* 6.264. Goudie: *Diary*, 185–7. Pitcairn: *Criminal Trials* 2.421–2. A marginal note tells us that Reid was found guilty and executed.

panel either in whole or in part, by unanimous or majority verdict. Torture does not seem to have been used with any regularity, except perhaps in some of the treason-trials of 1590–1, and even then needed the authority of a specific, short-term commission. The other, infrequent applications of torture to suspect witches were clearly illegal. The proposition that James VI introduced Continental theories of witchcraft into Scotland after his six months in Scandinavia is almost certainly mistaken, and the notion that waves of persecution of witches throughout Scotland were started by James's personal fears or the publication of his *Daemonologie* has little to recommend it.[113]

Those magical operations which are most commonly reported seem to fall broadly into three categories: (a) healing, (b) malefice, and (c) divination, with this last being carried out either by mechanical means such as the shears and riddle, or by consultation with spirits. Such spirits are usually interpreted in the records to mean 'evil spirits' or Satan himself even though it is clear – and would have been clear to the original actors – that many of these spirits were *sithean* or spirit-guides: and there seems to have been an almost wilful desire on the part of the authorities to misunderstand the involvement of magical operators with *sithean*, perhaps because *sithean* existed in a grey area of popular belief which, contrary to the comfortable doctrine of the Kirk, granted preternatural beings a permitted role as constituent parts of the natural occult order. That such beliefs and practices were popular in the widest sense of that word can be seen from the readiness with which the whole of Scottish society, from highest to lowest rank, was willing either to use or to participate in these various magical practices. The Kirk seems to have been inclined to look askance at this willingness, fearful lest many of those same beliefs and practices it deemed 'superstitious' turn out to be the same as those of remnant Catholicism and thus pose a threat to the rapid establishment of a new and reformed religion.

But neither Kirk nor state appears to have embarked on any witch 'hunt', certainly not in the manner of some of those hunts which disfigured one or two places elsewhere in Europe at the end of the sixteenth century, and although it is possible to suggest that both Kirk and state were not above using witchcraft trials on occasion to make political points to one another, on the whole it can also be said that both Kirk and state, through kirk sessions on the one hand and assizes on the other, made conscientious endeavours to try the crime of witchcraft with as much judicial fairness and equity as they brought to other capital offences.

---

113 Nor, as Larner has pointed out, can one make out a case for a connection between demographic disasters, whether famine or dreadful weather or plague, and surges in witchcraft prosecutions. See *Enemies of God*, 82–3, 204.

BIBLIOGRAPHY

Manuscript Sources

Aberdeen
Aberdeen Press 18/64

Dundee
Council Book, 1586–1603
Treasurer's Accounts

Montrose
MTH. Montrose mss. M/W1/15/6

St. Andrews
Anstruther Wester Kirk Session Records, CH2/89/3
St. Andrews Kirk Session Records, CH2/316/1
St. Andrews Presbytery Records, CH2/1132/1
St. Monance Kirk Session Records, CH2/624/3

Scottish Record Office (now National Archives of Scotland)
CH2/121/1
CH2/185/1
CH2/424/1
CH2/722/2–3
CH2/1081/3
GD16/25/4, *Airlie mss.*
GD188/25/1/3
GD406/1/56
JC1/12
JC2/2&3
JC2/10
JC6/3
JC26/1
JC26/2/1–30
JC26/2: *Earl of Bothwell, Conspiracy*
JC27/27
JC27/32
JC40/1–2
JC49/7

Primary Printed Sources
Aberdeen Council Letters, ed. L.B. Taylor, Vol. 1 (Oxford University Press 1942)
Accounts of the Treasurer of Scotland, Vol. 12, ed. C. Thorpe MacInnes (Edinburgh 1970)
Adamson P: *De Papistarum superstitiosis ineptiis* (London 1618)
Ayr Burgh Accounts, 1534–1624, ed. G.S. Pryde (Edinburgh 1937)

Balfour J: *Historical Works*, 4 vols. (Edinburgh 1824–5)
Bannatyne R: *Memorials of Transactions in Scotland, AD 1559–1573* (Edinburgh 1836)
Birrel R: *Diary*, in J. Dalyel: *Fragments of Scotish History* (Edinburgh 1798)
The Book of the Kirk of the Canagait, 1564–1567, ed. A.B. Calderwood (Edinburgh 1961)
The Book of Perth, ed. J.P. Lawson (Edinburgh 1847)
The Booke of the Universall Kirk of Scotland, 3 vols. (Edinburgh 1839–45)
Bruce R: *Sermons Preached in the Kirk of Edinburgh* (Edinburgh 1591)
Buchanan G: *Ane Detectioun of the Duinges of Marie Quene of Scottes* (London? 1571?)
————: *The History of Scotland* (London 1690)
Burne N: *The Disputation concerning the Controversit Headdes of Religion* (Paris 1581)
Calderwood D: *The True Historie of the Kirk of Scotland* (n.p. 1678)
Calendar of Border Papers, ed. J. Bain, 2 vols. (Edinburgh 1894–6)
The Calendar of Fearn, ed. R.J. Adam (Edinburgh 1991)
Calendar of the Writs of Munro of Foulis, 1299–1823, ed. C.T. McInnes (Edinburgh 1940)
Canisius: *Ane Cathechisme or Schort Instruction of Christian Religion*, in T.G. Law (ed.): *Catholic Tractates of the Sixteenth Century, 1573–1600* (Edinburgh 1901)
The Catechism of John Hamilton, ed. T.G. Law (Oxford 1884)
Carmichael A (ed.): *Carmina Gadelica*, 6 vols. (Edinburgh 1928–71)
Chambers D: *De Scotorum fortitudine doctrina et pietate ac de ortu et progressu haeresis in regnis Scotiae et Angliae libri quatuor* (Paris 1631)
The Chronicle of Aberdeen in *The Miscellany of the Spalding Club*, Vol. 2 (Aberdeen 1842), 31–70
The Chronicle of Perth, ed. J. Maidment (Edinburgh 1831)
Correspondance diplomatique de la Mothe-Fénélon de 1568 à 1578, ed. T.H.A. Teulet, 7 vols. (Paris-London 1838–40)
Cramond W: *The Records of Elgin, 1234–1800*, 2 vols. (Aberdeen 1903–8)
Dunbar W: 'The Tretis of the Tua Mariit Wemen and the Wedow', in Hope: *A Midsummer Eve's Dream*, q.v. 270–299
Erskine J: "Ane epistill wrettin to ane faythfull brother be John Erskyne of Dwne, 13th December, 1571", in *Spalding Club Miscellany* 4.92–101
The Exchequer Rolls of Scotland, Vol. 16, ed. G.P. MacNeill (Edinburgh 1897)
Extracts from the Council Register of the Burgh of Aberdeen,, ed. J. Stuart, 2 vols. (Aberdeen 1844–8)
Extracts from the Records of the Burgh of Edinburgh, AD1589–1603, ed. M. Wood & R.K. Hannay (Edinburgh 1927)
Extracts from the Records of the Burgh of Stirling, ed. R. Renwick, Vol. 1 (Glasgow 1887)
St. Andrews Formulare, 2 vols., ed. G. Donaldson and C. Macrae (Edinburgh 1942–44)
Goudie G. (ed.): *The Diary of the Reverend John Mill* (Edinburgh 1889)
Herries, Lord: *Historical Memoirs of the Reign of Mary, Queen of Scots, and a portion of the reign of King James the Sixth* (Edinburgh 1836)
Hibbert S: *A Description of the Shetland Islands, comprising an account of their Geology, Scenery, Antiquities, and Superstitions* (Edinburgh 1822)
Highland Papers, ed. J.R.N. MacPhail, Vol. 1 (Edinburgh 1914)
The Historie and Life of King James the Sext (Edinburgh 1825)
Hume D: *Commentaries on the Law of Scotland*, 2 vols. (Edinburgh 1797)
James VI: *Basilikon Doron*, ed. J. Craigie, 2 vols. (Edinburgh & London 1944–50)
————: *Daemonologie*, ed. G.B. Harrison (reprint Edinburgh 1966)
————: *Letters*, ed. G.V.P. Akrigg (Berkeley 1984)
Keith R: *History of the Church and State in Scotland*, 3 vols. (Edinburgh 1844–50)
Kirk R: *The Secret Commonwealth of Elves, Fauns, and Fairies* (Edinburgh 1815)
Knox J: *History of the Reformation of the Church of Scotland*, 2 vols. (Dundee 1812)
Leslie J: *The Historie of Scotland*, 2 vols. (Edinburgh & London 1888–95)
Lindsay of Pitscottie R: *The Cronicles of Scotland*, 2 vols., ed. J.G. Dalyell (Edinburgh 1814)

Low G: *A Tour Through the Islands of Orkney and Schetland, containing Hints relative to their Ancient, Modern, and Natural History* (Kirkwall 1879)

MacKenzie G: *The Laws and Customs of Scotland in Matters Criminal*, in *Works*, 2 vols. (Edinburgh 1716–22)

Martin M: *A Description of the Western Islands of Scotland* (London 1703)

Melvill J: *Diary, 1556–1601* (Edinburgh 1829)

Melville J: *Memoirs of His Own Life, 1549–1593* (Edinburgh 1827)

Minutes of the Synod of Argyll, 1639–1651, ed. D.C. MacTavish (Edinburgh 1943)

Miscellany of the Spalding Club, Vol. 1 (Aberdeen 1841), 83–193 = Aberdeen witchcraft trials

Monro D: *Description of the Western Isles of Scotland*, ed. D. J. MacLeod (Edinburgh 1994)

Moysie D: *Memoirs of the Affairs of Scotland* (Edinburgh 1830)

Napier J: *Folk Lore, On Superstitious Belief in the West of Scotland Within This Century* (Paisley 1879)

Nau C: *The History of Mary Stewart*, ed. J. Stevenson (Edinburgh 1883)

Newes From Scotland, printed in Pitcairn: *Criminal Trials* 1.2, pp. 213–23

Pennant T: *A Tour in Scotland and Voyage to the Hebrides, 1772* (Chester 1774)

Pitcairn R (ed): *Criminal Trials in Scotland*, 3 vols. in 4 (Edinburgh 1833)

R.S: 'The legend or discourse of the lyfe and conversatione and qualiteis of the tulchene Bischope of Sanctandrois', in Dalyell q.v. 2.303–44

Records of Inverness, 2 vols., ed. W. MacKay and H.C. Boyd (Aberdeen 1911–24)

Records of the Meeting of the Exercise of Alford, 1662–1688, ed. T. Bell (Aberdeen 1897)

Records of the Presbyteries of Inverness and Dingwall, ed. W. MacKay (Edinburgh 1896)

Records of the Synod of Lothian and Tweeddale, 1589–1596, 1640–1649, ed. J. Kirk (Stair Society, Edinburgh 1977)

Register of the St. Andrews Kirk Session, ed. D.H. Fleming, 2 vols. (Edinburgh 1890)

Registers of the Presbytery of Glasgow, November 1592–March 1601, in *Miscellany of the Maitland Club*, Vol. 1 (Edinburgh 1840), 53–96

Registrum Magni Sigilli Regium Scotorum, 1580–1593 (Edinburgh 1888)

Rentale Sancti Andree, ed. R. Kerr Hannay (Edinburgh 1913)

Robe Stene's Dream (Glasgow 1836)

Sanderson W: *A Compleat History of the Lives and Reigns of Mary Queen of Scotland and of her Son and Successor, James the Sixth, King of Scotland* (London 1656)

Satirical Poems of the Time of the Reformation, ed. J. Cranstoun, 2 vols. (Blackwood, Edinburgh 1891–3)

Scot J: *The Staggering State of Scots Statesmen* (Edinburgh 1754)

Scot R: *The Discoverie of Witchcraft*, ed. B. Nicholson (London 1886)

Shaw L: *History of the Province of Moray* (Edinburgh 1775)

Shaw M.F (ed.): *Folksongs and Folklore of South Uist* (Oxford 1977)

South Leith Records, ed. D. Robertson (Edinburgh 1911)

The Spottiswoode Miscellany, ed. J. Maidment, 2 vols. (Edinburgh 1844–5)

Spottiswoode J; *The History of the Church of Scoland*, 3 vols. (Edinburgh 1851)

Statutes of the Scottish Church, 1225–1559, ed. D. Patrick (Edinburgh 1907)

Stirling Presbytery Records, 1581–1587, ed. J. Kirk (Edinburgh 1981)

The Warrender Papers, ed. A. J. Cameron, 2 vols. (Edinburgh 1931–2)

Secondary Printed Sources

Anderson P.D: *Black Patie: The Life and Times of Patrick Stewart, Earl of Orkney, Lord of Shetland* (Edinburgh 1992)

Anderson W.J: 'Narratives of the Scottish Reformation I: Report of Father Robert Abercrombie, SJ in the year 1580', *Innes Review* 7 (1956), 27–63

Anglo S (ed.): *The Damn'd Art* (London 1977)

Ankarloo B. & Henningsen G. (edd.): *Early Modern European Witchcraft* (Oxford 1993)

Anon: *A History of the Napiers of Merchiston* (London 1921)

Bardgett F: 'John Erskine of Dun: a theological reassessment', *Scottish Journal of Theology* 43 (1990), 59–85

————: *Scotland Reformed*, (Edinburgh 1989)

Barrow G.S: 'Land routes, the Mediaeval evidence', in Fenton & Stell, q.v. 49–66

Barry J, Hester M & Roberts G (edd.): *Witchcraft in Early Modern Europe* (Cambridge 1996)

Bawcutt P: 'Elrich fantasyis in Dunbar and other poets', in McClure & Spiller: *Brycht Lanternis*, q.v. 162–178

Bawcutt P. & Riddy F. (edd.): *Longer Scottish Poems I, 1375–1650* (Edinburgh 1987)

Beasley A. W : 'The disability of James VI', *The Seventeenth Century* 110 (1995), 152–62

Behringer W: *Witchcraft Persecutions in Bavaria* (Cambridge 1997)

Beith M: *Healing Threads* (Edinburgh 1995)

Beyer B: 'A Lübeck prophet in local and Lutheran context', in Scribner & Johnson, q.v. 166–182

Bingham C: *James VI of Scotland* (London 1979)

Black G.F (ed.): *County Folk-Lore, Vol. 3: Orkney and Shetland Islands* (London 1903)

Briggs K: *A Dictionary of Fairies* (Harmondsworth 1976)

Brown J.M. (ed.): *Scottish Society in the Fifteenth Century* (London 1977)

Brown K.M: *Bloodfeud in Scotland, 1573–1625* (Edinburgh 1986)

Burns J.H: 'The political background of the Reformation, 1513–1625', *Innes Review* 10 (1979), 199–236

Campbell J.G: *Superstitions of the Highlands and Islands of Scotland* (Glasgow 1900)

————: *Witchcraft and Second Sight in the Highlands and Islands of Scotland* (Glasgow 1902)

Cassirer M: 'ESP in post-Mediaeval witchcraft', *Journal of the Society for Psychical Research* 55 (1989), 350–359

Chambers R: *Domestic Annals of Scotland* 3 vols. (Edinburgh 1859–61)

Clark C: 'People and languages in post-Conquest Canterbury', *Journal of Mediaeval History* 2 (1976), 1–33

————: 'Nickname creation: some sources of evidence, 'naive' memoirs especially', *Nomina* 5 (1981), 83–94

Clark S: 'King James's *Daemonologie*: witchcraft and kingship', in Anglo: *The Damn'd Art*, q.v., 156–178

————: 'Protestant demonology: sin, superstition, and society (c.1520– c.1630)', in Ankarloo & Henningsen q.v., 45–81

————: *Thinking With Demons* (Oxford 1997)

Cowan E.J: 'The darker vision of the Scottish Renaissance: the Devil and Francis Stewart', in I.B. Cowan & T.D. Whyte q.v., 125–140

Cowan I.B: 'Church and Society', in J.M. Brown, q.v. 112–135

————: *The Scottish Reformation* (London 1982)

Cowan I.B & Shaw D. (edd.) *The Renaissance and Reformation in Scotland: Essays in Honour of Gordon Donaldson* (Edinburgh 1983)

Cowan I.B. & Whyte T.D. (edd.): *The Renaissance and Reformation in Scotland* (Edinburgh 1983)

Cowan S: *The Ruthven Family Papers* (London 1912)

Dalyell J.G: *The Darker Superstitions of Scotland* (Edinburgh 1834)

Davidson H.E (ed.): *The Seer in Celtic and Other Traditions* (Edinburgh 1989)

Davidson J: *Inverurie and the Earldom of the Garioch* (Edinburgh 1878)

De Blécourt W: 'On the continuation of witchcraft', in Barry, Hester & Roberts q.v. 335–352

Dodgshon R.A: 'Livestock production in the Scottish Highlands before and after the Clearances', *Rural History* 9 (1998), 19–42

Donaldson G: *Scotland, James V to James VII* (Edinburgh & London 1965)

Dunlap R: 'King James and some witches: the date and text of the 'Daemonologie', *Philological Quarterly* 54 (1975), 40–46

Eerde K.S. van: 'Robert Waldegrave: the printer as agent and link between sixteenth-century England and Scotland', *Renaissance Quarterly* 34 (1981), 40–78

Fasti Ecclesiae Scoticanae, 8 vols. (Edinburgh 1915–1961)

Favret-Saada: *Deadly Words* (Cambridge 1980)

Fenton A. & Stell G. (edd.): *Loads and Roads in Scotland and Beyond* (Edinburgh 1984)

Ferreiro A. (ed.): *The Devil, Heresy, and Witchcraft in the Middle Ages* (Leiden 1998)

Ferrier W.M: *The North Berwick Story* (North Berwick 1980)

Findlay B. (ed.): *A History of Scottish Theatre* (Edinburgh 1998)

Foster W.R: *The Church Before the Covenants* (Edinburgh 1975)

Fraser A: *Mary, Queen of Scots* (London 1969)

Fraser G. MacDonald: *The Steel Bonnets* (London 1971)

Gentilcore D: *From Bishop To Witch* (Manchester 1992)

Gowling L: *Domestic Dangers* (Oxford 1996)

Graham M. F: *The Uses of Reform* (Leiden 1996)

Grant I.F: *The Social and Economic Development of Scotland Before 1603* (Edinburgh 1930)

Green C. & McCreery C: *Apparitions* (London 1975)

Hastings A: *With the Tongues of Men and Angels, a Study of Channelling* (Fortworth 1991)

Hay G: *History of Arbroath to the Present Time* (Arbroath 1876)

Hewitt G.R: *Scotland Under Morton, 1572–80* (Edinburgh 1982)

History of the Napiers of Merchiston, (London 1921)

Hope A.D: *A Midsummer Eve's Dream* (Canberra 1970)

Hornell J: *British Coracles and Irish Curraghs* (London 1938)

Houston R.A: *The Population History of Britain and Ireland, 1550–1750* (Cambridge 1995)

Hutton R: *The Stations of the Sun* (Oxford 1996)

Ives E.D: *The Bonny Earl of Murray* (East Linton 1997)

Kamen H: *The Spanish Inquisition*, 2nd revised ed. (London 1997)

Kelsall H. & K: *Scottish Lifestyle 300 Years Ago* (Edinburgh 1986)

Kieckhefer R: 'Avenging the blood of children', in Ferreiro q.v

Kyle R.G: *The Mind of John Knox* (Kansas 1984)

Langbein J.H: *Torture and the Law of Proof* (Chicago 1977)

Larner C., Lee C.H., MacLachlan H.V: *A Source-Book of Scottish Witchcraft* (Glasgow 1977)

Larner C: *Enemies of God, the Witch-Hunt in Scotland* (Oxford 1981)

———: *Witchcraft and Religion* (Oxford 1984)

Lee M: *John Maitland of Thirlestane and the Foundation of the Stewart Despotism in Scotland* (Princeton 1959)

———: 'King James's Popish Chancellor', in Cowan & Shaw, q.v. 170–182

Legge F: 'Witchcraft in Scotland', *Scottish Review* 18 (1891), 257–288

Lynch M: 'The Scottish early modern burgh', in Wormald: *Scotland Revisited* q.v. 73–81

———: *Edinburgh and the Reformation* (Edinburgh 1981)

MacClure J.D & Spiller M.R.G. (edd.): *Brycht Lanternis: Essays on the Language and Literature of Mediaeval and Renaissance Scotland* (Aberdeen 1989)

M'Crie T: *Life of Andrew Melville*, 2 vols., 2nd ed. (Edinburgh 1824)

Macculloch J.A: 'The mingling of fairy and witch beliefs in sixteenth and seventeenth century Scotland', *Folklore* 32 (1921), 227–44

MacDonald A.R: *The Jacobean Kirk, 1567–1625* (Aldershot 1998)

MacDonald F (ed.): *Island Voices* (Irvine 1992)

MacDonald Fraser G: *The Steel Bonnets* (London 1971)

McInnes J: 'The seer in Gaelic tradition', in Davidson: *The Seer*, q.v. 10–24

MacKenzie A. & Sutherland E: *The Prophecies of the Brahan Seer* (London 1977)

MacKenzie W: 'Gaelic incantations, charms, and blessings of the Hebrides', *Transactions of the Gaelic Society of Inverness* 18 (1891–2), 97–182

MacLagen R.C: *Evil Eye in the Western Highlands* (London 1902)

Maclean-Bristol N: *Murder Under Trust: the Crimes and Dath of Sir Lachlan Mor Maclean of Duart, 1558–1598* (East Linton 1999)

MacLeod Banks M: *British Calendar Customs: Scotland*, Vol. 1 (London 1937)

MacPherson J.M: *Primitive Beliefs in the North-East of Scotland* (London 1929)

Maloney C. (ed.): *The Evil Eye* (New York 1976)

Marwick E.W: *The Folklore of Orkney and Shetland* (London 1975)

Mason R.A: *Kingship and the Commonweal* (East Linton 1998)

Matheson W: 'The historical Coinneach Odhar and some prophecies attributed to him', *Transactions of the Gaelic Society of Inverness* 46 (1969–70), 66–68

Mathew D: *James I* (London 1967)

Maxwell S. & Hutchison R: *Scottish Costume, 1550–1850* (London 1958)

Maxwell-Stuart P.G: 'The fear of the King is death: James VI and the witches of North Berwick', in Naphy and Roberts: *Fear*, q.v

————: 'Witchcraft in Aberdeenshire, 1596–97', *Northern History* 18 (1998), 1–14

Merrifield R: *The Archaeology of Ritual and Magic* (London 1987)

Monter W: *Ritual, Myth and Magic in Early Modern Europe* (Brighton 1983)

Morrison I: 'Evidence of climatic change in Scotland before and during the age of agricultural improvement', *Scottish Archives* 1 (1995), 3–16

Muchembled R: *Culture populaire et culture des élites* (Paris 1978)

Mudie F. & Walker D.M: *Mains Castle and the Grahams of Fintry* (Dundee 1964)

Mullan D.G: *Episcopacy in Scotland* (Edinburgh 1986)

Murray M: 'The 'Devil' of North Berwick', *Scottish Historical Review* 15 (1918), 310–321

Naphy W.G. & Roberts P: *Fear in Early Modern Europe* (Manchester 1997)

Neill K: 'Spenser's Acrasia and Mary Queen of Scots', *Publications of the Modern Language Association of America* 60 (1945), 682–688

Normand L. & Roberts G: *Witchcraft in Early Modern Scotland* (Exeter 2000) (this title appeared too late for me to use it in this book)

Parry M.L. & Slater T.R: *The Making of the Scottish Countryside* (London 1980)

Pócs E: *Between the Living and the Dead* (Budapest 1999)

Purkiss D: *The Witch in History* (London 1996)

Radin D.I. & Rebman J.M: "Are phantasms fact or fantasy?" *Journal of the Society of Psychical Research* 61 (1996), 65–87

Reyes Garza J.C: 'Del de amores y de otros males: curanderismo y hechiceria en la villa de Colima del siglo xviii', *Estudios de Historia Novohispana* 16 (1996), 83–99

Riddle J.M: *Eve's Herbs* (Harvard 1997)

Ridley J: *John Knox* (Oxford 1968)

Romeo G: *Inquisitori, esorcisti e streghe* (Firenze 1990)

Rorie D: *Folk Tradition and Folk Medicine*, ed. D. Buchan (Edinburgh 1994)

Ross A: 'Reformation and repression', *Innes Review* 10 (1959), 338–381

Ross W: *Aberdour and Inchcolme* (Edinburgh 1885)

Rushton P: 'A note on the survival of popular Christian magic', *Folklore* 91 (1980), 115–18

Sanders A: *A Deed Without a Name* (Oxford 1995)

Sanderson M.H.B: 'Catholic recusancy in Scotland in the sixteenth century', *Innes Review* 21 (1970), 87–107

————: *Cardinal of Scotland* (Edinburgh 1986)

————: *Ayrshire and the Reformation* (East Linton 1997)

Sanderson S: 'A prospect of fairyland', *Folklore* 75 (1964), 1–18

Scott H: *Fasti Ecclesiae Scoticanae*, Vol. 1 (Edinburgh 1915)

Scribner R. & Johnson T. (edd.): *Popular Religion in Germany and Central Europe, 1400–1800* (London 1996)

Seton G: *A History of the Family of Seton*, 2 vols. (Edinburgh 1896)

Simpkins J.E: *County Folk-Lore*, Vol. 7 = Fife (London 1914)

Simpson J: 'The weird sisters wandering: burlesque witchery in Montgomerie's Flyting', *Folklore* 106 (1995), 9–20

Steuart A.F: 'The Scottish 'Nation' at the University of Padua', *Scottish Historical Review* 3 (1906), 53–62

Stevenson D: *The Origins of Freemasonry* (Cambridge 1988)

————: *Scotland's Last Royal Wedding* (Edinburgh 1997)

Stone J.C: *The Pont Manuscripts of Scotland* (Tring 1989)

Sutherland E: *Ravens and Black Rain* (London 1987)

Thompson F: *The Supernatural Highlands* (Edinburgh 1997)

Tiryakian E.A: 'Towards the sociology of esoteric culture', *American Journal of Sociology* 78 (1972), 491–512

Tolbooths and Town-houses: civic architecture in Scotland to 1833 (Royal Commission on the Ancient and Historical Monuments of Scotland 1996)

Truckell A.E: 'Unpublished witchcraft trials', *Transactions of the Dumfriesshire and Galloway Natural History and Antiquarian Society*, 3rd series, 51 (1975), 48–58

Tyson R.E: "Household size and structure in a Scottish burgh: Old Aberdeen in 1636", *Local Population Studies* 40 (1988), 46–54

Walker D.M: *A Legal History of Scotland*, Vol. 3: *The Sixteenth Century* (Edinburgh 1995)

Watson G: *Bothwell and the Witches* (London 1975)

Watt E: 'Some personal experiences of the second sight', in Davidson: *The Seer* q.v. 25–36

Whittington G. & White I.D. (edd.): *An Historical Geography of Scotland* (London 1983)

Whyte I.D: *Scotland Before the Industrial Revolution* (London 1995)

————: *Scotland's Society and Economy in Transition, c.1500–c.1760* (London 1997)

Williamson A.H: *Scottish National Consciousness in the Age of James VI* (Edinburgh 1979)

Willis D: *Malevolent Nurture* (Ithaca 1995)

Wormald J (ed.): *Scotland Revisited* (London 1991)

————: 'The witches, the Devil and the King', in T. Brotherstone & D. Ditchburn (edd.): *Freedom and Authority in Scotland, c.1050–c.1650* (East Linton 2000), 165–180

Wyness F: *More Spots From the Leopard* (Aberdeen 1973)

INDEX